The Deplorables

America Interrupted

Q

ISBN: 978-1667800295

ISBN: 978-1667800301 (ebook)

To all of the cripples, bastards and broken things
that make this a beautiful world

A review by David Masciotra as published on the *Daily Ripple*

Author of *I am Somebody: Why Jesse Jackson Matters and Melllencamp: American Troubadour*

"*The Deplorables: America Interrupted* is an interesting and righteously indignant tour of the monstrous Trump base, and how exactly they threaten to transform the United States, a flawed multiracial democracy, into a neo-fascist state.

How to restrain people who not only defend and encourage neo-Nazis, but aspire to destroy America's democratic system is currently the most vexing and troubling political project.

The author never falls for the trap of right wing commentary and mainstream analysis by breaking out the world's smallest violin to depict Trump supporters as harmless and misguided proletariats. The author of *The Deplorables* never even entertains – and good on him for it – that the people chanting "Send Her Back!" and "Build That Wall!" are reincarnations of the Joad family.

The author understands better than most media commentators, that the Trump cult and neo-fascist movement is about the preservation of white power, and the protection of America, according to their bigoted ideology, as a white, Christian and heterosexual nation. He accurately diagnosis the disease: "This is not a collegial bunch. Like their de facto cult hero, they will respond to your misplaced passivism with a bare knuckles beat down. Left to their own devices, they will tear to ground every vestige of a civilized America."

As if there were any room for doubt, the attempted coup d'état of January 6th, and the subsequent assault on the American electoral system, with massive voter suppression laws and the Trump-led attempt for partisan officials to take command of state and county election offices, confirm the harsh, but correct assessment of the author.

It is unclear if American democracy will survive the right wing assault. The author of *The Deplorables: America Interrupted* has made a valuable contribution to the democratic-preservation effort."

Contents

Foreword

Read <u>The Deplorables!</u> Who is the author, Q? I don't know. To me, knowing his identity is less consequential than heeding his warning about the bare-knuckled fistfight already in progress between Commendable and Deplorable forces.

Embark on Q's compelling, chilling, and critical journey through our recent history. Meet the key influencers and formative leaders, including the reviled and the adored. Learn about America's expanding network of underground extremist groups — their genesis, growth, gatherings, goals, and their guns. Gain perspective on the social and historical context underlying recent events. Get informed about the powerful, dark web of social media and the dangerous information/disinformation they disseminate. Laugh and cry at the comic and tragic dimensions of "this American life." Re-live recent key events with an informed, attuned eye and ear.

Why MUST you read <u>The Deplorables?</u> Because if, like me, you have willfully ignored the news that distresses you, or complacently lived your life in your own bubble, or pollyanna-ish-ly assumed that "all will work out in the end," you need to wake up and face the reality that Shakespeare understood more than 400 years ago: "...what is past is prologue."

The past that Q centers on in <u>The Deplorables</u> is not distant; rather, he focuses most of his book on the period of the Trump administration (2016-2020). For Q, it was in these four years that the emboldening and empowering of The Deplorables occurred: These insidious, dangerous, anti-immigrant, defiant, violent, anti-Semitic, white supremacist, Islamaphobic, aggressive, hate groups emerged from dark places into the light of day. Fueled by social media chat rooms in which rumors and conspiracy theories abounded, fed by radio/TV talk show hosts promoting an "us vs them" divisive mentality, and nourished by the tweets and actions of Donald Trump, their secular savior, The Deplorables pumped up their demands for power and attention. And despite Trump's loss in 2020, The Deplorables are not going away.

So, if past is indeed prologue, what does a future with active Deplorables look like? Not good, according to Q. If we, The Commendables, do not know our enemy, or if we do not take seriously the threat the Deplorables pose to our multi-cultural citizenry and democracy, we will lose the fight for American exceptionalism. Q shows us that the Deplorable vision of our future is a nightmare of ignorance, violence, bigotry, and division.

But Shakespeare's quote provides another path: "...what is past is prologue, what to come, in yours and my discharge." THAT is Q's urgent message and urgent call to action in <u>The Deplorables</u>: The past may be written, but the future is ours to influence. The informed choices we Commendables make and the informed actions we take are absolutely and undeniably critical to creating the "City on the Hill," the American society of our dreams.

Get off your duff; leave your comfort zone; take off your rose-colored glasses; prepare to laugh at the absurdities and gasp at the travesties of "Deplorabilism," and dive deep into the words and images and ideas that Q has written for you. Going along on Q's personal and public journey is sure to test your ability to face our societal problems head-on, but reading The Deplorables will ultimately strengthen your character, your compassion, your understanding, and your resolve.Read The Deplorables!

J.A., A Commendable

Chapter One

Like Oxygen

She could have sploshed me with three pounds of stewed tomatillos. She could have split my lip with the knotty side of a rotted old two by four. Maybe she could have set my balls on fire. But, as it happens, old married couples are rarely that subtle. Instead, on a crisp but barely white Christmas morning 2018, my lovely wife sucker punched me with a photo taken exactly 30 years earlier. A younger, simpler me, positively bursting with possibilities, stared back at a grayer, world-weary me posing with the *Donald J. Trump Art of the Deal* board game mere inches from his smug face. "What an asshole," I thought as I tried to hide the sudden shame you might feel if caught banging the cat at your own surprise birthday party.

In fairness, 30 years before then, neither I nor the Donald could possibly have imagined what a malignant dirt bag the brash 42 year old real estate tycoon was well on his way to becoming. Certainly, I had no idea I would not soon become the next brash young billionaire dirt bag. So, you could say, he and I were on perfectly parallel life paths in those heady days. Why quibble over the marginal difference a $400 million dollar head start might have made? Anyway, after admitting that my taste in rich, powerful men back in the day was as bad as Anne Boleyn's, I felt I owed an explanation to my adoring loved ones as they were now crying from laughing so hard at the picture. "You realize," I whined like Charlie Brown surveying his bag full of Halloween rocks, "The Trump U victims thought old Cheeto Jesus walked on water, too, before he cleaned out their piggybanks." Humans are marvelously adaptive mammals, who predictably move through progressively more evolved stages in life from barely coherent, to mostly functional, from being aggressively boned by reality every now and again. It takes time! When I was 26 years old, all I wanted was to get laid every few hours and make shit tons of money, rinse and repeat as necessary. Life for me was either game on or game off. Trump was always winning, so who was I to question the product?

It took a few swift Booyahs to my boys below and the soul crushing weight of marriage and fatherhood to develop that uniquely adult thing known as a conscience. Conscience is nothing more than your inner shrew reminding you that when you are shitting on the carpet in public, there may be a more appropriate time or place for such behavior. That epiphany would have come in handy in college, by the way. For the 30 intervening years, between unwrapping my secret weapon for success, the *Art of the Deal Home Edition*, and Christmas, 2018, I watched as the Donald shit on many carpets publically and destroyed lives like I destroyed public toilets after heavy binging back in the day. So, naturally, I outgrew the Donald long ago. That's not to say I didn't still fantasize about a jet setting lifestyle or wallowing in the Benjamins. Hell, I'd massage Mitch McConnell's obstructed bowel today if the money was right, I just felt there must be a less slithering way to achieve greatness. The point is, who in their mid-fifties didn't realize the Donald had long since become an

14

unmitigated disaster and likely mobbed up crime figure by the time he announced his presidential candidacy? Apparently, this constituency was far larger than I imagined.

Certainly, the age of Trump in America, has launched a vicious death match between reality and madness, but this story is not about Mr. *Art of the Deal*. Unless the Universe itself is an impish gaslighter, his freak show should come to a merciful end in January of 2021. This story is about a consequential fist fight, surely already in progress, between commendable and deplorable forces.

In this story, Donald J. Trump is revelatory of a far graver malaise. Like Shakespeare's poor bit player, he has strutted and fretted his unhinged hour upon the stage with mind numbing sound and fury since 2016, but may leave an inconsequential legacy. Aside from a footnote about joining only two other US presidents to be impeached, or the first and only to be impeached twice, what will history really say of him? What will last other than the malodorous vestiges of his attacks on American meritocracy? Today, he receives all of the headlines as we pray for the resilience of our institutions against illiberal incursions, but isn't it the primordial material itself, forever malevolent, which will remain combustible? Is it this evil that commendable people have always aimed to beat back, which has coalesced more formidably in the age of Trump? Are we all rushing headlong toward a final Freudian reckoning between society's good and evil impulses? Who will emerge victorious when the battle field is cleared of so much bloody wreckage and death? Are we aware enough, and resolved enough, to reset ourselves on an axis tilted toward our better angels, or will we be dragged beneath the sticky goo by bottom feeders attempting to rewrite our bedrock principles?

15

There is no time left for indifference and the kind of lethargy that has accumulated, like mildew and mold, over decades and left us vulnerable and afraid. Surely it is time for us to refresh the tree of modern American liberty and wage figurative, if not literal, war against the tyranny of small minds that have become violent of late.

Webster's defines deplorable as "Deserving censure or contempt," which seems pretty Jell-O and pudding to me when you consider many of the synonyms for the word: despicable, "grubby," "mean," "nasty," "pitiable," "scummy," "scurvy," and "wretched." The point is, we only use the word "deplorable" to describe purely awful people with awful values, awful intentions, and hell bent on doing awful things. To regain our righteous footing, we will need to render these heinous creatures impotent. Our recent pre-Trump past provides some direction. Before the slurry of social divisions between commendable and deplorable sorts crested about 12 years ago, the two factions coexisted grudgingly but peacefully. The war was mostly symbolic and didn't change the conduct of anyone's daily life consequentially. We all mostly lived only a step left or right of a functional center save for the truly radical anarchists.

Our first step will be to resist the centrifugal force that angst from a consistently changing reality exerts. For many, hate and bigotry is a natural defense mechanism during tectonic shifts in modern society. Faced with what they don't know, they retreat to the familiar, and urgently lash out against perceived threats. Counterintuitively, this moves them, not toward the center again, but thrusts them to the extreme margins where they can find other maladapted kindred spirits. At the margins, bigotries only intensify. Fears only become more unhinged. Like anyone suffering from addiction, congregating only with other destructive addicts is a recipe for disaster. The thread of real decency runs though the commendable gooey center where the tastes of either side are neither too sweet nor too sour. We must always seek to live in that commendable gooey center.

Step two, we must decapitate the head of the rotting fish who would either tacitly or overtly permit the assault on our small "d" democratic Republic. This is done, not violently, but electorally and legally. Holding the leader of a radicalized cult responsible for the flock's behavior won't arrest the disease, but it will help to delegitimize the movement and drive it back where it belongs to the radical fringe. No Bully Pulpit credibility, no acquiescence from a subservient political party, no statist media echo chamber to anoint this as anything but madness. On January 20, 2021, we assume the first part of this solution will be enacted. Thereafter, when Trump's immunity from prosecution on the basis of OLC guidance ends, we are already aware of several factions waiting in line to litigate against him civilly and criminally.

Step three, we must always strive to stash away the social anarchists among us in dark places where they exert little to no influence on polite society, and where they can be easily sniffed out by law enforcement when necessary. This was once much harder, but now can happen simply by stepping out of their way as they naturally gravitate toward places that coddle subversive impulses. In recent years, the Deplorables have raged against a "Deep State" that would do anything to suppress their movement, and most media are seen as the face of this resistance. The "mainstream media" has become like Kryptonite to people who just can't handle the truth anymore. Even Fox News itself, long a basic food group for Deplorables seeking escapism, has now been ostracized by the tribe. In the aftermath of the 2020 election, in which Fox dared to call the results when the results were evident, and not when a story could be concocted that better aligned with their candidate's baseless allegations, they committed an unpardonable sin in the estimation of this clan. In its place, Newsmax and the OAN networks have emerged as more resilient Rightwing prevaricators, and ratings for each have trebled as a result. Indeed, each of these networks resisted calling the outcome of the 2020 election for well over a month, finally relenting, when doing otherwise, would look purely conspiratorial. Let the Deplorables march unencumbered toward this mecca for the misinformed and maladapted. Every moment spent trying to channel them into more socially acceptable venues is a moment you can't get back and will cause only twice as much backlash. For even the Kumbaya obsessed, just let them live in infamy elsewhere.

As modern media has splintered into an endless number of special interest niches, many of which are purely indecent, those who fear and loathe the mainstream will be ministered to by a recognizable set of agitators and charlatans seeking to exploit counter decency. We want to stash the social anarchists there, not because we are against free speech, but because they won't stop shouting "fire" in the crowded public square. It is better that these alarmist messages echo among the likeminded than escape to pollute our children's impressionable minds. Hopefully, as the crazy ricochets so wildly among the faithful here, they will all drive themselves to madness. Within these destructive echo chambers, we can easily identify those who must be sanctioned for their dangerous incivility and violent tendencies. We can also more easily identify opinion leaders from the group who may be a disproportionate threat. These will be the agitators creating the discussion threads and inciting violent opposition, not the sheep following them with wild eyed affirmations.

What is, and is not, protected speech has only become more complicated in the age of user generated Social Media. Do "citizen journalists" have any responsibilities at all when publishing content that is dangerous and misleading? If you are my age, and you remember the truth in advertising dilemmas of the 70s and 80s, you couldn't help but feel corporate interests bear some responsibility and that consumer protection legislation should reflect that responsibility. It was purely unconscionable what tobacco and large chemical interests foisted on an unsuspecting public. But does the average Joe share that responsibility to society when all we want from Facebook is affirmation that "*doggone it, people like me.*"?

Aside from blatant harmful exploitation, do even the Social media platform owners themselves bear any further social responsibility? The relative merit of freedom of expression versus social responsibility is tending to neatly divide commendable and deplorable people. One side naturally understands the responsibility we all should share in polite society to be accurate and truthful with all publicly relevant reporting. The other side finds pleasure in doing the exact opposite. Commendables seek to win over their opposition and build consensus whenever possible. Deplorables seek to confuse and destroy their opposition; finding consensus, on even mundane matters, seems ill advised and threatening. One side uses persuasion as a tool; the other side uses it as a weapon. Commendables understand there is real danger lurking in the kinds of purely inflammatory lies the Deplorables use willingly to achieve social dominance. As unpopular as this sentiment is, I generally think it has become best if we agree to disagree and steer completely away from each other on social media. I would advise you to leave 4 Chan, 8 Chan, Parlor and Gab, which all hide behind their promise of unfettered freedom of speech, to anarchists seeking anonymity for the crimes against society they plot online

Clearly, social media has failed its original intent to bring us all together and is now actually a new lever used to pry us apart over any number of inconsequential ways we differ in beliefs and social mores. But what about politics, which should be more burdened by the goal of promoting domestic tranquility? For years, it seemed we were moving slowly but reliably toward a defined center which worked more or less equally for all. But now, modern politics has become unbearably polarized. The flashpoint seemed to be how our people responded to the election of our first black president in 2007. It was the first time we were tested by the theory that we as a nation had become color blind. Slightly over half of us passed the test, but, slightly under half failed miserably to accept any challenge to the normalcy of white privilege or even white supremacy in America. For many this was little more than an amorphous tingle that something was slightly amiss. For others, it became a personal affront to the racial caste system they always imagined should exist in "their America." It is toward this more resentful constituency that opportunistic politicians anew have sought to exploit the endemic fear and hatred. Moreover, they encouraged a new counter decency movement that helped draw the lines between sides more indelibly. Commendable people are aghast at how an entire political party has allowed its most recent standard bearer to cater almost exclusively to white malcontents, and inspire truly dangerous anarchists along the way.

20

Trump represents circumstantial evidence for human life without conscience or gray matter, but he is not central to the plot. He'll make frequent walk-ons, but mostly as an excuse to ridicule his heinous cultists for whom he'd become an unlikely Svengali figure. Trump is the original "empty barrel," absent any principled ideology. He is a shape shifter, entirely malleable, and a cunning manipulator as his ambitions require. He is a mindless predator who will mercilessly destroy opponents without conscience to suborn his own lawless pursuit of riches. As a hopeless narcissist, with a bottomless need for adulation and self-aggrandizement, he is the perfect wiki node for "useful idiot." Without so much as a blush, he will collaborate with malign interests, both foreign and domestic, on a wink and an eight figure check and will leave the consequences for others to launder. We wonder, as we acknowledge these things so easily, how so many others among us can look at these same facts, not as sure signs of a defective product that is quite harmful when used as directed, but instead, as positive features of a product most useful for the times we live in. To me, this would be like buying a vicious Rottweiler you found gnawing on a Toy Poodle at the pound to bring home to your baby girl, and expecting good things to come of it. We also wonder what forces allow those who have seen this show for years, to disregard all semblance of critical thinking for populist hero worship. For some people, maybe the precarious times we live in require moral and spiritual subjugation to a ruthless father figure who will keep all of the scary threats at bay as long as we promise to always love him very much. Maybe they are just envious of the "Teflon Don" for doing whatever he pleases, whenever he pleases, and facing no consequences. There is a certain rugged American appeal for figures we imagine are simply superior to mere mortals like ourselves.

Perhaps we feel they should lord over the rest of us with complete impunity. Surely we all knew just as clearly in 2015 where this would lead by 2020, right? Anyone with even a casual acquaintance with the world around them must have realized everything that would happen over the next four years was inevitable. That this would end with death and destruction. What type of person, with what type of personality disorder and confused belief system would take that leap and never stop to question the abyss below no matter what happened on the way down? Yes, we are talking about deeply flawed human beings, precious few of whom are redeemable in any way I can imagine.

This is a good time to make an important caveat. I don't want what follows to devolve into a politically correct screed that imagines racism lurking behind any and all of our nation's shortcomings. A message like that delivered by a middle aged successful white male will rightfully seem contrived. Let's agree to focus exclusively on those who have used racial divisiveness as a weapon to achieve social dominance and would use all manner of violent retribution to achieve their ends. We are buoyed in this perspective by the indisputable fact that our own FBI has identified rightwing extremists and White Supremacists as the premier threats against our homeland and have begged for years for laws and policies that could help them contain the damage. Regretfully, a failure of imagination in this society has led most of us to ignore a storm that has gathered for years in plain sight. Like so many other things, we have lacked the political and social will to accept our greatest challenge. At times, we will laugh out loud at the Deplorables' ludicrous belief systems and commitment to unhinged conspiracy theories. At other times, we will look with total sobriety at the panoply of their dangerous behavior. In either case, we aim to undermine the

Deplorable movement before it latches itself to our majority, silent or otherwise.

The villains in this story are the millions of lost souls, racked by immeasurable rage against the American principles of equality and tolerance for all, who used Trump as an avatar for the face of their counter decency movement. The leader's place at the bully pulpit provided a thin schmear of respectful cover that coaxed them from hiding, but otherwise never changed the terms of their enduring struggle against "others" for whom they have nothing but antipathy. For them, Trump served as a construct for better organizing their rage and directing it at a half dozen convenient targets for their deep disaffections. However, this has progressed to a point that, with or without our 45th president at the helm, all of the psychopathologies and general malcontent will continue to remain as destructive as ever.

Trump's legacy is simply a cringe worthy reality docudrama that perfectly captured the stench rising up from the very dregs of our society. These bottom feeders and misfits who, until recently, had the courtesy to live in the dank spaces beneath our refrigerators with the other cockroaches, now feel emboldened to find the light of day again. As a country we fought for hundreds of years to render these gruesome creatures a harmless curiosity, but now they feel they deserve to walk among us again. Hell, they even refer to themselves as the "Silent majority" to burnish their tarnished street cred.

As US history has surely leaned forward toward a more perfect union, with equal opportunity and justice for all, the Deplorables have been a gale force headwind. For the entirety of our nation's history they have weaponized the abstract concept of race, for strategic social and political advantage, by linking it with the skin color of culturally disparate peoples. Until the late 1700s, when an enterprising slave holder, convinced other enterprising slave holders to divide their indentured workforce on the basis of skin color against rebellion, the idea that black and brown folks were inherently inferior didn't exist. Indeed, it was the fear of an Oreo insurrection from the collective violent bargaining of poor European whities and African darkies that provided the original inspiration for racism. Until then, privilege was predicated strictly on having or not having property and wealth, not on being or not being white. By bestializing the black man, the idea that hatred between the pasty and pigmented was righteous, became inviolable for many. Today, for many, we can't separate this inglorious pairing of virtue from race with an atom splitter. Nothing galvanizes the Deplorables more than opining about the general superiority of the white man's response to our nation's woes and how black folks in general respond like criminal thugs to the same stimuli. It represents a thoroughly deplorable lack of empathy but is hardly a new bug. When has a plurality of whites in America ever been comfortable with the uprising of angry minorities and not sought to quell protests in the public square before they gain broader mainstream credibility? Hell, they surveilled and then killed Martin Luther King Jr. over such "radicalism." In their estimation, it is never the right time or the right place for blacks in America to petition their government for any redress of grievances. Indeed, they don't even accept the basic terms of the grievances themselves. By their reckoning, there is an inviolable caste system in this country which must be protected by law enforcement, our military and our court system. When any of these vital institutions refuse to veer, even marginally, from the ideal of equal protection, the Deplorables blame liberalism for encouraging a false sense of entitlement. In response, a

24

breathless call for civil war rises from the ashes of their defeat. Unlike other creatures on the planet, which imagine themselves of only one race, social anarchists within the human race have the unique capacity to imagine that all are not from the same seed of civilization and will always aim to divide and conquer on that basis.

So why flog this old mare about original racist sin so hard, especially in our post racial present? I'll leave the hobgoblinism of the post racial meme aside for now and focus on why "otherism" is foundational for the Deplorables. You simply cannot understand what makes these creatures tick until you realize everything for them is about in-group superiority and their fear of marginalization. Simply put, they are hard wired for white power. Being white and Christian and male dominated are table stakes they expect to be spotted from birth. "I realize I am a miserable failure in life, that I have no discernable skills, the education of a 12 year old, have made poor life choices since kindergarten, am enthusiastically stupid, am equipped with only three functioning teeth and smell like rancid vinegar, but by gum, I am better than anyone darker than sand." For them, the "superiority" of white Europeans over black Africans was not just circumstantially pragmatic, it was axiomatic. They adopted a rigid code of magical thinking to convince themselves there were obvious biological and theological bases for their unearned privilege. For them, it was ordained as the natural order of things that no matter how unintelligent, how unsuccessful, how uneducated they were, they still were superior to people of color. Though the number of white folks riddled with this cancer has dwindled significantly over the centuries, these cultural dissidents still represent a highly coveted constituency for politicians, and surely are the clearest threat to our country's noble mission.

25

Spoiler alert, not all Trump voters are created equal. It is true that not all of those who voted for Trump are vicious sociopaths drunk on white power, but all of the domestic terrorists who have total antipathy for "others" surrendered their souls to the petulant Man Baby in Chief. There's a decent slice of party voters who are not awful, even if their choice in leaders is atrocious. These are not the folks whose agenda we fear. Our focus in on the Deplorables, those who have desecrated the very idea of Making America Great by expressing how vile they are at White Power MAGA rituals. No matter how broad this MAGA crowd claims their agenda is, this whole Trump wave is based on one thing only, the supremacy of, and perceived threats against, white Christian identity in America. The alternative truth, as Kellyanne Conway might dub it, is a canard that most home schooled fifth graders have already taken a hard pass on. No, Trump is not the anointed one for Deplorables because of his mad business skills or his independence from the evil machinations of swampy elites in favor of the common man. And it was not for the delectable gooey center of his moral convictions, or his commitment to family values that he was elevated. No, the Donald won over the Deplorables because he mobilized the vote among a remarkably large number of "white victims" thrilled with how he pledged to shit all over the same marginalized people they would if they had power. For the Donald, this is performance art; for his disciples, it is oxygen.

Life for the Deplorables is a zero sum game that neatly separates winners from losers. The American pie is one fixed size that does not fit all. Social imagination and diplomacy be damned when rivals must vie for a bounty that simply cannot be shared equitably. Losing became more self-evident for these pariahs with each tick we made toward equal rights and opportunities for all. Surely, they imagined, progress made by any rival tribe would come at their equal and opposite expense, and so they grappled with society at large, like a sweaty game of tug of war, to drag America back from the tolerant abyss. At the limbic level, they realized they were indeed inferior, not superior combatants, and therefore were terrified of becoming as marginalized as their imagined replacements if forced to play by the same rules. The Tiki Torch brigade in Charlottesville revealed the full Monty on this with their "Jews will not replace us" genocidal grievance chants. Clearly for White Supremacists, "Jews" may be replaced with any number of other non-white or non-Christian nouns for equal effect. So, the Deplorables became increasingly unnerved by how precarious their circumstances had become in an increasingly diverse and tolerant country. The last thing these "competitors" wanted was a level playing field, and the idea of a tide lifting all boats made them vomit a little bit in their mouths. It is all the hyperbolic drama around the threat to white supremacy in the US that has always given these soulless monsters agita. For them, Barack HUSSEIN Obama was like a ball peen hammer blow to the amygdala, triggering their fight or flight response and leaving them dizzy and confused. To regain stasis, they added the first African American president to the tippy top of their list of existential threats which must be neutralized at all costs to restore natural order. Because this struggle was life or white genocide for them, they carried out their mission with no civilized rules of engagement. On one end of this spectrum was the joy of wallowing in hate and outrage porn on social media 24/7, garbage in, irradiated garbage out. On the other end, an actual desire, and a few half-baked plots, to eliminate the threat(s) with extreme violent prejudice.

Most of us remained detached or just moderately amused for years, watching how far down strange rabbit holes the Deplorables would plunge themselves without rhyme or reason, instead of grasping the gathering threat such mass hallucination could unleash. Perhaps this came from how irreconcilable the Deplorable's world view, and the psychopathologies driving it, were with our sense of normalcy. Even the commendable struggle with empathy when the subject matter is so convoluted. Perhaps it came simply from complacency or the politically correct notion of false equivalency. However it came to be, it is time to wake from our sleepy dreamy slumber and mobilize as our rivals are already awake and very active.

Chapter Two

Facebook Fun

"There are many things of which a wise man might wish to be ignorant"

Ralph Waldo Emerson

I was a very late Facebook adopter. In fact, it was actually the Deplorables that drove me to make my first regular appearances only 11 years ago. After a few years of semiannual visits to discover which of the juvenile delinquents I ran with back in the day were either dead or in prison, I stumbled upon a post from one of my few Facebook "friends" that I simply couldn't resist responding to. Apparently Christians believed that the then recently elected president, Barack HUSSEIN Obama, was the Antichrist and heralded the coming Apocalypse. And to think I believed he was just a one term Democratic Senator from Illinois who won the 2007 presidential election.

My friend demurred by inquiring simply "Do you believe...?" as in, I'm not sure I do, but maybe others may look at dumbfukery less skeptically, especially if it provides the only explanation for why their children haven't called them since 1992 though they live only 3 doors down. It was the very first response to this tease that caught my eye. "If Barack Hussein Obama is Mabus, or the Antichrist himself, as predicted by Nostradamus hundreds of years ago, shouldn't he be hanged?" He actually wrote "hung" but why quibble over grammar with a poster who would put a bullet through my head just for mentioning it? Plus, five other words were butchered anyway. Talk about a religious experience! At this point, the discussion thread had amassed over 4000 comments, and this gentleman collected 360 likes for cheerleading the hanging of a sitting president. So that happened, and not under extreme duress in a police interrogation room either. Maybe I am a glutton for punishment but, in that moment, I had to determine if the participants knew their comments were actually visible. A few immediate questions occurred to me. Who was this "Christian"? Was he a danger to himself and others? Was he riddled with drug induced PTSD? Would the authorities soon be battering open the door to his double wide trailer? Once inside, would they find 1000 pounds of fertilizer, 150 AK 47s, 10,000 rounds of ammo, and a hairless cat in a Christmas vest? I was so blown away by the anti-social carnage of his comment, I forgot how hundreds of likeminded lepers had already high fived him for this hate smut. Immediately overcome with morbid curiosity, like from following an 80 year old man in yoga pants and a fedora through an Alabama Walmart, I began picking through the wreckage that followed. Certainly, this comment was the proverbial red headed step child, and every other post would be iced tea, hopscotch and poodle skirts, right? Next, a helpful middle aged white lady from Ashtabula reminded us that *Revelations* told of the Antichrist being a leopard descended from Nimrod and born in Kenya. "Obama was born in Kenya" offered the next 3 posters within seconds of each other followed by two "Amens." Slowly, others joined in to piece together

30

the story, as they had understood it, from a sketchy email they all happened to receive but failed to question why. The anti-Christ will be a man, in his 40s, of MUSLIM descent, who will deceive the nations with persuasive language, and have a MASSIVE Christ-like appeal. He will promise false hope and world peace, and when he is in power, he will destroy everything. Is it OBAMA? Yes it is Obama." "Obama." "Obama." "Barack HUSSEIN Obama" followed by a few more "Hang him"(s) and "Amens." After absorbing this moving gospel, I offered a playful quip; "How do you know the antichrist isn't really Foghorn Leghorn just pretending to be Obama?" Apparently, my fellow posters resented the levity I brought to this weighty existential matter as they began pelting me with baseless accusations of crimes I allegedly committed against humanity including pedophilia, terrorism and worst of all, being a libtard! One pleasant lady even said this: "Oh shut up, you are coming back as an illegal and hope they find you soon. Get the F off of this page if you don't support it." Yes, she actually attacked me for not supporting the idea that we should hang the sitting president of the US for being the Antichrist!!

Another alert poster pointed out Obama's uncanny resemblance to a Zulu witch doctor and illustrated this with a picture in case we weren't clear on the reference. On cue, several folks dropped heart like emojis in celebration. Now, in fairness, maybe these outwardly aggressive comments were not racist at all. I mean, when I inquired, they were quick to point out how only the libtards played the race card for every little thing, and that any real racism was hate directed at the white man or the Christians these days. Then they told me to go fuck myself so I am sure I was just being a little too sensitive. Welcome to the cesspool where the dregs of society, the misfits and the bottom feeding degenerates come to wallow in outrage and hate porn. Some onlookers might have fled from this freak show in horror, or phoned the authorities at least. Not me, I was reeled in like a guppy on a 100# steel braided test line. I am a sucker for a dumpster fire.

Being gob smacked like that by such blind rage and hate was a little disconcerting for this mild mannered Middle-American suburbanite, but the social scientist and sadomasochist in me was hooked. The comments were hazmat for sure, but what of the creatures who oozed this toxic waste so unapologetically? Were they unwitting victims of their social environment, or were they actively and willfully creating their own unhinged reality? Along my journey, I had to trash my first thesis that they were simply empty receptacles strategically injected with an outrage virus bomb by their intellectual superiors for political gain. Certainly, cunning rightwing talking heads staked their eight figure empires on mobilizing reliably awful people for influence and huge ratings. But this gunk also appeared to be pretty foundational for them like reading, writing and 'rithmatic. There is an absolute wasteland of pseudo intellectual rightwing goo vying to impregnate impressionable, small, and hateful minds. And, there is endless tin foil-hat-wearing conspiracy activating the circulatory system of this body politic. But, there is innate evil lurking there, too. The question is, would the barely literate and bigoted among us simply open a perfectly good vein and mainline this with uncritical abandon, or must they be inherently flawed children of a lesser God? Maybe they were thalidomide babies who ultimately succumbed to a host of psychological personality disorders. Perhaps they were the tragic result of a genetic experiment gone horribly wrong. Chicken or egg? I came to learn all of this is likely at play and has created a positively electric feedback loop. And nothing lubricates this supercharged track slicker than the fragility of white identity.

Years later, as I viewed the Deplorables through the lens of their cult hero, Donald J. Trump, much of this became better contextualized for me. Unlike their new de facto leader for whom performance art was about building the image of a predator, the Deplorables had nothing tangible to gain from publically flaunting their loathsomeness. They came by their awfulness naturally. When the Donald spoke to their very souls by baselessly accusing the 44th president of the US of secretly being a Muslim born terrorist and illegitimate holder of the office, the cult leader knew what the cult did not. That it was pure bullshit. Indeed, the Deplorables believed exactly what they wanted to believe, not for personal aggrandizement, but because it was deep in their genes to regard the very idea of a black president as something threateningly evil. As such, long after Trump admitted Obama was born in America, debates still raged in rightwing chatrooms about the fraud of Obama's birth certificate and how his Muslim ancestry surely made him a terrorist sympathizer, or terrorist himself. We live in a purely vulgar age, and no one channels the vapid and vulgar imaginations of the perpetually outraged like Donald J. Trump. But it is the willful ignorance of those consumed with amorphous rage over lost privilege that has perpetuated so many vicious fictions that will long outlive Trump's leadership.

Another lie the Deplorables feasted upon, courtesy of Trump, was the notion that brown immigrants, Mexicans specifically, meant them both physical and economic harm. They were rapists and murderers who wanted to suck up all of our tax dollars and social entitlements. We certainly would have no way of sussing out Trump's true feelings on this matter, but we know the Deplorables only approve of legal white immigrants for whom they feel they have far more in common with and assume don't want our riches. Immigrants, illegally here or otherwise, from Central and South America are scary brown people who want to invade our nation and take by force what the white man has earned. For political correctness the Deplorables will insist they only oppose "illegals" but then will show 100% support for general anti-immigration legislation that has made legal immigration and asylum a living nightmare. Clearly, they believe in white supremacy and essentially excising from our country all people of color before building an impenetrable fortress locking "others" out permanently. Is it really unfair to simply call this out for what it is? The Deplorables willfully and unapologetically have remained outnumbered on the wrong side of history since the days of Jim Crow. Even facing growing opposition for years, they remained irredeemable no matter how uncomfortable that became. They may have become bolder in the age of Trump to admit their bigotries, but their disease didn't just magically metastasize when Trump assumed significance in their lives. We only blame their opportunistic hero for mining their endemic hate and outrage to divide and conquer the country for his own enrichment. This cancer is not going into remission any time soon.

After a month or so of having heated exchanges with the Deplorables wherever I encountered them on social media, and getting my ass handed to me regularly, I resolved to develop more of a game plan. I learned a few tricks from the few reliable liberal trolls I met. First, I realized that if I really wanted to gain insights from a hostile hive, I needed to establish more than one online identity. Scrumming with my diametrically opposed foes, was personally amusing, but I was getting constantly dinged by cowardly opponents and receiving Facebook jail time for my troubles. You can hardly win against rivals who make you take a month long seat on the bench whenever you've scored more points than they in battle, and they can convince the community standards police you were spamming or being unacceptably rude. For more staying power, I engineered 3 additional aliases with corresponding avatars thanks to a creepy AI generated website called Thispersondoesnotexist.com and some basic stagecraft. My four identities were pretty similar philosophically, and politically, but at least I could always have a round in the chamber as my alter egos fell in battle.

I also learned about metrics, particularly those available on Facebook. At first I was a bit Jell-O and pudding about "likes" and "shares" and "emojis" and mostly just aimed at discussions with the highest numbers of comments accumulated. The sheer number of comments a discussion attracted was a good indication of how passionately the commenters felt about the topic, and so I generally threw myself into those with big boy numbers. If I took note of how long ago the thread was launched, I could get an even better bead on enthusiasm; the higher the velocity, the more passion, leading to an intimate understanding of abiding themes the participants embraced. When a topic gained a thousand comments in less than an hour, I felt I found a main artery to troll. The final set of metrics, the likes, shares, and types of emojis used for likes was pay dirt. An experience I had a couple years ago on the Sean Hannity Facebook page I frequented is a good way to illustrate these tools in action. It was the 50th anniversary of the assassination of Dr. Martin Luther King Jr., and Sean Hannity's staff felt it was appropriate to launch a thread so fans could pay their respects. The thread stayed up for 3 days and gathered a sum total of 412 comments, 645 likes of various emoji types, and exactly 31 shares. To put that in perspective, a Facebook page frequented by well over 3 million users, routinely generates thousands of comments with tens of thousands of likes within a 24 hour period for topics embraced by posters. Because the premise was to pay respects to the civil rights icon, one would assume the 412 comments would reflect strictly heartfelt tributes and fond memories. In fact, of the 412 comments, only half were of this variety, while the other half were snarky; "MLK would roll over in his grave over Obama's racism" posts. More of the thumbs up and heart emojis were tagged to the snark than to the respects paid. During the 3 days this thread lived and breathed, the Hannity crew launched several other threads all seeking to have fans opine about black and brown folks "behaving badly." Within hours, each dwarfed the MLK tribute by a factor of 5X. At the risk of over generalizing, this amateur anthropologist concluded that the Hannity tribe just wasn't that into the good Dr. King. And, even more obvious, they loved to wallow in outrage over the conduct of "others," particularly black and brown others.

In time, I developed my own metric. It was not the most scientific, but it amused me like no other. I called it the awkward pause. If I joined the Deplorables in full melt down mode online and timed an irreverent truth MOAB response just right, I could produce a cringe-worthy pause in the festivities. Once you realize how the conformity of opinion along very narrow parameters creates its own predictable rhythm, it's easy to create a collective synaptic misfire by simply speaking truth to the power of dumbfukery. I would sense a preponderance of agreement among the clan, often expressed in a cacophony of "Amens" and "Bingos!" about some unquestioned Deplorable alternate truth, and simply break the spell with a true

36

statement and a citation from a neutral news source. The neutrality of the journalistic reference was important to ward off an immediate "fake news" retaliation. But, when you force non thinkers to think, you can create an excruciating vacuum they will need time to fill. A good metaphor is troops needing to reload after a devastating attack has left them scrambling and exposed. I imagine in those moments a hundred hapless contributors pausing to say "why I oughta'..." before accepting how the rhetorical cupboard is bare. I would simply compare the time it took for the very next snide comment to how rapidly comments were made before I rocked their Casbah. After a few juvenile retorts, eventually some brave soul would step forward to restore order with his own hyper partisan citation. The best examples were times I forced a complete shutdown of discussions that were fast and furiously collecting comments, likes and shares for hours before. In those cases, I could measure the devastation by simply noting the number of frowny face emojis they left me on their way out.

One week, another of my alter egos joined an AOC hit and run in progress on Hannity to slime the freshman lawmaker for her "radical Socialist agenda." Nothing seems to terrify the Deplorables like the threat of becoming Venezuela because, of course, our country like Venezuela, has seized control of our largest corporate entities for state run hegemony. Oh wait, never mind, I just Googled to find how Amazon is still owned by Jeff Bezos and Facebook by Mark Zuckerberg and all of the rest of our economic lynchpins seem to be owned and operated by Wall Street investors. Gosh, even Google is owned by Google it turns out! Hell, I even found out how the wealth from those companies is equitably split on a 99 to 1 percent basis between the owners and the workers, making it clear that laborers are fully in control over the means of production in this country. But how can capitalism survive on the basis of the minor detail that our currency is the reserve currency for the entire world? Not very comforting considering how George Soros wants to create a New World Order, and a United States that becomes Venezuela is instrumental in that pursuit. Yes, our resemblance to today's Venezuela is uncanny indeed. And George Soros is truly omnipotent. Anyway, within this mess about the Congresswomen's general Green New Deal, was a relatively minor bit on reparations. I guess this looney radical had the audacity to conclude we should at long last consider if it's possible to make good on our promise for handing over 40 acres and a mule to people we said we would hand over 40 acres and a mule to after the awfulness of slavery was litigated in the Civil War. Surprise, this notion threw pasty faced white victims into massive hissy fits.

A particularly aggrieved poster, from Titusville, FL, seemed to strike the prevailing chord when he offered this opening thought: "I have ancestors that died in the Civil War fighting to free slaves....I want her and her followers to pay me reparations." In only 12 hours, Chris H. was already staked to 1300 likes for this effort to rewrite history. In response, my Facebook avatar dared to suggest that the brave Union fighters, many of whom were in fact slaves gambling on a prayer for freedom, actually were ordered to turn back a secession movement of the traitorous Southern states to "save the Union" more than to make a principled stand against slavery. In fairness, I only based that theory on what motives have prevailed among American soldiers in every combat mission in our country's history, so maybe I was wrong in this case. I mean really, is there any chance we invaded and occupied Iraq in 2003 for any reason other than to liberate the oppressed Iraqi people? Also, it was odd that he seemed to want to frame this as a purely selfless labor of love, but retroactively make it a mercenary mission instead, and still receive credit for his ancestor's gift to humanity. An attentive lady from Lenett Alabama summed it up this way: "We as whites need reparations because my ancestors helped free the slaves... but didn't own any!" Not to nitpick, my alter ego responded, but doesn't that statement prove my point about why the Union soldiers fought? In fairness, I am sure, her complaint was animated by the decades of systemic disadvantage her race has dealt with since the late 1860s. Surely, she should be made whole for the wealth and equality gap white Americans have struggled against since the Civil War. "Typical libtard white guilt," she replied. Likening today's "blacks" to kidnappers who would never be satisfied with the ransom paid, DWM said "If reparations were paid, they would always want more." Finally, to gift wrap the whole caboodle, KD warned "No protected class for you, only genocide in the end." Perception is funny. Where all of these agitated posters found great comfort in the "heroism" of their ancestors in beating back the scourge of slavery, I found baseless excuses for people who simply had antipathy for an entire race that was not their own. I resisted the urge to say I bet they would own people of color today if they could. But, because that is not legal, they would be satisfied if only we could drive all of the "others" they object to out of the country and then maybe build a big wall around white America. Just spit balling.

Inquisitive readers might wonder why I trolled Hannity so relentlessly in the early years. Others may ask, why troll "Conservative" social media at all if you are so virulently opposed the messaging that festered there daily. The second question is easier to answer. I believe in the adage about "*keeping your enemies close.*" But why keep such a vigilant eye on the Hannity Facebook page specifically? Studying the intrinsic hate of this species in its natural habitat would be as easy as getting laid at an all-women's prison with a handful of pardons if I simply entered the worm hole that is InfoWars or The Daily Stormer (until it shut down). But, I needed to keep tabs on what I imagined were the least extreme elements of the Deplorable's movement to find out how deep in the genes this disease went. What better way than eavesdropping on those I imagined were the least infected? It is also important to underscore how Deplorablism had been a defective cog in the American machine long before the term was popularized in 2015/2016.

By the time Trump and his opponent began campaigning, I had had eyes on the Deplorables for 6 years, and the whole thing had become as monotonous as power watching Scooby Doo reruns. My early adopter status helped me understand what would surely happen over the next 5 years. The through line glowed with urgency. So, I guess I kind of felt like a counter terrorist officer monitoring subversive anti-American chatter before imminent attacks occurred. When friends suggested I was overstating both the breadth and depth of a noxious modern strain of White Supremacy in America, I could say *"Let's see how this goes."* If all the poison had been relegated exclusively to the fringe, I might have agreed I was being too hyperbolic. But, another even more troubling dimension of the problem, revealed itself in 2015. An unmistakable thread of overheated conspiracy theorizing became visible in the mainstream and was used consistently to construct an entirely new alternative reality that was kinder to counter decency in general. As the Deplorable faithful insisted that what we saw and heard with our own eyes and ears should be regarded as "fake news" that would undermine America, my eyes and ears opened wider than ever. I began to take great interest in the idea of using actual fake news as a counter insurgency tactic for unearthing the conspiratorial roots of the Deplorable's baseless beliefs. Just how much unhinged fantasy could they be talked into if it came from the "right sources"? Certainly, the seeds of massive discontent were being watered regularly, why couldn't I be the constant gardener? My second question was how does this kind of vapid slop achieve such a Kung Fu grip on the new breed of "conservatives?" I am far from an expert on mass hysteria, but assume it is based upon very primal needs of very needy people.

Listen folks, if we want to treat the disease that is beginning to metastasize again within the unhealthy Deplorables, we will need to be ruthlessly honest about what ails them and how the sickness spreads whenever we become complacent. No time for infinitely splitting hairs or being inordinately polite to excuse a wide swath of Deplorables for condemnation on the basis of their degree of sickness. This is not a collegial bunch. Like their de facto cult hero, they will respond to your misplaced passivism with a bare knuckles beat down. Left to their own devices, they will tear to ground every vestige of a civilized America. Current Covid-19 guidance is social distancing and PPE protection, and is partially predicated on the notion that the infected may or may not be visibly symptomatic but may still be carriers. The Deplorable malaise is a little trickier. While steering clear of the infected is wise, and encasing them in an impermeable plastic waste bag very tempting, don't we really need to shine the brightest spotlight down upon them? In fact, shouldn't we encourage them to identify themselves for closer scrutiny so appropriate antigens can be developed and then injected into our society's bloodstream to inoculate the rest of us against the spread of virus?

We must never surrender to the put-on that their movement isn't completely animated by antipathy for non-white, non-Christian "others." We must not assume their numbers are still dwindling in modern times. For every five people insisting White Supremacy in America is a relic, one of them is a White Supremacist and another one or two are happy to benefit from the movement. We witnessed this dynamic during slavery when even the poorest Southern whites, without the wealth to own humans themselves, were thrilled to soak up their elevated status over "inferior" Negroes. Pay attention to the through lines for almost any issue that is aggressively debated between deplorable and commendable people, and you will find the same underlying cancer. The hate and fear cocktail is indeed quite potent. There is no time left for giving the benefit of the doubt to people who have shown us every one of their cards for years.

So, with some trepidation, I wandered into a few of the more radical rightwing platforms with 3 shiny new conservative identities so I could do as the Romans do. As a likeminded soulmate, I could descend, like Colonel Kurtz before me, directly into the heart of darkness. At first I was as awkward as Donald Trump holding a bible, like it was a pitchfork, in front of St. John's Episcopal Church. Thankfully, my new friends were not a cerebral bunch so orientation week was easy peasy. I made fast friends with people desperate to find real community with others as gripped by rage and boundless hate as they were. I quickly learned the painfully simplistic language and the syntax of the few basic themes upon which their entire identities depended. I also gained an awareness for another troubling dimension of their character, a veneer of phony religious and nationalist piety spread thinly over the rage. Was this with the hope of providing respectable cover for a worldview even they realized was strictly counter culture? Indeed, I learned it was, and this provided a pivot point for them to turn any number of vicious fictions into "facts." I took full advantage of their capacity to believe even the most outlandish fairytales served up by malicious propagandists. By injecting my own little fictions, like blood dye, into the Deplorable's circulatory information system, I could see in real time how receptive they were to really subversive ideas; how quickly these ideas moved through the hive. For all my revulsion to the tenets of their faith, I must confess their message discipline was as impressive as any devotion I could imagine. Their own radical jihad lived just below the more placid surface of their public selves. Once an idea gained credibility with the flock, it could not be dislodged by even an earthquake. This is what makes them the ideal conduit for spreading misinformation widely, and foot soldiers for the kind of creeping fascism we used to universally abhor.

In time, I began dropping bread crumbs, tiny fact free fabrications, to lead them into the wilderness. Instead of bowing under the weight of preposterous unhinged satire, they absorbed the lies, and amplified them, as they sought ever more validation for their insider's street cred. For them, I believe, the very fate of humanity was at stake, and their faith that this insider's wisdom would reset the world on its righteous axis was absolute. If only they could decipher the cryptic clues dropped by charismatic charlatans, they could ward off so many domestic threats. They needed a grand unifying theory for their alternate reality, and I obliged. Where rational thought was lacking, and logical syllogism was absent, I supplied random data points to jury rig a more elastic explanation for otherwise manifest causes and effects. For the true believers, opponents weren't acting in contrary ways because they had legitimate differences of opinion, they differed from the Deplorables because they were inherently evil and were summoned

43

from the bowels of hell to bring pestilence down upon God's children. If, by dint of your mainstream upbringing, that statement made you go "*huh?*" I would suggest you read it again. Many things were just too terrifying to fully absorb but became central to the plotline that followed. It was purely fortuitous that the new president was as dedicated to appropriating sheer nonsense to prey upon his supporters' weaknesses as I was to bash them for it. From the biggest most visible bully pulpit on the planet, Donald J. Trump amplified many of the very fabrications I sowed to an adoring audience, and they lapped it up like Kobe Beef.

So, in November of 2017 I dropped this bomb on 4Chan. "Patriots, the end of this nightmare is near at hand, soon Hillary and her satanic Deep State benefactors will be in custody at last for their crimes against our children, Gitmo is about to get very crowded." The prevailing response to this purely fabricated quip was; "Thanks Jesus and Donald Trump for removing these evil pedophiles and cannibals from our midst. Lock them all up and throw away the key, surely they will all burn in hell for their crimes." Just how profoundly deep seated must one's rage against normalcy be to willfully absorb this disturbed fiction as fact? We saw in the aftermath of the Pizzagate dumbfukery just how dangerous these unhinged delusions can get as one confused victim of the conspiracy set out to murder what he imagined were members of Hillary Clinton's inner circle running a child sex trafficking ring from the basement of the Comet Pizzeria in DC. Current advisory from the FBI, that conspiracy theories like this one could fuel "extremist" violence, adds more context to the tinderbox of raw emotions that come from deranged hate and fear. Adding more combustible dry rot to the mix were the talking heads like Alex Jones, with his myriad false flag pronouncements, and Sean Hannity for promoting a Russian Intelligence originated conspiracy alleging the Clinton campaign murdered campaign staffer Seth Rich. Where would all this hyperbole lead?

People already sacked by unimaginable rage, appear powerless to fend off farfetched nonsense as long as it channels their essential grievances and fragile identities. These are society's outcasts and misfits and they represent a legitimate threat to our nation's security. These days the threat is even more elevated as it becomes clear how easily persuadable they are by malign influencers both foreign and domestic. I think we will soon conclude this is a far greater danger to our country than Islamic terrorism. The question is, will we take the same focused nonpartisan approach to solving the problem?

In fairness, I suspect the Deplorables believe, with heart and soul, their struggle against progress and equal opportunity for all is patriotic. After all, most regressive attitudes are easily mistaken by some as "traditional values." Most confrontations with Deplorables devolve into good versus evil standoffs, and they always co-opt the usual symbolic trappings of Americana in their defense. A life of willful ignorance is grand when the entirety of civilization can be dumbed down to a bumper sticker. They simply lack the mature capacity for discernment most people develop by early adulthood. They remain convinced that certain powerful individuals, and even entire organizations, are hell bent on altering the entire conception of America for their own nefarious purposes and to create a totalitarian New World Order that will sap their motherland of it exceptionalism. While most of us imagine American exceptionalism means freedom, liberty, justice for all, and representative democracy, for them, exceptionalism is really a euphemism for exclusion and refers to the rightful supremacy of white Christians over those underserving of the American dream.

Conspiracy theory around the so called New World Order has consistently tweaked the hyperventilated imaginations of militant anti-government rightwing nut jobs. Tragically, in the age of Trump, the number of violent white nationalist, militia and "patriot" groups exploded. Recruitment among them is at a 50 year high. Moreover, NWO fever has gripped fundamentalist Christians too, for their irrational fear of the End Time's emergence of the Antichrist. On either account, this substance is purely incendiary and is leading more frequently to unimaginable carnage perpetrated by disciples. It really must be eliminated from civilized society root and branch before our liberal democracy comes to a catastrophic end. I can't tell you how disturbing it was for me to realize that among my new "friends" lurked many true sociopaths committed to this kind of anarchy with more fervor than Islamic extremist terrorists have for their cause. There is quickly becoming an overpowering lust for violent resolution, and it has seized the mob.

My strategy was to separate from the herd the truly dangerous, reveal their identities, and shame them so they could be neutered by polite society. I also hoped to become a human speed bump that might slow the total indoctrination of sociopaths in training to mitigate the escalating threat. I borrowed and created a few purely fabricated conspiracies as bait.

Chapter Three

Hypocrisy, what hypocrisy?

"If you're gonna be two-faced at least make one of them pretty."

Marilyn Monroe

The Deplorables only demand moral and ethical consistency from their opponents, not from themselves. When it comes to their own compasses, there is no True North, only what is circumstantially useful in the moment to win that moment. In the very next moment, they may find the same argument less useful. As such, you will find them to be avid hypocrites and the most untrustworthy of negotiators. You mustn't expect they will even try to square their deeds with their words because, to do so, means admitting they are wrong sometimes. Deplorables never admit they are wrong. Far better, in their estimation to gaslight opponents whenever possible to shift the burden of accountability. Think rope-a-dope.

2014 was a particularly tumultuous time for this country with respect to race relations. As we were nearing the end of our first African American president's tenure, the chasm between norms and standards for how people were treated on account of their skin color had regressed under the antipathy so many had for Obama and what he represented. This was stunning considering how that moment in history capped decades of substantive progress on civil rights and equal opportunity for our people regardless of their race, religion, sexual orientation or creed. Most progressive thinkers imagined an Obama presidency could only improve upon this progress. We can debate whether the president was culpable for shining a light on the few remaining inequities instead of celebrating the fruits of our better angels, or simply had become an obvious lightening rod for the hate from his detractors gathering potency under his first several years in office. What is harder to debate is how the issue revealed hypocrisy among those most animated by racism in general.

In that year, three high profile cases of police confrontations with unarmed black men ending in homicide sparked nationwide protests. These were marked by extreme tension between protestors and law enforcement for heightened emotions on each side and concerns for the safety of citizens and property. Sometimes things got out of hand, and clashes between the sides broke out, property was destroyed, and even a few injuries resulted. Some would argue this was more a consequence of deliberate decisions in some locales for a more militarized police presence, some argued the protestors were criminal by nature, and behaved in kind. Supporters for the cause of the protests were measured in their response. They acknowledged how mostly things remained peaceful, but regretted that some bad apples escalated tensions through isolated lawless behavior. It is generally believed that anarchists will always glom onto visible protests to sow....wait for it...yes, anarchy. Still supporter's empathy for the issue reminded them how the participants came to this moment with heavy hearts and considerable pent up frustration, and so they assumed some minimal skirmishes would occur and managed to place the few outlying instances in context. Certainly none of the supporters felt the protests could be characterized as riots.

By contrast, the Conservative media framed these events as highly dangerous riots and sought to assign blame to agitators like Black Lives Matter and the general lawless behavior we should expect when people of color petition their government for redress of grievances. For them the medium was exclusively the message. Many white people, it turns out, have always been fearful of agitated blacks and would prefer putting down any congregation of dark faces in the public square summarily rather than judge a cause on its own merits. Surely, some still heard the faint echoes from a Jim Crow past when they simply didn't need to put up with this kind of "radical" behavior. More outrageous was their suggestion that protestors didn't even know what they were protesting and participated only to cause trouble, destroy property, and loot local businesses. Nowhere in their analysis was an intelligent discussion of the issue that drove thousands into the streets in the first place, or any call for empathy for fellow citizens who felt wronged and powerless. The whole spectacle came off as an opportunity to bash black folks for "behaving badly."

As usual, it was within the Rightwing freak-o-sphere where perceived anonymity permitted truly awful people to speak freely about what they witnessed. Among all of the expected admonishments for uppity blacks disrespecting their own communities, aggressively disregarding law enforcement, and generally acting like animals, many expressed truly violent fantasies for how the "rioters" should be treated for their transgressions. Even in the most innocuous of places like the Hannity or Fox News Face Book pages, posters advocated for an aggressive beat down of people pleading for attention to their cause. In response to the protester's anguish, they should be neutralized by tear gas and rubber bullets before they could mobilize and cause more havoc. Quickly, calls for stronger police response went from militant, but non-lethal, to purely lethal. Yes, people actually suggested that to save some businesses from being vandalized by folks protesting the shooting of unarmed black people with impunity by law enforcement, the unarmed protesters should themselves be shot dead or, as one artful poster put it, mowed down by armored riot vehicles to make a point.

All of these glorified violent fantasies are motivated by the same basic view that law enforcement exists solely to protect the white "silent majority" from the inherently lawless thuggish minorities who aim to take what they have earned. The Rightwing spox will dust that basic turd with so much powdered sugar that the majority of Deplorables will gobble it up uncritically. But what of white Christians behaving like lawless thugs? How should law enforcement approach these miscreants? And, must white folks even have to answer for the misdeeds of their brethren?

That same year, 2014, we learned about Cliven Bundy, an unapologetically racist cattle rancher from Nevada. Bundy had been battling with the United States Bureau of Land Management for 21 years over $1million in grazing fees he owed for using federally owned land adjacent to his own. Mr. Bundy believed for some crazy reason, it was unconstitutional for the federal government to own federal land he deemed "public." Neither the Bureau of Land Management nor the District Court of Nevada happened to agree. This 21 year standoff on paper became a standoff in person in March of 2014 when BLM officials and federal law enforcement showed up and began rounding up the offending livestock as collateral for Bundy's unpaid debt. The standoff quickly escalated as heavily armed friends of Bundy, mostly militia nuts, came to protest the seizure and confront the Feds directly. The tense standoff lasted two days, during which, many of the armed protesters took sniper positions along the highway overpass, and various places along the land and in the brush, with law enforcement agents literally trained in their rifle scopes. One photo that went viral was of one of these dudes aiming his long range rifle directly at the BLM base camp.

I vividly remember taking to the Fox News Facebook page expecting to read comments from the reliable law and order crowd excoriating the protesters in this case for so brazenly resisting law enforcement and indeed, even placing them in harm's way over old man Bundy's baseless grievance. After all, unlike the unarmed black folks gathering to protest against police, these guys took their cause to a violent new level by taking up arms against duly sworn officers of the law. This wasn't about a handful of petty crimes committed amidst an otherwise peaceful gathering, this was about creating circumstances that presented a clear and present danger to all involved. It was pure intimidation through an overwhelming show of force without regard to the personal safety of either protesters or officers. Another theme prevalent on Fox is personal responsibility. It was expressed consistently during the protests against police homicides, how people must do as authorities demand or face the consequences. When asked to disperse, these folks had better damn well disperse or it's game on. Certainly Bundy's bunch didn't heed the commands of all those federal agents demanding they drop their weapons and surrender peacefully. Certainly the dispute over which this chaos ensued was pretty inconsequential compared with pleas against police brutality and senseless death.

The comments stunned me. A measured response among them was scarcer than a Deplorable with a library card as not a single one took issue with the essential lawlessness that occurred at the ranch. Indeed, quite the contrary. One after another focused instead on the overreach of the officers and the Federal Government in this particular case. No admonitions about doing as you're told by law enforcement to avoid tragic consequences, no calls for mowing down crazed lawless protesters with extreme prejudice for the threat they represented to lives or property. In their estimation, this risky anti-establishment behavior was completely justified and excusable and Bundy himself, was elevated to hero status for standing up against "oppression." Hell, they even said the Feds' choice to finally stand-down to avoid bloodshed was proof they were in the wrong over the dispute.

As I said, this dispute was relatively inconsequential other than for the danger it posed to life and limb for the immediate participants. I brought it up to simply illustrate the typical hypocrisy of the Deplorables. It was the theme about government tyranny, and the nature of those pushing back hard against it in this case, that spooked me most. There have been several times in our recent history when this same sentiment led to unimaginably violent outcomes.

In 1995 two men, both former US Army soldiers, carried out the bombing of the Alfred P. Murrah Federal Building in Oklahoma City, OK leaving 168 dead. The two had served meritoriously in the Persian Gulf War in 1991 but managed to become increasingly radicalized in the years following over unfounded suspicions of the Clinton administration for overreach, particularly on gun rights. Two events really crystalized their anti-establishment sentiments. First was the shootout between federal agents and militant survivalist Randy Weaver at his cabin in Ruby Ridge ID. Weaver, who had ties to the Aryan Nation, had threatened former president Reagan but was never charged with a crime. In 1989 Weaver was scooped up by the ATF in an illegal firearms sting. After skipping his hearing and taking refuge as a fugitive off the grid with his family at Ruby Ridge, the US Marshall's service planned his apprehension. This would be quite dangerous in light of Weaver's weapons arsenal and virulently anti-establishment leanings. Their first incursion upon the cabin ended in bloodshed as a shootout left Weaver's son Sammy and one of the Marshalls dead. The next day hundreds of US law enforcement and federal agents, led by the FBI, converged upon the cabin to force the surrender of the Weavers and friends holed up inside. Next to die was Weaver's wife Vicki from sniper fire meant for one of the male aggressors. Mercifully a Special Forces soldier arrived on the scene the next day and finally persuaded Weaver to surrender before further blood was shed. For Randy Weaver, his supporters and most especially Timothy McVeigh and Terry Nichols, this incident confirmed their darkest suspicions about the federal government.

In February of 1993, the federal government led by the ATF raided a compound in Waco Texas which was home to the Branch Davidians, a Millennial Christian Sect led by David Koresh. Koresh and his disciples were violating multiple firearms regulations and were to be peacefully apprehended that day. But instead, 4 ATF agents and 6 Davidians were killed during a gun battle that occurred before a cease fire was finally negotiated. 900 more law enforcement officials, including the FBI, showed up and surrounded the compound while 85 Davidians holed up inside for 51 days. On April 19, FBI agents rode two tanks through the front of the building to deposit 400 canisters of tear gas inside with the hope of finally ending the siege. Soon after, several fires were set simultaneously, and some gunshots were heard coming from within. Nine Davidians managed to escape, but the rest, about 76, including 25 children, remained within to perish in the flames.

These two events describe either egregious examples of federal overreach or the tragic consequences of delusional people making bad lawless decisions and paying dearly for them. Whichever explanation is most comfortable for you, they both highlight many troubling parallels with more recent events. Increasingly, people with a certain point of view and with certain deeply held convictions feel under siege by forces beyond their control. Is it a lack of alignment with an evolving reality that provokes such violent backlash, or is it intrinsic hatred for "others", and those who would champion the causes for those others that stokes such pent up hostility? What should we make of the message Timothy McVeigh wore on his T-shirt when apprehended; *"The tree of liberty must be refreshed from time to time with the blood of patriots and tyrants."* Surely Thomas Jefferson was speaking out against rebellion and not in favor of it. Yes, wars must be waged, from time to time, against outside aggressors even at the expense of blood and treasure but never should home grown insurrection be glorified. McVeigh's act of domestic terrorism was essentially the opposite of what Jefferson meant. In fact leading up to that passage of his letter, Jefferson said this; *"The people cannot be all and always well-informed. The part which is wrong will be discontented in proportion to the importance of the facts they misconceive."* However passionate citizens become over internal grievances, remedies other than violent sedition are available in these United States. So, isn't he saying rebellion is more the effect of ignorance than enlightenment? Many of our people today are

54

tragically misinformed or completely ignorant on matters of great importance. Actions motivated by Ignorance, willful or otherwise, never end well. "Patriots," who would lash out in violence against their fellow man from an ignorance about events that confound them are not heroes, they are enemies of the State and must be dealt with accordingly. Surely a tenet of our legal system is that ignorance is no defense.

Mindless destruction springs eternal when those with muddled ideologies champion poorly understood causes. Today, a new version of the conspiracy of "cultural Marxism" has animated the Deplorables to imagine all kinds of multi-cultural threats which don't exist in the real world. All of their disillusionment and resentment from social and cultural misalignment with their times gathers into a vicious knot of pain begging for primal relief. They are literally killing themselves with drugs or handguns or depression when they are not visiting violence upon others. The whole thing is a seething cauldron of fury and violence which used to be checked by a polite society but now flows freely throughout the insulated vulgar spaces they inhabit. The stories are becoming all too familiar. White rightwing fanatics taking up arms against Jews or Muslims or Hispanics as they imagine these groups as threats to their livelihoods or physical safety.

Chapter Four

Divide and Conquer

"Perhaps travel cannot prevent bigotry, but by demonstrating that all peoples cry, laugh, eat, worry, and die, it can introduce the idea that if we try and understand each other, we may even become friends."

Maya Angelou

The Deplorables insisted Barack Hussain Obama set race relations back a generation. Then they watched, willfully oblivious, as their cult hero Donald Trump pulverized the notion that nothing could get any worse. No one could divide an entire country like our 45th president. Stoking culture wars to divide and conquer an unsuspecting nation was the whole zeitgeist of the Trump movement. If you were categorically and philosophically opposed to "others" Trump was your Earth Angel. If you were commendably tethered to the notion of American exceptionalism, you prayed he would soon serve prison time. Obama's mere presence may have amped up racial resentments, but this consequence was a reaction not an intention. It is when racial and social strife became exactly what was intended, that we felt that kind of pre-lightning tingle crawl up our arms. Nothing scratches the itch for Deplorables like the opportunity to wallow in

56

self-righteous condemnation of ideological rivals. For them it's like pounding snowflakes flat with a meat mallet. No opportunity to ever inflict pain seems too excessive. As most in our country were horrified by the naked politics of 45 cleaving to the racial resentments of a malcontented minority to hold his office, and further enrich himself, millions of Deplorables were as committed as ever to the cause of white supremacy. While much of the racial unrest toward the end of Obama's second term tweaked the conscience of America, nothing overtly systemic took root with regard to how we would treat our more vulnerable citizens moving forward. It wasn't until late March of 2020 when a truly horrendous incident galvanized a spirit, which existed only for the most committed equal rights advocates among us, and created a majority movement.

On the evening of March 25 2020, a black man named George Floyd was apprehended by Minneapolis police for allegedly passing a counterfeit $20. As they handcuffed him and pulled him from his vehicle and threw him aggressively onto the pavement, one of four officers on the scene knelt upon Floyd's neck to subdue him. Horrified by how violent this apprehension quickly became, onlookers filmed the next 10 minutes of the encounter. As a thoroughly incapacitated suspect lay face down on the ground and handcuffed from behind his back, the suspect began pleading with the officer that he could not breathe. Onlookers protested; one of the other 3 officers protested too, but still, Officer Derek Chauvin was unmoved and continued to choke the life out of Mr. Floyd from his knee firmly pressing against the suspect's neck. As Floyd continued to beg for his life, even crying out for his mother, he soon was rendered unconscious from the ultimately lethal deprivation of oxygen. The sheer depravity of this officer's willful disregard for the life of George

Floyd, captured on cameras, was somehow a rawer portrait of the inhumanity of our times than anything we'd seen before. I have no doubt that this vulgar moment echoed with so many other incivilities of Trump's America that a greater sense of urgency welled up among the Commendables that enough was finally enough! Sadly, even now, in our country it still takes the consent of the white majority to define right and wrong before the legitimacy of any given cause can gain currency. However, this little slice of pure wretchedness captured the majority of our people white, back and otherwise in a sea change that would wash across the country and indeed across the entire world. When millions of all races and creeds took to the streets to protest, I prayed we were finally turning the tide against the Deplorables for good.

When it is said, "black lives matter," most of us are aware of the hidden "too" dangling from the end of that statement. No decent person believes anyone's life is not precious. But, we say it that way because it often seems less than obvious when compared with our society's reverence for white lives. So, it is a distinction we make for added urgency when so many black lives are snuffed out with what appears to be depraved indifference. It is that truth that makes the knee jerk reaction "all lives matter" or "blue lives matter" seem callously indifferent. Imagine if we were talking about a Christian living in a predominantly Muslim country and it was said of this person "Christian lives matter" would anyone really take umbrage? Would we really think the unstated "too" was necessary to articulate the point? Isn't it true that by immediately responding "all lives matter" we are indeed undermining the very premise of the statement? Is this kind of nuanced understanding beyond the reckoning of the Deplorables? The ignorance often seems willful, like so much of what Deplorables do for effect, as if maybe this could "trigger" the more enlightened among us to be offended, and therefore offer them smug self-satisfaction.

That kind of "Whitesplaining" is irritating but not overly consequential. However, what happens when the Deplorables offer tortured explanations for why a particular black life really doesn't matter? How do we square their assessment that "all lives matter" with the litany of reasons a particular "thug's" life does not? From every account in recent memory of an unarmed black man either gunned down or beaten or choked to death by rogue members of law enforcement, the Deplorables respond as if a reward depended upon it, how this person's criminal past, or aggressive behavior in the present, justifies and excuses the outcome and holds harmless the officers responsible. Blue lives always matter more when they are protecting white America from those deemed inherently lawless. Law enforcement overreach could apply only if violence wasn't endemic to the black man. At will, Deplorables are able to dehumanize the victim and therefore feel zero empathy for him and/or his cause. The circumstances of a troubling encounter fade quickly when rationalizations are applied. Often a preponderance of even civilized people remain neutral until the results of an investigation or trial are known. But how can real justice exist when Deplorables insist Lady Liberty remove her blindfold? Even when a tipping point is reached, and most observers conclude an injustice has occurred, 100% of all Deplorables remain overwhelmingly unsympathetic to the dead black man. And yet they say "all lives matter." Is it a leap of faith to conclude that these people simply don't believe all men are created equal?

So, when they are done trashing a black victim for his past transgressions or his present resistance to the thin blue line, the arguments Deplorable's make become even more tenuous. Surely the relative infrequency of blue on black violence pales by comparison with black on black crime of all stripes, right? There is no question that more white people in America are shot and killed by police anyway, right? Surely more brown faces are in prison for violent crime than white faces, right? These facts can be explained without resorting to ill-fitting Straw Man arguments, and often are by Commendables. The Deplorables will always remain unimpressed with circumstantial evidence that does not comport with their bigoted caricatures and will insist on having antipathy for an entire race of humans instead. When the hatred is so vivid, we must reject the lipstick for the pig. As Deplorables insist their double standards have nothing to do with racism, aren't they just whitewashing their own hypocrisy? The social pain of publicly admitting their bigoted hate moves them to create baseless excuses for the underlying illness. Otherwise, the consistency in their response to these events would be puzzling.

Ultimately, racially charged incidents, tipped so much frustration and pent up anger into the largest and most sustained protests in my lifetime as people of all races and creeds joined aggrieved blacks in demanding better all over the country. However, a president, fearing diminishing chances to achieve reelection, determined this was the perfect kind of social and racial unrest from which he could plumb reliable white grievance. At their core, his supporters have always imagined law enforcement exists exclusively to protect their white privilege from the "barbarians at the gate." So, Trump channeled a Nixonian law and order façade to consolidate support among his white genocide- fearing supporters, and hoped to attract fearful suburban whites, too. If he could show uppity blacks, and the liberal whites who champion racial justice, getting their heads cracked in the streets for their riotous uprisings, surely most whites would agree their interests were being met with extreme prejudice. His overwrought Gestapo- like response galvanized the reliably outraged, but failed spectacularly with educated people of all races. It turns out civilized people wish to remain civilized.

Chapter Five

Missing the Zeitgeist for the Trees

"It seemed to him a mistake that he strove to offer his thoughts to the world. The world could be moved by thoughts, but was it not like with the pendulum that one pushes with one's hand out past its two rest points? The clock would certainly not be affected by what happened beyond those points, but rather only by what happened between them."

Ernst Wiechert

Today our ratings driven media are fixated on "Breaking News" sensationalism and the politics of personality rather than on presenting their audience with perspective. No through lines or helpful themes are offered to help us contextualize the events of our time. No Edward R. Murrow to make sense of an increasingly senseless world as the media has splintered into thousands of special interest echo chambers, each remaining unimpressed with the others. Media either avoid weighing the tension between clearly defined protagonists and antagonists, to remain maddeningly agnostic, or they stake their reputation on siding exclusively with one partisan point of view or the other; they homogenize the prevailing mood of half of the country to maximize share points. To this end, the media ignores the proverbial forest for the trees and drives the civically curious to calculate for themselves what truth is. How are we surprised when people become more comfortable clinging to the thin shmear of faith-based propaganda? The public now gravitates toward or away from "fake news", and even defines for themselves what these two points of the pendulum represent.

The Deplorables cower behind the tortured reckoning that all opposing views, however moored to intellectual honesty, are merely a product of liberal bias. This may have been truer years ago but is less so now that "news" is more curated to appeal to narrow special interests, and infinite choices exist to feed all political and social niches. Defending turf at all costs is disingenuous and can become quite dangerous as we have seen in recent years. It is also among the most visible signs of a creeping Fascism that can submerge even the most buoyant of democracies. Today, threats to our liberal democracy and the rule of law, which have always distinguished the country as exceptional, loom larger than at any time in the last century. If the purpose of journalism is to empower the informed to make societally responsible decisions, mustn't journalists accentuate the consequences of wanton ignorance? Mustn't they have the courage to place truth above provocative headlines? We fear as powerful interests coerce a more opportunistic version of truth and cloak this in the name of a populist nationalism. Never has it been more important for the media to resist this impulse to publish relative truth.

Social media interaction has only made things worse. In chat rooms, all over America, "citizen journalists" are free to project vicious fictions with impunity to soothe the deep seated needs of their own damaged souls. Within these platforms, a commenter's allegiance is not to truth, or even to persuasion, but to fishing for affirmation among the likeminded. Honest debate between pro and con on any issue devolves into accusations of trolling, or worse, baseless allegations of criminal wrongdoing against opponents. Consensus is nonexistent and indeed, discouraged. There is no Socratic method behind the madness as combatants leave these encounters more galvanized in their beliefs than when they entered. This overwrought schism between people of differing perspectives is reaching a fevered pitch from which we may not recover.

So what's the big picture? I believe it is nothing short of a fundamental clash over what is meant by America. Was ours a daring escape from the bondage of European Aristocracy in pursuit of freedom, justice and equality for all? Or, for all our protestations to the contrary, are we inextricably bound to our European ancestry and doomed to a rigid caste system that will always favor the haves over the have nots? Is there even a place for non-European descendants to have an equal voice? Do we really believe in meritocracy, or will we always weigh one or more factions among us down with the baggage of low expectations? Surely, America is an idea first, and has always presented an ideal for those who would choose her. So why has the essential message of all men being created equal been so easily perverted? Why have so many fought so viciously against sharing our nation's bounty fairly? Sadly, it's deep in the species to divide and conquer, and that impulse is tempered only by enlightenment and the recognition of our codependence for living peacefully and prosperously. Fundamentally, we are divided over whether our strength comes from standing together or whether we feel only the strongest should reap the riches we all sow. We must imagine this essential dilemma has existed since the dawn of humanity. Today, do we believe in positive sum outcomes, greater through cooperation, or zero sum outcomes as inevitable, when resources are scarce and our imaginations are not equal to the task of creating alternatives for shared prosperity? From America's very beginnings, the idea of standing together united, versus interpreting our new found freedoms from the divided perspectives of the new territories, has defined our history. North versus south, the free man versus the enslaved, have always defined America's divided mind. This struggle has birthed our greatest accomplishments and our greatest shames. While most of our people have gracefully accepted the idea of becoming a more perfect union over time, tragically for others, early wounds have never healed. This divide has been handed down from generation to generation and exploited by political ideologues seeking an expedient plurality from the governed.

Today, we still struggle with our essential differences and still divide along rigid political, racial, religious, social and geographic boundaries, reinforcing convenient but unhelpful labels used to divide us even further. Rather than honoring our shared humanity and celebrating our diversity constructively the Deplorables still rage against our increasingly less homogenous European heritage. As counter intuitive as it may seem to rally behind the very concept of a society as stratified as that which we escaped from, the Deplorables still find deep comfort in the bonds of our heritable beginnings. For the Deplorables, the idea that one sect is not inherently superior to another is strictly heresy and becomes fodder for so many more zero sum struggles.

Chapter Six

Sign the petition already

I laughed like a baby chimp with his first pair of cymbals when my friend sent me a link to the petitions page on the Whitehouse.gov website in late 2019. This is where folks with a cause can petition for likeminded signatures, or reveal the depths of their mental illness publicly. If their pet cause can garner 100,000 signatures in 30 days, they win a response from the Whitehouse staff or maybe a pair of Trump steaks. In the age of Trump, the petitions page took a hard shimmy toward Never Neverland. Nestled between culture war fiddle faddle, like outlawing abortion, or enshrining the right of all to own Hellfire missiles, a few petitions expressed exquisite dumbfukery. One petition, which drew almost twice the magic number, caught my eye. It was a plea to impeach Nancy Pelosi for treason for a laundry list of offenses against our country. Apparently she gave aid and comfort to "invading Illegals," which are not to be confused with desperate refugees seeking asylum, so "these enemies of the State would bring drugs and terrorism causing catastrophic levels of death and crime to our people." If only she would have allowed POTUS to build that wall at enormous taxpayer expense, instead of pandering to the San Francisco Liberals, we could live in peace. Folks could sleep through the night, secure in the knowledge that only white rightwing fanatics, not brown terrorists, would slit their throats or make Swiss cheese of them from high velocity fire from AR-15s. If that wasn't grounds enough to remove her from office, how about not allowing POTUS to deliver his SOTU from her House in Congress? At least the petitioner showed great restraint in not advocating for a public hanging for these offenses. Who in civilized society would contemplate sending political leaders to the Gallows to settle ideological disputes anyway? Regretfully, four out of five Deplorables surveyed would show no such equanimity on the matter as social media posts in the rightwing freak-o-sphere would reveal for years. Within the first 15 days, the petition had only received 197,817 signatures, so maybe it wasn't yet a thing?

Apparently in his fervor to reorder the world's global power structure in favor of child eating elite pedophiles, George Soros applied Saul Alinsky tactics of creating and funding political organizations! Against this tyranny, 190,312 signed on the dotted line to strip him of his vast riches, RICO style, to save the children and save the planet. We must identify him as a domestic terrorist so we can seize all of his assets under our Civil Assets Forfeiture law. I know, who the hell is Saul Alinsky? This Q Anon fever remained pervasive among the Deplorables for years as they became increasingly uncomfortable with well-resourced opponents.

135,806 of our people believed Rashida Tlaib, the freshman Congresswoman from MI, must immediately be removed from office for her "inappropriate and unstable actions." Digging deeper we found the offense, according to this patriotic petitioner, was her profanity and rude display of a lack of respect for our vulgar Grifter in Chief at the time. 135,806 people agree this made her a grave security threat. Not to minimize the threat this brave patriot describes, but Tlaib's district represents the interests of approximately 700,000 people while POTUS represents 327,000,000. Did this make Trump's vulgarity and general disagreeableness toward opponents, unbecoming of a leader, almost 500 times more of a threat to national security? Indeed for the Deplorables, the point was moot simply because Tlaib is Muslim, and therefore undoubtedly a terrorist. Talk amongst yourselves.

Another Congresswoman the contestants on Whitehouse.gov Petitions Edition, wanted expelled from Congress was Maxine Waters, or as Trump referred to her, "Low IQ Maxine." Waters crossed the line when she called upon Americans to "push back" against Trump officials in public. The petitioner A.M. said this "It is especially dangerous to call for public attacks at a time in our country when Liberals are so wildly unhinged and violent, have no control over their emotions and are brainwashed by fake news and hoodwinked by lying, sleazy politicians like Maxine Waters." I think I will just let the rampant hypocrisy of this statement speak for itself. Nitpicking, I guess, but did Waters really call for an unhinged violent insurrection against the State or simply to verbally confront elected officials? You make the call.

A Q Anon gift, was the petition calling for accountability for Obama era government. Unless you live in a hermetically sealed Glad bag buried below the ocean's floor, you are aware how Trump Supporters believed it was Obama and his cohorts, not Trump and his, responsible for all the malfeasance and Russian collusion that the "fake news" foisted on us for 3 1/2 years. C.S. insisted our elected officials dedicate the same level of resources and accountability to investigating Trump opponents, provided, of course, the investigators could all be non RINO Republicans. The idea was simple. If we were committed to making the United States a Fascist dictatorship, shouldn't we haul before a firing squad, a raft of people who were not accused of crimes against the state, but would oppose a Totalitarian leader in accomplishing his agenda? The whole mishigas is balanced precariously on the notion of the "Deep State." To the Deplorables, "Deep State" means nothing more or less than Trump opposition. Republicans who remained unimpressed with the Dear Leader's antics were randomly lumped together with liberal Never Trumpers as part of the evil cabal. Indeed, the late Senator John McCain might have been singled out for treason had he not inconveniently died before the petition was written.

A petition signed by only a few thousand stalwarts called for simply removing all Muslims from political office nationally. Again, I am not sure what they imagined as the process, but this alert patriot felt the small handful of Muslims in Congress have disrupted the body, are responsible for dividing all 327 million of our people, and will surely bring Sharia Law to our communities and the next Islamic Jihad.

One petition, launched by W.C., on its surface seemed perfectly reasonable. W.C. strove to protect free speech in the digital public square. I agree, Mark Zuckerberg and Jack Dorsey should not be the arbiters of what is and is not politically appropriate. As our intrepid petitioner pointed out "banning users from their platforms, those corporations can effectively remove politically unwelcome Americans from the public square. That is repugnant to our shared values of free speech and freedom of the press." Bravo W.C., except that what Zuck and Dorsey have actually done is simply to impose standards of conduct in their spaces so that folks can use their products without the threats of harassment and indeed have violence rained down upon them for their mainstream political beliefs by the truly repugnant among us. Debate with your fellow man vigorously over

69

whether or not Hillary Clinton really was running a child sex trafficking operation from the basement of a pizzeria, but don't threaten to burn their house down and murder them and their children over the dispute. W.C. joined many of his politically disaffected ilk in believing all media, including the digital public square, is tilted against conservative thinkers. Principled debate is great, but plotting anarchy in the public square is not so great. These days, plenty of subversive rightwing echo chambers exist for people untethered by a moral conscience. Why not leave Facebook to cat lovers and amateur chefs? Another complaint the petitioner had, is that Twitter and Facebook accounts were taken down simply because they were coopted by Russian saboteurs during the 2016 election cycle. To that I have only one response, huh? For people obsessed with calling rivals "Commies," this too seems comically overwrought.

Another petition came from R.M. This petitioner's plea read simply "Sheriff Arpaio's Cold Case Posse found these to be forged documents, let's find out the truth!" Who can't get behind a call to continue litigating the fantasy that our 44th president was a Trojan horse born and bred in Kenya? Hawaii my ass! Perhaps no petition captured the very essence of the Deplorables quite like R.B.'s call to declare that mass immigration is "forced adoption" and "stop making whites pay for White Genocide." In fairness, R.B. did acknowledge some may label him a racist for thinking that integration of non-whites into this melting pot might "blend whites away."

Thankfully, a vehicle exists for folks with a bottomless pit of grievances to bring these to the attention of the White House. Who doesn't want to "blend out" all of the differences that threaten to make this country a many splendored thing?

In 2020, many were positively apoplectic over the Covid-19 pandemic either because they believed in science or because they did not. One concerned petitioner, C.S., gathered over 650,000 signatures for his call to investigate Bill and Melinda Gates' charitable foundation for medical malpractice and crimes against humanity. I wasn't aware they were even doctors and felt their only crime against humanity was releasing Windows 1.0. Anyway, inspired by some choice Q drops, C.S. was on to their crimes. One event in 2019 convinced our petitioner that Bill Gates was more Josef Mengele than nerdy philanthropist. It was a pandemic preparedness exercise held in New York to encourage public/private partnership to mitigate against major societal consequences of the next great pandemic around the globe. Not in 2019 but, over a year later, C.S. became outraged that Gates led a panel of likeminded Corona virus chasers that painted a picture eerily similar to the Covid-19 outbreak. Surely, his advance knowledge that Corona viruses even existed, let alone could spread to our shores, was too much of a coincidence to fathom. As the 45th President himself said many times "Who knew something like this could happen?" Certainly not someone who devoted much of his philanthropy in this very area. And the fact that Event 201 was held in Wuhan China was just the final straw. Wait, was it held in Wuhan China or Wuhan New York? The brochure just said New York. Is there a Wuhan New York? C.S. just said Wuhan. Bill Gates' main contribution to the event was to discuss effective vaccine development. The real kicker for C.S. was how he had heard Gates say many times how he hoped for a 10-15% decline in population growth worldwide and, obviously, a vaccine that reduced childhood mortality would accomplish just that. Wait a second, what? Yes, it is true, as Gates himself explained, in underdeveloped countries people don't birth eight babies because they want super large families;

71

they have many kids because they know many will die prematurely. Vaccinating the population against lethal virus relieves the anxiety posed by this sad fact. The whole thing is based upon some hinky idea that lower population could be economically beneficial for third world countries. Not on this petitioner's watch. Certainly the least affluent in the world should have hordes of children they can't afford to feed because God or Jerry Falwell Jr. said so.

Chapter Seven

How it started

"If someone has decided to drown, it's probably already impossible to save them."

Vladimir Putin

On June 16, 2015, the serially bankrupted long time real estate tycoon, and reality TV star Donald J. Trump announced his 2016 candidacy for President from the lobby of his offices at Trump Tower. He had toyed with the public about this ambition many times before as a way to rejuvenate his fledging brand, but now he felt he owed it to his country to assume control and restore greatness. After all, his brand had landed in the toilet many times over the last 30 years and so too had the fate of the country. Time to MAGA. In his speech that day he said, "When Mexico sends its people, they're not sending their best. They're not sending you. They're not sending you. They're sending people that have lots of problems, and they're bringing those problems with us. They're bringing drugs. They're bringing crime. They're rapists. And some, I assume, are good people." It had been almost 45 years since I sat in the back row of Mrs. Bell's history class in the eighth grade, but somehow the notion that Mexico was sending us their bad apples as a policy struck me as being dumber than a turd in the punchbowl. It's not that I believe Mexico is a utopian paradise in any way other than its majestic vistas and great weather. A weak government in general, and the spread of violent drug cartels specifically, have made much of the country a living hell for its law abiding citizens. But it is this lawless dynamic, within the country, that has led decent families to seek safety and opportunity from without, while the criminal elements have thrived from the very circumstances of criminality within. For a certain number of our citizens, Trump's speech was a xenophobic buzzer beater as they had prayed for decades for a firewall, real or metaphorical, against "invaders." They were never going to imagine the cultural assimilation of brown people represented anything but a threat. And they would never muster the empathy for fellow human beings who looked that different from themselves. In one rampantly hateful statement, Trump identified how he alone could neutralize the threats "others" always created for a white America. He would recycle that meme ad nauseam, for political capital, as long as he chose to appeal only to awful people. And, more disturbingly, he planted the seed for any number of violent take over fantasies metastasizing in the minds of the hopelessly incoherent haters he recognized as his base supporters. This indeed was a gift that would keep on giving. He had his flock of cultists at "Mexican's are rapists."

Also Trump leveraged the populist notion that a "Deep State" existed and was allied against the Deplorables for worshiping their God, loving their guns, believing in Capitalism, standing against abortion, and being White Nationalists in general. Relentlessly scratching the basic itches that have always animated their resentments, created millions of Deplorable arsonists willing to give no quarter in a truly violent American rebellion.

74

Chapter Eight

She said it first

"Once you defend a crooked, divisive, foul-mouthed, racist, sexist, xenophobic liar like Donald Trump, you have no standing to be outraged about anything anyone else says or does. Ever."

Keith Boykin

In a stunning, "Oh no you didn't girl" moment, Hillary Clinton said this in a September 2016 campaign speech, "You know, to just be grossly generalistic, you could put half of Trump's supporters into what I call the basket of Deplorables. Right? The racist, sexist, homophobic, xenophobic, Islamaphobic -- you name it." At that moment you could feel a discordant groove carve itself into the vinyl that was spinning so melodically. As someone who couldn't imagine a better explanation for why some would side with Trump, her comment was more precise than derisive about such a Rainbow Coalition of white grievance mongers drunk on hate. I would have added "heinous" and "bottom feeding cretins" somewhere in that description. But I am not a politician, so I have the luxury of speaking my mind freely, even when doing so causes my wife to toss all my belongings onto the front lawn. The point is, Mrs. Clinton said what was on the minds of at least 50%

of all functionally literate people in the country. In fairness, half of Trump's supporters would have amounted to less than a quarter all voters cogni-capable or otherwise. Is it fair to suggest a quarter of the electorate are irredeemably awful people? For about a week, it was considered decidedly unfair, as the howls whipped up from every corner of the alt-right universe to condemn Clinton for such a despicable comment about our country's true patriots. But, in short order, millions of our most detestable people stopped raging against Clinton's insult and embraced it instead as an emblem of proud irreverent defiance of liberalism that fueled a cottage industry of Deplorables T-shirt and hat vendors. Ironically, appropriating the term was a lot like black folks appropriating the N word back in the day, though the Deplorables couldn't explain the parallel with a gun to their head. Willfully identifying as a repugnant slob with total allegiance to their leader's vulgar and anti-brown agenda, was the surest way to beat back the American ideal of a tolerant multi-cultural society. But it was going to require supernormal message discipline to prop up their alternative reality against truth. From that moment on, everything became either Trumpism or "fake news".

It is rhetorically convenient for disadvantaged thinkers to simply dub every opposing view as a product of the liberal mainstream media's imagination. If you tell them Babies are among our youngest in society, expect they will blame you for allowing CNN to indoctrinate you. In a social media post, simply citing CNN, MSNBC, The New York Times or the Washington Post as a fact source disqualifies your comments. Certainly Breitbart, Fox News, The Daily Caller and InfoWars are less partisan arbiters of truth and have all the Pulitzer prizes to prove it. Wait, never mind.

Even more gaslighting occurs when they pan the very online Fact Checking sources, which must be used to settle partisan cable news grudge matches. These sources are situationally accepted by the Deplorables only in the rare cases they doled out their Pinocchios against liberal commenters. Otherwise, the very purpose served, separating fact from fiction, is for Deplorables, as contrived as anything else the liberal media would do to push an agenda. When the Washington Post sided with the Trump administration, and against opponents, their truth was unimpeachable, when they opposed, they were dubbed liberally biased enemies of the state. Certainly citing their hero for making an astounding 30,573 lies in 4 years, went over like a "fake news" lead balloon.

Even funnier is how the Deplorables elaborately layer all sources of opposing information into a single master conspiracy theory based upon the delusion that all of society is united in suppressing them and their beliefs. It is not just the Democrats and their fawning mainstream media co-conspirators, but it is an entire political infrastructure of elected and unelected power elite, the swamp, who are dedicated to a New World Order and destroying opposition to the Deep State. Indeed, even our 3 letter intelligence agencies were in on the heist. Instead of realizing they are just wrong, the Deplorables would continue to torque this counter intuitive narrative to the breaking point. Because they would sooner huff asbestos than admit rhetorical defeat, they turned the spotlight from their own tragic ignorance outward with the hope of stoking collective resentment.

Conveniently, all survey research companies too are accused of being in the tank for the Democrats – especially after their dismal performance in calling the 2016 race. Fair observers might admit

Clinton's defeat in the 2016 campaign hinged upon many factors not related to Trump's stable genius. Gallop, not properly weighing the impact of the Bernie Bros backlash or Comey's announcement to reopen the email scandal may each have influenced the outcome. Why was the assessment that Clinton was still a few points ahead, in the home stretch, regarded as another liberal plot of the Deep State? Collectively, the Deplorables spent the preceding 6 months preemptively soothing Trump's vainglorious heinie ahead of the likelihood of Mrs. Clinton's handing it to him on November 8th. Could we have imagined, on that night, the fictions our 45th President would concoct 4 years later as his own candidacy for reelection was even more in doubt?

Everyone, including Trump himself, assumed a loss until election night. Years later, as the aggregate of all polls still placed Trump's approval underwater and unmovable, Deplorables assumed the polls must all have been suspect except for the single outlier that always said Trump was only despised by half of the electorate. If the polls weren't in on the conspiracy, surely Trump's approval would have been in the 80% range and any election a landslide in his favor. The Deplorables are simply unaware of how uniquely wired their world view is.

In the aftermath of the election, the Deplorables wallowed in their self-fulfilling fantasy that the razor thin margin validated their malignant worldview as the prevailing mood of the country, despite how their guy actually lost the popular vote by millions. From that moment on, the world was split for them between the patriotic us vs the anti-Trump them with all of the baggage you might imagine coming from that zero sum assessment. The inconvenient fact that the anti-Trump camp was already larger and would only become larger still, would be chalked up to an all-encompassing conspiracy against their duly elected champion. As much of that swelling margin came from newly disaffected, formerly loved Conservatives, the argument became increasingly thin. Republicans with impeccable conservative credentials were now as much a part of the Deep State as vilified Democrats were, simply for parting with the party boss on matters of civil and racial decency. Indeed, the conservative principles the Deplorables claimed to espouse a single election cycle before, like the Tea Party crowd did, were dropped like a flaming turd in favor of Trumpism. Hate sells and unhinged hate sells even more. It is an article of faith among Deplorables that any unkind word about Trump must be bought and paid for by George Soros, who had apparently become party blind enough to finance any "Never Trumper" group that would promote the swampy New World Order. So they became focused on what they assumed was a popular mandate to reorder the world and defeat the Deep State as a nod to white power. Inconveniently they forgot they were opposed by 60% of their fellow citizens. Just imagine the frustration from being really loud, but now only a minority in these United States.

Between assuming facts not in evidence, and suppressing facts that were in evidence, the Deplorables erected their own metaphorical wall against all "others" whose ideals were less sympathetic to the cause of re- whitening a browning America. Yes, the Deplorables are racists. They deftly suppress all empirical evidence, however statistically relevant, that runs contrary to their beliefs about the evils of cultural assimilation while cleaving to outmoded fictions. The hypocrisy is so deeply cynical when the objective of debate is simply winning at all costs. We know, for example how immigrants, illegal or otherwise, are vastly less likely to commit violent crime. This is especially true when

79

compared with people who are politically, ethnically, religiously, socially and racially more like themselves. So they cherry pick the instances when "others" commit gruesome violent offenses as if for the survivor's loved ones, the racial identity of the perpetrator is more relevant than the finality of the outcome. Murder is murder until bogged down by the baggage of bigotry. Unless committed to a zero sum us vs. them existential struggle, would anything but the circumstances of the crime itself matter? Statistically each of us is several thousand times more likely to die at the hands of someone who looks ostensibly just like us than a savage Islamic extremist crying "Allahu Akbar." Yet somehow, for the Deplorables, all Muslims must wear the shame of the heinous terrorism of the very few and be treated like lepers for their faith. Indeed, the Deplorables sided with the Dear Leader on a proposed ban of all Muslims entering the country. Other races, ethnicities or faiths, too, are inextricably tied to the caricatures these white Christians ordain for them as if the righteous superiority of one sect over the other is unquestionable. They will hiss "all lives matter" reflexively when an opponent says "black lives matter" and then fabricate a dozen sketchy reasons why any particular black man's life will never matter. I think we all know this is not how honest brokers, legitimately interested in achieving peaceful and equitable outcomes, would conduct themselves. It does not speak to the kind of empathy we are all taught to believe is at the root of social harmony. This is more warfare than diplomacy. Must we really pretend otherwise when we know better? How about when their tactics become antisocial and violent?

Chapter Nine

Who are these monsters?

"Most Nazis, KKK members, MAGA minions, and other deplorable racists don't even know they're racists, because they don't know that the malicious lies they believe about other races aren't actually true."

Oliver Markus Malloy

What do we know about this species known as Deplorables and why should we be repulsed by them? The first thing that leaps out at the casual observer is how very white they are. As a white male myself, I don't find that as much objectionable, as it is curious, in the rainbow world we live in. At Trump rallies, finding legitimate black faces made *Where's Waldo* child's play. To me, it seems highly unlikely that anything truly commendable could appeal to only one race. When I visit Wrigley Field and bathe in the glory of a rocking capacity crowd, the faces seem roughly representative of the society around me. Isn't it this kind of true representative diversity that is supposed to be a commendable feature of our country? The whole extravaganza of a MAGA circle jerk is based upon the exact opposite of that ideal. So what were the Deplorables celebrating with wild eyed enthusiasm that folks not white or not Christian would not? More importantly, why were the crowds so openly hostile to the non-whites who were not on the guest list? Aside from Trump's "African American" of whom he was so very proud, what made "others" feel so unwelcome? And how is it possible in the Deplorable's monochromatic world, so openly hostile to "others," they felt it was they, as white Christians, who were the real victims of racism? To me, racism is a crime of opportunity committed by those who have many against those who have fewer. The power imbalance in a majority white country takes most of the teeth out of the argument that the poor white folk are being discriminated against. Yes, many of the Deplorables do, in fact, play the white victim card with hypocritical abandon. Will Commendables, the majority of whom are white, acknowledge and reject this unhealthy meme?

The Deplorables exhibit all of the signs of stage four malignant narcissism. They are anti-social sadists who delight in "triggering" the Libtards even more than binge watching Duck Dynasty reruns. They find it purely intoxicating to melt all of the "snowflakes" around them with the most ludicrous debunked talking points, long past their use-by date. Opponent's frustration with this inverted reality is like mother's milk supplying all of the nourishment necessary to sustain so many more wretched fantasies. No, the Uranium One deal struck between the US and Russia's nuclear energy agency for mining rights to 20% of junk uranium within this country was not a pay for play deal struck unilaterally by Hillary Clinton to enrich her charitable foundation. No, Obama was not a creature sent from the depths of hell, as prophesized by Nostradamus, to bring about the end of the world. If that wasn't obvious before, now after more than four years with a world still spinning luminously, the argument has worn a bit threadbare. To his cult followers, Trump was a religious Svengali figure who moved in mysterious ways to restore the natural order of things. He was a highly stable genius and business Jesus to his flock. Surely, his capitalist majesty would trickle down, like gold from heaven, to the deserving silent majority. If they still found themselves adrift in a world they were ill equipped for, he would at least help them manage their night terrors over diminishing unearned advantages in an increasingly brown world. He would take care of whitey unlike like that Kenyon Muslim terrorist he succeeded.

Voters in 2016 and 2020 who expressed deep antipathy and a hostile bias against nonwhites overwhelmingly chose the Donald. As it turns out, racism, sexism and nativism are the 3 basic pillars that define them. It was their deep fear of being replaced, or of having their social and political status diminished in a changing society, that drove them into a more deplorable fugue state.

It is essential that all Commendables understand that the Deplorables are fanatics. Fanatics and ideologues tend be absolutists, who wallow in self-affirming "truths" of their own making and will always wish to impose their toxic values on all, with an increasingly violent fervor. They remain disconnected from the consequences of their actions and beliefs because, like a drunk driver, they are convinced they are more than capable of driving while under the influence.

The Deplorables never met an intellectual superior they couldn't baselessly accuse of crimes against children. If they can't beat you on the merits, surely alleging you rape little babies will even the score to the satisfaction of their peers, especially if they can create actual legal jeopardies for you. They will spring this trap on anyone who cannot be coaxed toward acquiescence in the moment. Their lack of empathy for all who are not pasty faced and awful, isolates them within their own echo chamber of likeminded outrage porn. Within these places, they become even more hopelessly gripped by rage and the baseless paranoia that comes from battling the specter of racial equality. The torment from this loop feeds back relentlessly so that the only final reckoning they can imagine is a violent one. Imagine all this noise as one enormous rebel yell meant to intimidate Commendables while boosting the morale of their own troops. If we complacently ignore their growing numbers, or imagine they are countenanced only by laughable caricatures, more pitiable than potent, we will lose this battle. They see themselves as William Wallace from Braveheart, not as a punchline. Like their figurehead Donald Trump, they will relentlessly bang the drum over a half dozen white grievances and be willing to decimate opponents in a vicious game of thrones. As a nation struggling to regain our righteous soul, we must provide no quarter for this kind of basic indecency.

Chapter Ten

How the Commendables differ from Deplorables

"While it is well enough to leave footprints on the sands of time, it is even more important to make sure they point in a commendable direction"

James Branch Cabell

Speaking of the recently concluded Game of Thrones extravaganza, one line from the show stood out to me. The Imp, Tyrion Lannister, said, "I have a tender spot in my heart for cripples and bastards and broken things." Though the time and tone of this medieval drama were far removed from our modern Democratic Republic, the sentiment expressed by this elite but conflicted dwarf, about the violently unequal world around him, channels the essential difference between Commendable and Deplorable people. Commendables root for the underdogs and pray for equality and peace as they hope to close the loopholes that advantage the privileged over the underprivileged. For them, conquest over people is the opposite of human progress. While good versus evil struggles may advance the narrative of human history, they undermine the moral of the story about becoming a more perfect union of peoples. Commendables abhor the idea of zero sum outcomes and believe fervently that science and technology and other forms of human ingenuity will ultimately create the proverbial higher tide to lift all boats. They embrace the notion that bipolar labels are simply constructs, which ethically and morally inferior people have exploited to gain unearned advantages. Commendables revel in diversity and celebrate the very "bastards, cripples and broken things," among more fulsome and abundant angels in society, which represent our shared humanity. The Commendables are so done with all of the "isms" Deplorables have always used to divide and conquer us. Between peoples, who are remarkably similar physically or genetically, they find almost infinite cultural and metaphysical differences worth celebrating for their own uniqueness to create a more intrinsically interesting world. Quite simply, it is the appreciation, instead of disdain, for the ways we differ that separates Commendables from Deplorables.

In tens of thousands of online chatrooms this very minute, Deplorables are expressing deeply held beliefs, opinions, and world views that are outside of the main in society. Indeed on virtually every politically relevant issue worth arguing over, they find themselves in the minority, and increasingly more so with every tick we make toward a more tolerant and inclusive society. Put simply, they are on the wrong side of history always. And yet, they will insist it is they who best represent the tone and tenor of the country; the real patriotic red, white and blue flag waving, apple pie eating, Chevy driving, gun totting norm against which lesser creatures must be judged and vilified. For them "mainstream" is an illusion that applies only to ideas and attitudes that create the loudest thread in society for indoctrinated others, not for those who know better. The disconnect, as they see it, is that society's opinion leaders, the media, academia, the scientists, the elitists and even

86

Hollywood are in cahoots, snookering gullible liberals into believing untruths that they find personally repugnant. They believe truth is independent of most of what is seen and heard in conventional circles and resides instead in fantastical tales that manage to gather up all the dangling social modifiers into a unified theory at odds with what the rest of society would call "mainstream." So they rage against "fake news" simply because it always resists comporting with the fairytales that nourish their counter culture. If the mainstream media are pitching a reality the Deplorables cannot accept, it must be, as their leader contended, an enemy of the State.

We might respect them more if they admitted they knew they were marching to a different beat than the rest of us intentionally because they viewed progress as a threat and not an opportunity. Rebels with a cause worth fighting for. Instead they insist it is they, whose beliefs are consistent with the natural order of things and it is we, the "mainstream," who are hopelessly compromised. It is hard to have sympathy for willful ignorance. One thing is for certain: Perpetuating this farce is taking a toll, as the Deplorables are becoming increasingly unhinged and dangerous under pressure from the facts of life.

I was tempted to agree with some friends and family that maybe I was being a bit of a drama king to insist the Deplorables were extreme rightwing fanatics every bit as radicalized and dangerous as Islamic extremists. There are too few of them to be a real threat, I was assured. Then I read a leaflet published by the British Ministry of Defense called "Extreme Rightwing Indicators and Warnings" to warn military leaders of the threats posed by "patriots" who idealize "whites only Communities" Among the neon flashing, warning signs were these:

- Describe themselves as patriots

87

- Describe multicultural towns as "lost'
- Looks at opponents as traitors
- Make generalizations about Muslims and Jews
- Talk of an impending racial conflict or 'Race War'
- Threaten violence when losing an argument, although claiming that XRW groups protest peacefully
- Become increasingly angry at perceived injustices or threats to so called 'National Identity"
- Refers to political correctness as a Leftwing or Communist plot

It is politically incorrect to dare link real malfeasance to anyone who is sworn to serve and protect society, either from the ranks of the military or law enforcement. Certainly, among us, these servants are generally more shining examples of our nation's conscience. But, it is from that acme of our own exceptionalism that we find the few examples of bad apples even more alarming. Their allegiance to True North principles generally stands in stark contrast to the instances in which they ally themselves with evil impulses. But, we also must accept the fact that so many of our modern illiberal boogeymen came from those ranks. For decades, the FBI has routinely warned its agents that the white supremacist and far-right militia groups it investigates often have links to law enforcement. It is also evident that many veterans make up a large share of violent rightwing fascist groups like the Oath keepers and the 3 Percenters. If those who defend civil society become just as radicalized as the Deplorables writ large, we may have to rethink who the good guys are. Now is not the time to be seduced by symbolism alone. If there really is but a thin blue line between violent militia groups and former law enforcement and soldiers it will not benefit us to live in denial. We must never forget that Timothy McVeigh served meritoriously in the Persian Gulf War and earned a bronze star for serving a county he would later attack after becoming radicalized.

Indeed my fear, and the premise of this book, is that it is the growing acceptance of such vile ideology, and the radicalization among a sizable chunk of our own people, that looms menacingly as our greatest challenge.

So, imagine how quickly I recalibrated my opinion upon recognizing in this list the essential basic food groups of everything I have seen discussed on social media by the Deplorables. Every day for 4 years or more, I have beaten back these basic arguments from a remarkably large number of totally lost souls. For the last few years, I have watched helplessly as heinous acts of violence have been perpetrated by these radicalized haters. Not surprisingly, the report was swiftly denounced by rightwing media, the Republican Party, the Department of Defense and Donald J. Trump himself, as these traits became increasingly more descriptive of the sweet spot of their movement. Despite the feckless protests from GOP leaders that "This is not my party," it is in fact entirely emblematic of their party now. They romanced the monsters who became their constituents, and even amplified the Deplorables' grievances to draw more electorally significant boundaries. This is why, in large part, so many who lived their entire lives comfortably within the conservative constructs of Republicanism have fled the party in droves since 2017. It is now inextricably linked to the broader Republican caucus who are now beholden to the mob. The icing on this cake came as all of these usual rightwing suspects panned the report as "fake news" and a further proof of a conspiracy against "Conservatives."

The Deplorables' movement has created a counter culture singularity that could change American civilization permanently. As their opinion leaders and foot soldiers become more incensed over a world they are increasingly less able to navigate, the gravity of their hate will become more infinite; remedies even more extreme. Meanwhile, each year, we learn from FBI statistics, that it is people with this disease, more than radicalized Islamic extremists, who pose the greatest threat of violence to our homeland. Indeed, the Deplorables really have become a single issue motivated voting bloc, and the leaders of the party they favor wantonly pander to the white power movement.

The Deplorables world has become very small. They simply don't fathom that beyond their margins, "others" are as repulsed by them as they are of "others." Or, that they are no longer the "silent majority." The country is fast becoming majority minority and with that will come even more of the imagined marginalization they battle today. That one of two political parties has chosen to "mainstream" the tenets of white nationalism for electoral success only exacerbates the problem. This makes it imperative that good people consistently call out these toxic values as counter culture and extremist positions to excise the cancer before it spreads too wildly.

Chapter Eleven

Why must so many people die?

"Those who incite violence have no business lecturing others about unity."

DaShanne Stokes

On Friday, March 21st 2019, 19 year old Sydney Aiello, a Marjory Stoneman Douglas High School massacre survivor, died from a self-inflicted gunshot wound to the head a little more than a year after 17 of her friends were gunned downed. Certainly, the arc of her life, after the shooting, was irreversibly mangled, and we learned of her battles with soul crushing depression from guilt and PTSD ever since that awful day. This news broke America's collective heart. As a father and human being, I assume I don't need to explain how that news washed over me. What shook me even more was how my endless sympathy stood in stark contrast to a year of the most heinous reactions to the Parkland shooting by the Deplorables. As survivors struggled to make sense of the senseless in front of the media and the world, a theme rose from the ashes, "Never Again." However, in the hopelessly diseased minds of the Deplorables, the rallying cry from these victims of mass carnage, was dumbed down to an anti-Second Amendment ploy. Not only was this a well-orchestrated plot aided and abetted by likeminded adult accomplices, but the actual shooting was a false flag, they insisted. The survivors, who began gravitating to the media more frequently with their "Never Again" pleas, were called "crisis actors." Not content to simply fling this fact free human waste around recklessly, these animals began heaving death threats at the surviving teens and showering them whenever possible with vile hate speech. Yes, mindless tormentors tormented the already psychologically shredded survivors of a mass murder. As unimaginable as it sounds, the Deplorables found it quite easy to place their ideological imperatives above human tragedy and were chastened only when legal recourse was taken by the families involved.

A day later we learned the initial sketchy details of another Parkland student survivor to take his own life, and a day after that, the news of Jeremy Richland's suicide. Jeremy was 6 year old Avielle Richland's dad. Avielle was one of 20 precious first graders slaughtered that December morning in 2012 at Sandy Hook Elementary School in Newtown MA. The wake of destruction from these senseless massacres has laid waste to so many lives. That any of the parents of the victims, or the survivors, would have to fend off attacks from mindless pukes with an agenda is truly monstrous. The Deplorables willfully accepted the premise that this tragedy, too, was a false flag operation mounted by crisis actors as perpetuated by noted conspiracist Alex Jones on Infowars. After four years of near constant defamation and harassment from Jones and many of his heinous like-minded Deplorable followers, an emotionally shattered Jeremy Richland succumbed to all the torment and heartbreak by taking his own life on March 22nd 2019. Three days later, during his Infowar's broadcast, Jones added more conspiracy addled insult to unimaginable injury by suggesting Richland's death was

92

too coincidentally timed to coincide with good news coming from the Mueller investigation to be anything but a homicide. Maybe this too was just another liberal hoax? The whole thing made him wonder whether he could even get a fair hearing for multiple defamation and harassment suits brought by the other surviving families. When pressed during depositions for why he terrorized these families relentlessly for years with his baseless lies, Jones offered how he may have been suffering from psychosis. Isn't psychosis rather redundant for a Deplorable? I checked on Hannity's Facebook page for signs of sympathy for the three suicide victims, and principled shaming of Trump favorite performance artist Jones. The posters there were otherwise engaged shaming Alexandria Ocasio-Cortez, Ilhan Omar, Adam Schiff, and CNN for their hate Trump crusades.

While hundreds of thousands of Americans gathered all over the country at the March for our Lives protests and rallies, the Deplorables cursed them on social media, and in front of their TVs, for everything they stood for. Nine year old Yolanda King, MLK's granddaughter spoke fearlessly and eloquently of her grandfather's dream of judging men by the content of their character and of her dream of a gun free world while those assembled erupted in tearful thunderous applause. In contrast, like ghoulish serpents, the Deplorables hissed their disapproval for the message and messenger. While the Commendables felt goosebumps, the entire basket of Deplorables were nauseated by the "liberal" spectacle.

In the immediate aftermath of the 2016 election, one enterprising Trump supporter sent letters to 10 Islamic centers around the country calling for the genocide of our nation's Muslim population, referring to them as "Children of Satan." In a childish scrawl, this wingnut went on to suggest that our new leader, Donald J. Trump, should do to the Muslims what Hitler did to the Jews. For the observant reader, this begged many questions. Clearly the author was anti-Muslim, but wasn't he also likely anti-Semitic if he fantasized how a new fascist leader might heroically follow an old fascist's playbook in eradicating another entire group of people? And what was it he saw in Trump that led him to believe the president elect would want to do something as heinous as wiping out 3.5 million Muslims among us in the name of cleansing America? Like so many times before this, the sober fervency of the perpetrator was chalked up to mental illness more than ideological terrorism. For so many, Islamic extremism, or radical liberalism, are among very few movements which must be held completely accountable for their evil deeds. White Christians are not required to own acts of wanton mayhem by dint of either their race or religion. There is always an escape clause built into the very reckoning of these acts that has nothing to do with either of these characteristics. Worse than that, all of those identifying as members of the offending sects are expected to wear the condemnation as a scarlet letter, leading to only more amplified condemnation to be met with more violent retribution.

In September of 2018, we watched the more sensationalized parts of the confirmation hearing of Trump's Conservative wonder Jurist Brett Kavanaugh to the highest Court. This fitness test for a lifelong appointment to the Supreme Court was a bit contentious, first for some rather obvious perjured statements by the good Justice and then, more notably, for an accusation from his distant past about a sexual assault. Christina Blasey-Ford, a professor of psychology from Palo Alto University, reluctantly lodged an accusation against Mr. Kavanaugh originating from an encounter the two allegedly had in high

94

school. Almost immediately, the horribly confused Deplorables cried foul, maintaining how the legal standard of innocent until proven guilty was being trampled by aggressive Democrats in their enthusiasm for sacking Trump's SCOTUS appointment. The presumed innocent standard is one they apply liberally to friends, but withhold with extreme prejudice from foes. Apparently they believed this was a criminal trial in front of a jury and not a confirmation hearing in front of the Senate, premised strictly on the standard of determining competence, juris prudence and fitness for this kind of appointment to the highest court. As word of Ford's testimony was filtered through the gas lighting machine of the rightwing media, Dr. Ford began receiving numerous death threats to herself and her family, nearly intimidating her into silence.

Finally, Ford's testimony was negotiated on the promise of her security. The proceedings quickly became overwrought, and it was determined the alleged charges of this accuser, as well as other accusers, should be vetted by the FBI before rendering a judgment on the nominee's fitness and character. Rightwing social media became positively nuclear, filling chat rooms with constant vile attacks on the character and veracity of Kavanaugh's accusers, overshadowing the only real aim of the hearings. They baselessly alleged that Ford was being compensated for her testimony and was the worst kind of scum for daring to impugn the good justice with lies and suggested she should be locked up for her crime. Never mind how she had exactly zero motivation to insert herself into this madness. Set aside how her testimony would risk opening old wounds and bringing new shame after 30 years of healing from old shame. Conveniently overlooked was how a confirmation hearing has exactly nothing to do with any of the witnesses who testify either in support or in opposition to the candidate but about the candidate himself. And, never mind how regular threats of violence against her would discourage all but the most committed plaintiffs. Certainly, the claim she was paid for her testimony had no basis in fact. After the hearing, we learned that Dr. Ford unplugged from the grid and remains essentially in hiding from continued death threats to this day. How unholy must one be to justify such violent anti-social behavior toward another human being over politics? Many shameless Deplorables turned this upside down to claim the Ford testimony would ruin this good man's life. Is it awkward, that failing in his bid to achieve a life-time appointment to the SCOTUS would result in his continuing his life time appointment to the Federal Circuit Court while Dr. Ford was basically gutted in the public square? Even now, the Deplorables will use this instance as an example of liberal hypocrisy.

In March of 2019, we heard a guilty plea from the Florida Trump fanatic Cesar Sayoc who mailed 14 pipe bombs to Trump critics and CNN, the cable news outlet the 45th President and his faithful called "Fake News." Indeed, his hit list read like a regular Who's Who of whataboutism on Hannity's Facebook page. Hillary and Bill Clinton, Obama, Maxine Waters, George Soros, James Clapper, Tom Steyer, and others were sent IEDs for simply being the usual targets of Trump's twitter rage. Sayoc, who was a regular at Trump rallies across the country and rode around Florida in a white cargo van plastered with heroic images of Trump and images of his reliable critic's faces in cross hairs, pleaded guilty to 65 felony counts. Absent, of course, was a charge for domestic terrorism as remarkably, there is no standalone criminal offenses outlawing domestic terrorism in the United States, even though it is considered our gravest threat by the Department of Homeland Security and the FBI. On Facebook his account handles were things like #Killgeorge Soros and #Killall Socialists, which coincidentally, are meat and potatoes feedstock for almost all of the Deplorables. When the media linked Sayoc to his cult hero, this terrorist, who is a registered Republican and yuuuuge Trump cultist with a criminal record, was branded by the Deplorables as a Democrat simply because they could lie about it with impunity among friends. Like juvenile delinquents caught red handed shaving the dog's ass, the Deplorables will always assign responsibility for wrong doing involving their hero in the most creative ways. Trump fandom requires denying what they see with their own eyes and hear with their own ears in favor of the most elaborate Kabuki Theater.

In August of 2019 Sayoc was found guilty and was sentenced to just 20 years in prison. The judge cited the fact that his explosive devices were duds, and surmised that maybe this was a conscious choice. Never mind how this crime was undeniably a domestic terrorist attack meant to sow maximum fear and chaos. Must we even contemplate what sentencing would look like if Sayoc was Hussain and his roots could be tied to any Muslim majority country? What may be most chilling in context with the general thrust of the Deplorables' white power movement was this comment from Sayoc's attorney: "In this darkness, Mr. Sayoc found light in Donald J. Trump, He came to believe that he was being personally targeted for supporting Trump: Mr. Sayoc thought that anti-Trump forces were trying to hurt him and they were to blame when his van was vandalized." How many times must we suspend our disbelief when one violent domestic terrorist after another consciously credits Donald J. Trump for his motivation?

Ever since the day the 116th Congress convened, in January of 2019, a trio of freshman congresswomen have lived under the tyranny of constant rightwing extremist death threats. Alexandria Ocasio-

97

Cortez, Ilhan Omar and Rashida Tlaib are notable for a few reasons. They are part of the Democratic caucus in the most diverse Congress in history (no thanks to the lily white male Republicans). They are dynamic progressives. They are all women of color, and two are of Muslim faith. Their most dubious distinction is how all three receive near constant threats to their safety and even assassination threats according to Capitol Hill police and the FBI. This kind of wantonly destructive verbal terrorism from the radical haters takes a pick axe to the orderly cadence of polite society. Like so many instances of hate against "others" in the age of Trump, we continued to be blindsided by this incoherent rage. God help our beleaguered souls when we stumbled upon the usual outrage porn on popular Rightwing social media. Instead of reasoned rejection of the madness, we found amplification of the underlying grievances from disaffected misfits seeking to wage war against progressive sanity. The whole thing becomes more Petri dish than disinfectant. Between the baseless accusations of treason, and anti-Semitism, and regularly linking both Omar and Tlaib to terrorism with 9/11 imagery, the whole caboodle became just another object lesson in the kindred spirit of rampant bigotry.

In April of 2019, we learned of another Trump devotee, 55 year old Patrick Carlineo of Addison New York willing to bring ultra-violence to the cause of Islamophobia. It seems Mr. Carlineo phoned Representative Omar's office for general harassment. He asked a staffer why she works for Omar, said she "was a fucking terrorist" and added how he would "shoot her." When arrested by the Feds, he told authorities "I love President Trump" and added, he hates "radical Muslims." In March of 2020, during the sentencing hearing, Omar asked the judge for leniency for Carlineo. He was granted a light 12 month sentence.

Also in April of 2019, news of another Trump addled hater was released. Alonzo Bolin was charged with lying to the FBI when questioned about a conversation he had on Facebook with an associate about a desire to mass murder Muslim Americans in Baltimore. Bolin and his buddy, both avowed supporters of white supremacy, praised the recent carnage in Christ Church New Zealand.

Unless you live in a lead-lined hermetically sealed steamer trunk, you are probably wise to the viral wet dream bubbling up within the Rightwing Freakosphere over the next Civil War. Because the issue of slavery was settled in the previous civil war 156 years ago, this one will be waged over the less pernicious matter of liberal versus conservative ideology. Never mind how many of the issues which divide left from right still involve the treatment of people of color, civil rights and due process, this one will be blood sport between Democrats and Republicans simply because one side doesn't trust the electoral process to choose voting over mass carnage to get their way. The Deplorables are fed up with having their asses handed to them pretty regularly on social media, and in life generally, so now will act out in their typical mindless violent way against superior thinkers by threatening to kill them. This is nothing new for me as I could wallpaper my entire home with the IM death threats I've received from these intellectually challenged bottom feeders. The gist of their fantasy is that, now that the "real American patriots" have put up with liberalism so patiently and peacefully for so long, and still have not "taken their country back," enough is enough. They will organize and use their vastly greater share of the 400 million firearms in the country to make amends.

Speaking of taking their country back, in October of 2019, we learned of a thwarted mass murder plot of a domestic terrorist who was a former marine, is a self-described White Nationalist and, most recently, was a lieutenant in the US Coastguard. Apparently Christopher Hasson had drawn up a plan to eliminate well known anchors and hosts at MSNBC and CNN as well as a long list of prominent elected Democratic officials. Do I really need to list the names at this point? Anyway, Mr. Hasson wanted to kill as many traitors as possible from the ranks of "leftists generally." This man was hell bent on starting a race war but feared "much blood will have to be spilled to get whitey off the couch." Further, he hoped to capitalize on some already polarizing incidents to energize likeminded anarchists. As news of the Coast Guard's arrest blanketed the mainstream media, Sean Hannity's Facebook page launched 8 threads about the Jussie Smollet case in its stead, and exactly zero threads about this planned attack that, according to authorities, was "on a scale rarely seen." Nothing energizes the Fannities more than opining about black folks "behaving badly."

In the aftermath of his trial, this violent anarchist, who was arrested on firearms and drug charges, not for his domestic terrorism plot, was released from prison on his own recognizance pending future trial. For at least half of the American public, this legal ruling begs a simple question. If his name were Hussein or Hernandez instead, would he ever feel the warmth of actual sunlight again? Finally, in January of 2020, Hasson was sentenced to 13 years in prison.

Now that mainstream social media are beginning to develop a social conscience against the casual use of unrestrained hate speech, where can people with no conscience hang out to wallow in violent expressions of racism and harassment? Gab, which proudly boasts of

800,000 users, claims it is a champion of free speech in an age where Twitter and Facebook would impose upon your right to be truly deplorable. Gab is ground zero for coddling the damaged souls of Neo Nazis, White Supremacists and alt-righters. In October of 2018, an impossibly rageful monster entered the Tree of Life Jewish Synagogue in Pittsburgh and indiscriminately mowed down 11 worshippers during their Saturday Shabbat service with a semi-automatic AR-15 assault rifle. The shooter, Robert Bowers, who was an enthusiastic Gab user, blamed the Jews for giving aid and comfort to the migrant caravans that Deplorables have become apoplectic over in the last several years. He had recently posted a video that purported to show a Jewish refugee advocacy group HIAS on the US-Mexico border. With only slightly more animus than you would find in a discussion among Deplorables on Hannity's Facebook page, he described the efforts of the group as "sugar coated evil" and registered his approval for the trend of haters, calling the refugees "Invaders" instead of just "illegals." As he was poised to enter the synagogue, he made his final Gab post; "I can't sit by and watch my people get slaughtered. Screw your optics, I'm going in." In the aftermath of the carnage, Gab's domain registrar GoDaddy severed ties with them for their perpetuation of hate, intolerance and violence. In a response on Twitter, a Gab spokesman pleaded to Donald Trump for help saying "This is madness, I hope you are paying attention." Indeed, Trump was receptive to the cause of disaffected "conservatives" being mistreated by lying liberal media in general. In a Twitter rant less than a month after the shooting he posted this;

Facebook, Google and Twitter, not to mention the Corrupt Media, are sooo on the side of the Radical Left Democrats. But fear not, we will win anyway, just like we did before! #MAGA

101

It is important to remember that the Deplorables have existed in one virulently awful strain or another for decades. Many of the examples of unrestrained hate and violence we discuss here just happen to be recent and just happen to implicate the cult hero they found in 2016. There are many important instances of this behavior that occurred before Trump.

In June of 2015, a tragically lost soul named Dylann Roof entered the *Emanuel African Methodist Episcopal Church* in Charleston South Carolina and gunned down nine African American parishioners in a fit of White Supremacist rage. He was charged with 33 crimes and in April of 2017 was sentenced to nine consecutive life sentences for his unrestrained hate. Mr. Roof claimed in an incoherent rambling manifesto how he was "truly awakened" by the coverage of the shooting of Trayvon Martin and became obsessed, like so many of the Deplorables did, over the fairytale of rampant black on white crime. No one flogged the troubling circumstances of that 2012 Florida encounter between an innocent teen and his pursuer harder for effect than reliable outrage media jock Sean Hannity as he insisted on ascribing a motive other than self-preservation to the teen victim. His fans were positively exorcised over how Trayvon "ground and pound MMA style" poor defenseless George Zimmerman into the wet pavement. Anyway, Roof's motive for eliminating peaceful church folk that day in historic Charleston was to spark a race war. Sound familiar? In 2020, we learned of a group of online Right Wing Dylann Roof fan boys calling themselves the Bowl Gang as a tribute to the mass murderer's bowl haircut who were inspired to pick up where their cult hero left off. One of these degenerate anarchists, referring to his ambitions, said he wanted to "pull a Dylann Roof."

Tragically, this hate based ultra-violence stoked by rightwing white grievance is not limited to the US; it has reached all over the world now. In March of 2019, 28 year old Brenton Tarrant brought unimaginably violent mayhem to two mosques in Christchurch New Zealand as he livestreamed the slaughter of 50 defenseless Muslims on Instagram. Tarrant, described by authorities as a "rightwing extremist terrorist," was another asshole with a manifesto. In it was a series of unhinged tantrums about immigrants, Muslims and Jews, and he cited "white genocide" as his motivation. He said he was a proud racist and believed the American president Donald Trump was a worldwide symbol of "renewed white identity." He too imagined the next Civil war In America was coming.

Proving just how transnational violent Rightwing hatred had become in the age of Trump, just a month later we learned of a 19 year old, inspired by the events in New Zealand, who entered a Jewish Synagogue in Poway California and gunned down three during Passover with his AR-15. The attack left 1 dead and 3 wounded. This latest mayhem gathers so many of the threads we've been battered with from other racist, xenophobic bigoted attacks, to fit neatly within the jagged new reality we face. Not surprisingly we hear how John Earnest was a frequent 8Chan presence as that platform still allowed unmitigated hate speech at a time more socially responsible social media aimed to eliminate it.

Anyone familiar with the 1978 novel *The Turner Diaries* may know what is meant by the "Day of the Rope." *The Turner Diaries* is basically a White Supremacist's wet dream. It portends of a coming white supremacist overthrow of the US government to erect a Nazi regime. From it we learn the 14 words that have animated so much of the rightwing doctrine over these last 43 years. "We must secure the existence of our people and a future for white children." If this sounds familiar it's because it is. Clearly, it focuses on the appeal to preserve European ancestry against incursion by Jews and other non-white non-Christian people, and trades heavily upon the notion that without violent intervention, white Europeans may be replaced. The Day of the Rope is the day the fictional anarchists from the story will raid the homes of "race traitors" and drag them into the streets to hang them from lamp posts, signaling the beginning of a race war that will eliminate all non-whites. More currently The Day of The Rope has become an Alt-Right chat room mantra about killing journalists. In his 8 page manifesto, Earnest mentions his desire for the "Day of The Rope." As terrifying as this ideology has always been, it has been gaining more and more urgency over the last several years. The idea that rageful Deplorables will be moved by sinister forces to wage terrorism against fellow Americans is hardly farfetched, considering we have eavesdropped on their conversations about it for years.

Just when you thought we could take a breather from all of this senseless death at the hands of white power domestic terrorists, in early August of 2019 we sat shell-shocked absorbing the news of another mass murder by an ideologically driven young man in El Paso Texas. The suspect, a 21 year old, was found to have posted his attack plan on 8Chan hours before mowing down 22 souls with a semi-automatic civilian version of the AK-47, in a crowded Walmart located over 600 miles away from his home. You will hardly be surprised to learn that Patrick Crusius, who was charged with Capital Murder for this mayhem spoke of a "Hispanic invasion of Texas." He cited as inspiration for this horrific crime, the Christ Church Mosque shooting in New Zealand and a fear of white genocide. When questioned by police, he admitted he was specifically targeting Mexicans in this border town.

Tragically, violence committed in the name of hateful ideology has been a feature and a bug of our country from the beginning. The circumstances of our origins have made that somewhat inevitable. What is profoundly disturbing about the new instances of this virus is how it has been blessed as a political weapon at a point in our history when we had become so much better than this. Yes, there has always been vile hatred from some of our people, and yes, this has been manifested by atrocities committed in its service. But never has it been so overtly coaxed from the shadows where we had managed to stash it in recent years. It is nothing short of evil to exploit the endemic hatred so many have for "others" in the pursuit of power. But, isn't it more evil to willfully allow yourself to be exploited when the consequence is death and destruction? It is incumbent upon all decent Americans to call this out before we pass the proverbial point of no return.

These are but a few of the monstrous acts of violence that have seen committed by the emotionally and spiritually stunted Deplorables in the spirit of lost privilege within our increasingly inclusive and equal society. As we have noted, they dwarf the number of senseless violent crimes perpetrated against our citizens, on our own shores, by Islamic extremist terrorists but remain the subject of considerable political debate over how they should be categorized. Yes, Terrorism is a global issue, but in this country, rightwing terrorism has become our own Armageddon. Until we can all agree that terrorism is terrorism, and indeed, terrorism committed by our own people may be even more indefensible, the kabuki between sanity and insanity will continue. All of these seemingly disparate threads can be gathered into a single woven theme that threatens to rock the very idea of this great country unless we have the courage to call it out for what it is and tear it down without mercy. Will we, as a society, rise to the occasion to embrace our better angels or will we succumb to the willful distortion of our very principles? Either way, we must lobby our Congress to provide the Department of Homeland Security and our 3 letter agencies with the tools they will need to hold home grown extremists as accountable as Islamic terrorists for the politically or ideologically motivated killing of Americans. We pray it will not take an incident as horrific as 9/11 to convince us the threat is every bit as dire.

Chapter Twelve

The Turner Diaries

"One of the major purposes of political terror, always and everywhere, is to force the authorities to take reprisals and to become more repressive, thus alienating a portion of the population and generating sympathy for the terrorists. And the other purpose is to create unrest by destroying the population's sense of security and their belief in the invincibility of the government."

William Luther Pierce, The Turner Diaries, 1978

On April 19th 1995, Timothy McVeigh was apprehended by law enforcement the very day he brought unimaginable horror to Oklahoma City, OK from his bombing of the Murrah Federal building. A small white envelope was discovered in the front seat of his vehicle. Scrawled across the face of it was a chilling message "Obey the Constitution and we won't shoot you." Within were various rightwing propaganda screeds and several photo copied pages from the 1978 Dystopian white nationalist fan-favorite novel, *The Turner Diaries*. Written by William Luther Pierce, under the pseudonym Andrew Macdonald, the Turner Diaries quickly became the animating voice of the white nationalist movement and is still celebrated 43 years later by White Supremacists, militia members and other seditious agitators.

The story describes the dystopian aftermath of a massive federal government confiscation of all firearms led by blacks and Jews and describes the apocalyptic overthrow of the "System" by the militant White Revolutionary movement called "The Order," culminating in a race war that spreads across the entire world. McVeigh joins an infamous group of domestic terrorists influenced over the years by this fictional anarchy that has led to the murders of more than 300 Americans. History informs us that McVeigh drew parallels between the events in the Turner Diaries and events occurring in real time during the Clinton administration regarding government overreach and infringement upon 2nd Amendment rights. Within the envelope were also several news clippings about the events at Ruby Ridge and Waco Texas in 1992 and 1993 respectively.

What is most disturbing about all of this is how enduring the themes from the book are to this very day. All fringe movements distribute themselves along a standard bell curve from least to most radical, but one universal message seems to resonate quite vibrantly across the spectrum of those identifying as right leaning: virulent mistrust of federal oversight of firearms possession and regulation and violent fantasies about the inevitability of the next racial civil war. The Deplorables have mainlined hate and fear over minorities for so long that they readily accept the idea that their very survival as a race depends upon the expulsion, and even extermination, of malign "others." Along the continuum of radicalization, this manifests as a rejection of racial intermingling to an ultimate showdown between whites and all non-whites.

108

The mood among those who identify with these violent anti-social impulses seems to rest precariously at a tipping point. When anarchist passions explode into real world violence and death, we watch incredulously, as many of our fellow citizens offer endless apologies and excuses, and even blame victims over perpetrators. When the prevailing excuse for dangerous radicalism becomes he/she/they/it made me do it, we know the apologists have reached a point of no return.

It is very disconcerting that the same people who embrace the tenets of White Nationalist revolution were the most ardent supporters of our 45th President. Virtually all extremist Rightwing hate groups identify with the prevailing grievance agenda popularized by Trump and imagined their hero would make amends for years of disaffection with their government. It is unthinkable how many who commit atrocities inspired by Turner, also attribute inspiration to our last leader. Continuing to normalize this ideological allegiance is a perversion which must be resisted by all who are guided by a moral compass. During the 2016 election, shameless politicos and talking heads channeled the same distrust militants like McVeigh had about the Clinton administration in the early 90s to sow ominous new warnings about Hillary Clinton. In the aftermath of the election, when the new president and hordes of fervent believers chanted "lock her up, lock her up" an alarming number of Deplorables reached back in time to gather together decades of baseless fears about the Clintons in general as further justification for it. Where those efforts fell short of galvanizing the Deplorables, heinous new allegations of criminality were invented. For Trump this may have been an effort to neutralize political enemies, for his supporters it seemed far more personal. The rawness of emotion has primed the wick requiring vigilance from all who seek better for our union before we must endure epic conflagrations between good and evil

109

forces. White rage has welled up inside a significant number of the Deplorables and now threatens to overwhelm civil society. It is time to empower new Congressional leadership to hold accountable those who would attack our country to place their intrinsic needs above all others. Whether you identify as a Democrat or a Republican, if you are a Commendable person, it is time pause your support for Republican leaders until the party proves they can govern again and seeks to appeal to a country craving a center left or center right mooring. There is a place in America for all who love her but people who simply can't live peacefully within the melting pot, must be locked away with the same urgency we would lock away foreign born terrorists. Decoupling the Deplorable movement from the GOP will eliminate the thin veneer of respectability they have enjoyed for the last several years. Politics is a purely mercenary sport. Parties will only latch themselves to a counter decency movement if it represents electoral fortune.

Chapter Thirteen

He/she said what?

"Gaslighting is a distorted alternate reality."

Tracy Malone

Sometimes, the clearest understanding of the Deplorables came from measuring their reactions to the Mad King and his coterie of enablers. Otherwise, there would be no reason to dwell so frequently on such bit players. The contrast between how Commendables and Deplorables processed so much of the performance art that masqueraded as governance during the Trump term, revealed the depths of a disease which they would surely succumb to over time. The endless lies and constant gaslighting were like sea biscuits chummed out to the hungriest of deranged seals who always clapped madly for more.

For four years, it was great fun to watch Kellyanne Conway show up at CNN to gaslight. As a professional spin doctor, she has a very specific skill set which can transform the purely ludicrous into something more digestible for the mainstream while not offending those who abhor the mainstream. Once, when Trump was given a chance to clean up his comments from 2 years earlier, when he said there were "very fine people" on both sides during skirmishes at the Unite the

Right Rally in Charlottesville, Kellyanne was asked to weigh in. Because apologizing for Trump is like setting his own balls on fire, he chose to conclude how his response then was "perfect," and went on to explain he meant all of the folks there who were in favor of preserving the *Robert E. Lee Confederate Monument* were very fine people. This was fundamentally understandable, considering how everyone says Lee was among our very best generals, even though he led a traitorous secessionist insurrection against our Republic back in the day. Plus, any insurrectionist who fought for inequality was aces to the Deplorables, who only wished they could find new "patriots" to perform a modern rebel yell. Anyway, unbeknownst to Trump, the Unite the Right rally was a White Supremacist rally organized by White Supremacist Richard Spencer to promote, wait for it, yes, White supremacy. The pasty- faced gnomes Trump identified as fine people, had gathered that day to pay their respects to the very fine general while chanting how the Jews will not replace them. The Jews certainly were a treacherous lot, in the estimation of the Deplorables, for the aid and comfort they have always given the liberal New World Order. Apparently Trump heard "You will not replace him" which is understandable considering how he is not getting any younger and often says very simple words in odd ways.

Usually when folks join a peaceful rally in support of a cause they hold dear, they arrive bearing brightly painted signs expressing their love. Oddly the very fine White supremacists came cloaked in Nazi attire, carrying semi-automatic weaponry and tiki-torches instead. Why quibble to say this looked more like a planned rumble than a campfire Kumbaya when the president assured us otherwise? After all, he had condemned the White Supremacists, Neo Nazis and KKK a couple of times before, after mere days of not doing so when asked to. In fairness, it's not always easy to articulate such nuanced positions as condemnation for racial anarchists. And when those racial anarchists represented the president's most electorally significant consistency, the matter must be handled delicately or not at all.

When cornered by Jake Tapper to explain the president's self-flagellation, Conway reminded us how clear Trump is on matters like this even when the media, the people, and even members of his own party are stumped. "Kellyanne it's a simple question" the host pleaded, "was Trump's response perfect?" How could he possibly know he'd have to ask the same thing multiple times against an onslaught of off topic rope-a-dope from the president's senior advisor, or Blueberry, as they called her in the Whitehouse? Thankfully, we did learn, how the economy was booming and, more importantly how AG William Barr's 4 pager had completely exonerated Trump for all crimes he's ever been accused of, except the one time he jaywalked to avoid confronting a sketchy black dude at a crosswalk. She proceeded to run out the clock attacking Joe Biden for daring to bring up Trump's Charlottesville mess and then Hillary Clinton for no apparent reason other than preventing another question, and because bashing Hillary was like snorting Meth Amphetamine for the Deplorables.

Soon we discovered from Rightwing chatrooms just how crystal clearly their hero's prevarication landed with Deplorables and how, they too, would rather set their own genitals on fire than admit otherwise. But, admitting there were fine people on both sides was a bridge too far. In their estimation, the counter protesters were Antifa or Black Lives Matter agitators who clearly are always the terrorist provocateurs. The fact that one of the "very fine people' struck and killed Heather Heyer, by ramming his car into the BLM crowd, had to be made benign somehow. After the murder, Heather's mom captured the stench rising

113

from this rotting fish when she said "A white girl had to die for people to pay attention." Certainly standing against hate unacceptably infringed upon the hater's 1ˢᵗ Amendment rights to hate and kill. Ms. Heyer must be viewed as collateral damage in the Deplorable's primal need to rewrite the history of the Confederacy.

By the way, during another exchange between them, Tapper asked Conway whether Trump still believed his comment made six weeks earlier, that Rightwing extremist violence was not on the rise, and only amounted to few "really sick people" in light of multiple massacres committed by Rightwing fanatics since then. Tapper resisted the temptation to point out a common theme for many of the attacks were specific props given by the perpetrators to one Donald J. Trump for their inspiration. Kellyanne said the president has been clear...

The Unite the Right episode was a text book example of gaslighting. Commendables who recognized that evil forces among us were beginning to coalesce again around the most shameful parts of our history, were accused by Deplorables of wanting to cancel that history. But, we know history is recorded in many ways and historians will choose how exactly we will document the events of our times. It must be terribly inconvenient for those protesting in favor of preserving monuments to dead secessionist leaders of the Anti-American cause, that these men were commemorated, not in the immediate aftermath of the Civil War, but long after it, as a nod to Jim Crow. Do we really choose to support this kind of enduring intimidation?

Because we know the history of the Civil war is indelibly captured in history books, perhaps we can continue to lobby our local government to remove the faces of its awful legacy, that cause so many people so much pain, from the public squares where it continues to

114

inspire such ugliness. That this seems to inflame the passions of people for whom our last Civil War was a prelude for our next Civil War, may be justification enough.

Chapter Fourteen

Mueller weighs in

"When (former Attorney General) Jeff Sessions told the President that a Special Counsel had been appointed, the President slumped back in his chair and said, 'Oh my God. This is terrible. This is the end of my Presidency. I'm fucked.'"

Mueller Report

As we examine so much of the malfeasance that took place over four years of the Trump administration, it is important to remain clear eyed over the implications. Again, we care about how malodorous Trump himself was, but we care more about assessing the threat his flock will represent until they are politically and socially neutralized. Every crime Donald Trump has been accused of since he was elected president has created much of the tension between the Commendables and Deplorables, as protagonists and antagonists in this account. We must remain vigilantly aware how so much of this truth jockeying had become cannon fodder for epic confrontations to come.

In April of 2019, the Entertainer in Chief took to the stage in Grand Rapids to invite thousands of pasty faced-friends of all stripes to

116

gloat over his "complete and total EXONERATION" from charges of collusion and obstruction of justice. This latest circle jerk among the Trump faithful came within a few days of the release of a Cliff Notes pamphlet sized assessment from the president's hyper partisan new AG, summarizing in 4 pages, the 400+ pages of findings from nearly two years of investigation. The general idea was to high five each other long enough in advance of the actual release of the Mueller Report to fabricate a kinder alternative reality from what we might someday learn. Yes, Trump was an irredeemable dirt bag, lacking even the pretense of allegiance to truth or a fealty to our Constitution, but he wasn't locked up for his crimes so there's that. To a wildly adoring crowd of misfits who still chanted "Lock him up" and "Lock her up" and "Build that wall" incoherently, Trump worked up an orange faced flop sweat scattering new conspiratorial breadcrumbs around the arena and asking to hold accountable any "pencil necked" opponent from Congress and our Intelligence agencies for treason. The crowd went wild. Their stable genius was always playing 3 dimensional chess, and would soon hold accountable for crimes those trying to hold him accountable for crimes.

But, at the risk of being redundant, I will remind my readers, this story is not principally about Trump, or anyone within his criminal cabal. With the kind of certainty we know Scooby and the gang will eventual stumble upon a local businessman in wingtips impersonating a scary ghost, we know Russia attacked our democracy and will continue to do so. Our intelligence community made that manifestly clear years ago. It is only toward viewers of the episode who remained on the edge of their seats rejecting the obvious throughout the Special Counsel's investigation, that we are puzzled or repulsed. Suborning all of the unhinged madness through mindless adoration of a conman simply because he claims, like you, he is disturbed by how multi-cultural and

117

multi-racial we are becoming is the real crime against humanity. The entire purpose of appointing a Special Prosecutor in the Russian investigation was to remove an administration, possibly complicit, from adjudicating the very crimes which may have been committed. The purpose really wasn't so the Deplorables would discover a new boogey man they could vilify for years. Allowing a kindred spirit of an Attorney General to provide a summary interpretation of the conclusions instead of immediately releasing the report itself to Congress, for proper oversight, and swift release to the broader public, was simply indefensible. So, on cue, the Deplorables defended it. They had forgotten, or willfully disregarded, that the entire reason Mueller was appointed was that Trump fired his FBI director "Over this Russian thing," for not administering his will to shut it down. For the bipartisan remedy of appointing Special Counsel, the Trump supporters vilified the former decorated marine and lifelong Republican public servant leading the investigation.

The standoff between Congress and the DOJ would surely languish long enough for Trump to win the narrative that this was the "witch hunt" he had called it from the beginning. Witch hunts for the Deplorables are like bobbing for apples for the Commendables; sports offering good clean fun and a participation prize for participants.

Anyone with a mammal's noodle knows that indicting and convicting a sitting president is almost impossible. The standard for bringing a criminal indictment against Trump was simply never going to be achieved without witnessing him shooting a man dead on Fifth Avenue. Mueller's mandate did not include murder, and the broader question of treason was never in play. Conspiracy to defraud the United States was, and even a smoking gun surrounded by hundreds of

118

expended shell casings was too circumstantial a case over which to upend our Constitutional republic. We would come to find out that even that impossible standard was more impossible because Mueller was guided by Office of Legal Counsel guidance against indicting a sitting president. The Deplorables jumped the shark entirely by insisting the lack of bringing an indictment, when you are expressly prohibited from bringing an indictment, is proof of no malfeasance. The Deplorables always made the Special Counsel's case exclusively about their hero, and they rejected even the premise of "collusion" as a Deep State conspiracy. So, they attacked every 3 letter institution viciously, without regard for many real crimes that were uncovered and showed no remorse for the patriotic public servants whose lives had been ruined to perpetuate the fairytale. Distinguishing right from wrong is quaint, but the Deplorable's only allegiance is to winning over losing, and winners must take all, no matter what ethical dilemmas must be suppressed. Even nastier was rejecting how Russia, a Donald Trump benefactor, remained a principal enemy of our great country. Spoiler alert; In the fevered imaginations of the alt-right, Russia is regarded as more of an ally than foe, in promoting white supremacy, which is the very blood that courses through their veins. This fact makes baseless counter claims of Russian collusion with Obama and Hillary Clinton a laughable dodge. Welcome to Adventures in Alternative Reality.

Throughout this sordid scandal, rightwing social media were positively ablaze with phony outrage and the kind of Whataboutism young children have always used to make their parents crazy. "Ok, so I microwaved the cat, but what about Suzy putting the fire out with the garden hose?" For every new revelation from mainstream "fake news" casting shadows on the anointed one, the Deplorables insisted on counter factual claims against Obama or Hillary Clinton, or Mueller or

Strzok, or Rosenstein, or Adam Schiff and or even the Obama's dog Bo. Flinging their own incoherent "facts" around wildly like diseased feces was their antidote to dealing with manifest reality. Certainly, their gold plated icon was as pure as a virgin in the driven snow and guiltless of anything more than jaywalking. After all, in 40 years in the public eye, who could take issue with a single angelic thing Trump had ever done? As the purview of top law enforcement expanded to consider much more than Russian Collusion, and the accusations become far harder to defend, the Whataboutism only intensified. So, Trump leveraged the Whitehouse for personal gain; what about Hillary Clinton's pay-to-play leverage from the Clinton Foundation? So, Trump used his charitable foundation as a personal piggybank; what about the Clintons, how do you suppose they became so filthy rich? So, Trump wouldn't reveal his taxes after promising to do so when the IRA concluded their audit; what about Obama and his birth certificate and college transcripts? So, Trump met secretly with Vladimir Putin on multiple occasions without witnesses; what about Obama's hot mic moment with Medvedev promising "more flexibility" once reelected? So, Trump wanted to foster stronger bonds with the Russian government; what about Clinton selling them 20% of our uranium in exchange for mammoth donations to her foundation? So, Trump was a serial sexual predator; what about Bill Clinton? So, Donald Trump enacted a zero tolerance policy toward "illegals," and separated children from parents of "invaders" to discourage migration; what about Obama beginning that practice years before? Wasn't it he personally who built the cages in his own workshop? You get the gist.

None of the counter claims could withstand basic scrutiny without the blanket protection of vilifying the mainstream media as "fake news" and enemies of the state. None of the dots could be

120

connected to the satisfaction of society's disaffected Deplorables without willfully undermining any and all of the institutions of our justice system and our intelligence apparatus. Alternative reality, as a coping mechanism, continued to animate the cult, now completely gripped by Stockholm Syndrome as their charismatic leader demanded they take another for the team. The unifying conspiracy theories about the patriotic greatness of their hero covertly beating back a Deep State takeover of the country loomed larger with each new scandal. Violent fantasies about how they would support an America First agenda against the will of the majority found broad acceptance within the tribe. The rhetoric throttled ever higher, the violent imagery became more vivid, the chasm between left and right widened. This was quickly escalating toward all out anarchy.

Regardless of what we finally learn from the Mueller Report and what comes of multiple other Congressional and Attorney's General investigations, the Donald has been a bad boy by any objective reckoning. The remedy for grifting off of America and distorting her principles can't be the near impossible standard of criminal indictments. It can't even be the remedy of convicting an impeached president, as a divided Congress makes this impossible too. No, the reckoning for his endless malfeasance must be settled at the ballot box in 2020. The wrecking ball he has willfully taken, for his own enrichment and amusement, to all of the societal norms and principled institutions that make possible our Constitutional Republic, must be stopped. His unconscionable undermining of traditionally marginalized and easily vilified "others" in the name of making America great again is nothing short of horrific and must be atoned for in a polite society. Anything short of excising this cancer from our body politic will only bend back the arc of our history toward a darker less enlightened age.

Our fight will be met squarely by soulless partisan hacks both within our government and from a subservient statist Rightwing media machine. Our biggest struggle will be against hate incarnate among a sizable share of our own people, who are convinced their very survival depends upon defeating progress. Buckle up Commendables; this will be a wild ride indeed.

Nearly three weeks after Barr's synopsis of the Mueller Report, instructing the public exactly how all of the material should be interpreted, and pronouncing his boss "exonerated" for collusion and obstruction of justice, a heavily redacted version of the report was finally released to the public on April 18th 2019. Barr had already led up to this moment with lots of gaslighting about counter investigations he might endorse for how the FBI indeed did spy on the Trump campaign, only backtracking when the media pointed out how loaded the term "spying" was to describe what actually happened. Besides actually appointing a special prosecutor to throw shade on the origins of the Russia investigation, in the end, the politically motivated gambit fell short and was not even concluded before the 2020 election. It may have been awkward too that the idea that Clinton, Obama, Comey, McCabe, Strzok, Rosenstein, and Mueller himself, may all still be indicted some day for treason was eventually put to rest. No one but Barr and the administration itself knew why exactly another Cliff's Notes regurgitation delivered 2 hours before the actual release was necessary other than to thoroughly confuse the matter. We also learned the White House had a thorough read through of this material before this day, which seemed odd considering Barr insisted they would not get a sneak peek. Things seemed clearer when we realized their attorneys had already completed their 30 page rebuttal several days before. Anyway, finally the public could waltz through most of the

Special Counsel's account of the Trump administration's complicity in the Russian hack of our election and the endless attempts of an allegedly innocent president obstructing justice whenever possible. This report was anything but pretty.

Before the release, most alert humans were already a bit skeptical that Barr's 4 page "in depth analysis" of the nearly 468 page report really captured all of the important nuance inherent in the Special Counsel's investigation and the basis for his recommendations. Using the word "exonerated," when the report took unusual pains to say the President was not, muddied up the waters a bit. I am no legal beagle, but to me, after slogging through this trove, the take away was pretty straightforward. Trump and his associates were willfully involved in many illicit activities, and then covering up for them, but, because Mueller could not indict the head of the rotting fish, he would leave punishment for the crimes to Congress if they wanted to impeach Trump or to other prosecutorial bodies to indict once Trump was out of office. The fact is, there was mounting pressure for Mueller to wrap up far sooner than most investigations of this kind do. While Mueller's investigation was always a thorn in the Republican Congress' side, it was the next presidential election looming less than 2 years out that really prodded the release of the report.

Spoiler alert, even though Mueller's findings were highly disturbing, and painted a picture of a lawless leader, an EKG machine couldn't detect any change in the Deplorables' hearts. They were reliable cheerleaders throughout for every loophole, every "scandal" that misdirected, and every questionable ruling throughout the investigation that favored their side with exactly zero regard for right or wrong. In a very real sense, they mounted their own obstruction of justice campaign on social media. Though the spoils were largely symbolic, we cannot underestimate the influence of the public opinion generated. Their message discipline about their hero was rock solid. The only thing that varied for them was who among Trump's inner sanctum deserved the same reverence as their hero, and that teetered and tottered exclusively on the whims of the Dear Leader, which teetered and tottered on how stable a genius he seemed at any given moment. So many within Trump's orbit during this ordeal were irredeemable dirt bags start to finish. But, over time, their acceptance or rejection by the Deplorables hinged exclusively on how loyal they seemed to be to the president and not at all on their character or lawfulness. It would be like saying; "I realize John Wayne Gacy raped and murdered 33 teenagers, but shouldn't we really wait to see if he supports Trump before judging him harshly?" Perhaps the Deplorable's calculation is even more cynical. Maybe it is more like; "I won't judge the child rapist murderer at all until my hero, a cult father figure to me, tweets his disapproval or approval." Either way, the Deplorables assessments of good versus evil remained highly mercurial.

At long last, Mueller himself, stepped before the cameras to deliver an 8 minute synopsis of his findings. He addressed an American public split almost evenly between those understanding the conclusions from the report, and those remaining clueless about a report they wouldn't read themselves under threat of an unsedated colonoscopy performed with a whaling harpoon. Certainly for the Deplorables, ignorance was more blissful than listening to Mueller's 'but seriously folks' reiteration of his principle conclusions. Mercifully for the Deplorables, Mueller disappeared as quickly as he arrived, taking no questions from a media eager to ask him how pissed he was by Team Trump's Creative Exoneration theory. As they listened to the Special

Counsel insist he was guided by the infamous Office of Legal Counsel in recommending no indictments, despite enumerating over a dozen offenses that 1000 current and former prosecutors insisted were indictable offenses for anyone other than a sitting president, they heard "blah, blah, blah, we wasted your tax dollars for this Deep State witch hunt." Only in TrumpLandia is the evidence of a rampant crime spree less relevant than whether or not the perp can be held accountable. And only in TrumpLandia must perpetrators aligned with the cause never be held accountable for their crimes.

The Deplorables were unamused by Mueller's insinuation that the crimes committed should be taken up by another body, namely Congress, which could hold the Grifter in Chief accountable. Even less gracefully accepted was the hint that Trump might indeed be culpable upon leaving office. So all this was hung out to dry like soiled knickers on a clothesline for the public to stew over in chat rooms around the country as the Deplorables clung to their messy delusions. The prevailing genius edition talking point was "there can be no obstruction of justice, if there was not an indictable underlying crime" as if an enterprising suicide bomber couldn't be scooped up by law enforcement if he only discussed his plan with FBI agents but didn't send himself and hundreds of others to Kingdom Come. Torturing that metaphor a little more, it seemed the Deplorables also believe that firing the cops who are investigating your plot to bomb a middle school is perfectly reasonable if you have the authority to fire any law enforcement official you want to. Why quibble over underlying motives or the natural laws of cause and effect, when the perp gets away with his crimes? Hell, why even quibble over the fact that crimes were committed? Apparently, fealty to truth and justice is only commendable when it works against your adversaries, not when it places your hero in the cross hairs. Clearly hoping their hero gets away with all his crimes remains the animating force in TrumpLandia, where the existential struggle for unearned privilege demands having the champion for their cause remain free from incarceration.

The House of Representatives took Mueller's bait. They were already embroiled in their own cat fight over whether or not to bring an impeachment inquiry against Trump and hauling Mueller himself before multiple committees seemed a reasonable stepping stone. In July of 2019 they would seek to have Mueller expand upon his cursory comments in front of an American public who overwhelmingly resisted the temptation to read 468 pages of legalese for themselves but would be delighted to watch the video version. They would never admit it, but this development threw the Deplorables into yet another hissy fit. They knew more than anyone that seeing and hearing Mueller speak for himself might be a game changer. Time to further muddy up the reputation of a Purple Heart and Bronze Star recipient for meritorious service in Viet Nam, with the sole purpose of providing cover for their cult hero.

The Deplorables are always more impressed by the sizzle than the steak. Simply slather enough creamy sauce over barely edible meat and viola, a culinary delight. So, when Mueller finally offered testimony to the Intelligence Committee, but came off more like a reluctant, doddering old man than the mastermind for a meticulous case against the 45th president of the United States, appearance was all that mattered. When Mueller reiterated in significant detail how he was constrained in leveling criminal charges against Trump by the Office of Legal Counsel memoranda, the Deplorables heard "no Collusion, no Obstruction." The fact that William Barr had already stated these conclusions brought

126

instant rigor mortis to the exonerate first, ask questions later, crowd. Anyone on intimate terms with these hobgoblins knew, from that moment on, what the rightwing narrative would be. For two years preceding this day, Deplorables nationwide were positively religious in proclaiming how "Collusion" was not an actual crime. Now, they insisted the word was 100% synonymous with Conspiracy, a charge Muller felt he could not adjudicate for lack of access to the perpetrator in determining his motivation. I vaguely remember an aging old goblin named Giuliani reminding us until our ears bled, he couldn't find "collusion" in the federal code with an electron microscope and therefore his client must walk among angels. Maybe I am paraphrasing a tad but, the post Mueller corollary was how the Special Counsel agreed 100% and that's why "Collusion" must now be called "conspiracy" to connect dots that were always hopelessly parallel for the benefit of people who cannot even be bothered with dots at all.

Chapter Fifteen

Bill got it wrong

"There are schizophrenics with Tourette's who are more in control of what comes out of their mouths than Donald Trump"

Bill Maher

I am a huge Bill Maher fan, but on one thing, I couldn't disagree with him more. He says, "You can hate Trump but you can't hate his followers." For Maher, who abhors the politically correct, this seems a bit of a fumble to me. I realize his statement is more about pragmatism than whether or not he condones the legions of Deplorables energized by 45. He fears that ostracizing them will only stoke their enthusiasm for being even more awful. Does Bill really imagine we didn't cross that threshold years ago? Where he confuses forest from trees is in diagnosing where the real evil in our country exists. Yes, Trump is a truly awful specimen. Something that the Cologuard people would return postage due if he was sent to their lab. But realistically he is first and foremost a shameless opportunist and self-promoter. It was the day he identified a constituency large enough, and dumb enough, to endorse him as an unlikely hero for the cause of white supremacy, that he pieced together an ad hoc agenda to turn out their vote. He may or may not own all of his visible gunk but that is the precisely the "'art of the deal". Like any grifter, much of what he says and does is performance art, malleable as necessary, and sensitive to the feedback he receives from fanatics.

Respectfully, I would suggest that Bill Maher not obsess over the inevitable. Whether or not we hate on the haters who love what Donald Trump sells, they will continue demanding it and buying it from the next dealer anyway. They will also react as violently and stupidly as ever when the supply side is threatened.

Still I will show my Bill Maher love with this homage to his signature "I don't know it for a fact...I just know it's true" bit.

I don't know it for a fact but...I just know it is true:

- The CDC will contact trace 5 million Covid infections back to Trump's final five MAGA super spreader circle jerks.

- White suburban women would rather fellate thorny porcupines than ever vote for Trump again.

- When the Deplorables wore masks in public places it was only for fear the blue hairs at Aldi would throat punch them if they weren't. And even when they did, they left one strategically important orifice or another uncovered.

- That millions of the Deplorable's children are currently enrolled in paramilitary militia training in Wilcox County, Alabama.

- When Donald Trump ralphed up a hair ball, the secret service doused it with hydrochloric acid to remove it from the Oval Office carpeting.

- That tens of thousands of Deplorables are plotting violent crimes against their liberal tormentors at this very moment.
- That at least 1000 Deplorables have injected themselves with Clorox Bleach, or stuffed a UV light up their poop shoots at the first sign of a 100 degree high fever
- The people who give Trump his glorious orange spray tan will spend a lifetime trying to unsee that.
- Every Deplorable in America will choose herd mentality over any Covid vaccine endorsed by either Dr. Fauci or Bill Gates
- That still no Deplorables have actually read the Mueller report though all are 100% sure about what it does and does not conclude.
- The Deplorables would sooner toss dwarfs than listen to a symphony when asked to choose a culturally uplifting activity.
- That with Trump's loss in the 2020 election, the My Pillow Guy will lapse back into heroin addiction and then die from an overdose of oleandrin.
- Some Deplorable from Franklin Kentucky is plotting the assassinations of Tom Hanks and Celine Dion.
- That within the last few days of the election cycle, Mitch McConnell wanted to drown Trump in the Potomac.
- That Sean Hannity piddles a little when Trump pets him on his head.
- Joe Biden's new Secretary of Defense, will raid Mara-a-Lago and remove Trump at Gun Point for masquerading as the president.
- That well over a million Q faithful are contemplating suicide now that the nothing burger Durham Report landed after the

election, and Rudy Giuliani may lose his law license and land in prison because he couldn't prevent Joe Biden form becoming our 46th president.

- Just for shits and giggles, a few clever Deplorables are organizing their own MAGA rally to be held inside a phone booth and attended by 60 mask less MAGATs to protest against human intelligence.

- That Donald J. Trump wears Superman Underoos.

- The Deplorables will run out of sports to watch, and companies to patronize, long before they realize Colin Kaepernick disrespected neither the flag nor our soldiers the day he quietly took a knee in protest.

- Deplorables who attended MAGA rallies found Waldo 3 or 4 times more than actual black faces.

- That 3 of 5 Deplorables will attend a white's only Nationalist meeting this week, while the other 2 lament how there is not one within 100 miles of their home.

- A dozen angry Trumpers have added Savannah Guthrie to a list of liberal targets to kidnap and try for treason.

- That 10 of 10 Deplorables will draw a black face when asked to jot down what they think of first when they hear the word "thug".

- Donald Trump is privately shitting his britches over the prospect of being imprisoned sometime in 2021.

- A dozen Deplorables are asking other Deplorables right now "why do black thugs get to call each other the 'N' word but we do not?"

- Trump asked the Secret Service to put down a Snickerdoodle that wandered onto the Whitehouse lawn.

- The FBI will question a dozen Deplorables over their excessive preoccupation with pedophilia.

- There are more pipe bombs under construction than residents now living in Miami, TX.

- 200,000 Deplorable kids are convinced their MAGA hats will protect them from Covid infection more than wearing masks.

- A couple thousand people in America just said "wait, what did Trump say about our vets?"

- Millions upon millions of Deplorables are posting on Facebook right now without the foggiest notion of which is the correct homophone to use for there/their/they're and will use them randomly and interchangeably in the same post.

- Most Deplorables are boycotting Wayfair for the online retailer's nasty habit of trafficking young children to pedophiles and cannibals.

- Donald Trump would insist he wouldn't know Mary Trump if she was standing right next to him.

- 9 of 10 Deplorables believe extra-judicial violence committed by white militia groups is simply not the same as the mayhem Antifa sows but can't explain the reason why except among themselves behind closed doors.

- Donald Trump has as much contempt for his supporters, the "disgusting people" he chose Covid infection over, than they do for "illegal invaders".

- A couple million Deplorables are still excluding all of the unarmed black males killed by rogue police from their list of all lives that matter.

- Every Deplorable in the country assumes it will be Kamala or Kamala-mala-mala, who takes the presidential reins from Biden sometime in 2021.

- The Deplorables will soon run out of "others" to blame for their hero's incompetence, catastrophic failures, and mounting legal jeopardy. At which point, they will consult the Greek alphabet for new names to use in random incoherent hate posts.

- Virtually all of the voting aged Deplorables will find voting by mail a perfectly respectable alternative to voting in person, from now on.

Chapter Sixteen

So, Immigration is a threat now?

"Remember, remember always that all of us, and you and I especially, are descended from immigrants and revolutionists."

Franklin D. Roosevelt

A reliably divisive issue in America has always been immigration, both legal and Illegal. Hidden within the legitimate issue over protecting the sovereignty and security of our border lurks a darker divide over which peoples in the world our citizens believe are worthy of exploring/attaining the American Dream. It is undeniable many have hoped our leaders would gerrymander the acceptable mix of different peoples and different cultures, and it is clear that this has overwhelmingly been premised on the basis of racial purity. Though our country is ostensibly committed to the idea of a harmonious melting pot that remains more an ideal than an historical fact, many believe this country remains of, by, and for the white man. Where this gets really ugly is when the White Supremacists define multi-racialism and multi-culturalism as threats to our survival as a predominantly European white Christian country. For these Deplorables, brown and black outsiders are reframed as "invaders" and regarded as violent and uncivilized animals seeking to infiltrate our land by force to rob us of our riches. The Deplorables actively imagine all kinds of sinister plots to overwhelm the natural order of things in favor of the invaders and against the viability of "traditional" America. Peaceful coexistence would depend upon a plus-sum assessment of US migration, which doesn't exist for Deplorables convinced that forces beyond their control aim to replace them and create a new world order for non-white hegemony. At its most extreme, the accusation is white genocide. When the aimless and disaffected speak in terms of genocidal threats to their own kind, you can bet violent backlashes will follow. It is not coincidental that the more fervently they hold racist and xenophobic biases, the more likely people will insist "others" are violent predators. The idea of exterminating this threat is mainstreamed among the Deplorables.

Life for decent families in Honduras, Guatemala and El Salvador has become so untenable in the last few years that a historically large number have fled their homelands. Abject poverty, unimaginable violence and food insecurity have forced hundreds of thousands of families to trek thousands of dangerous miles to our Southern border for a 3.7% chance at salvation through asylum. Not only are they fleeing violence, but they also are actively protecting their children from gang recruitment and sex trafficking exploitation. Is it because their struggles have left them like "bastards and cripples and broken things," that the Deplorables are so easily able to dehumanize them? Since when has it been anything but uncharitable to feel so little for the tempest tossed?

For four years, the Trump administration implemented a series of policies designed to discourage this desperate mission and to choke off what small hope for success families clung to by criminalizing the previously orderly and lawful process of petitioning for asylum. They actively sought to make the consequences for escaping hell an even greater hell. Where once entering the country illegally and then petitioning for asylum brought misdemeanor charges, quickly dismissed, now asylees are immediately charged with an aggravated felony, which virtually always prohibits them from petitioning. This was a blatant attempt to drastically reduce the number of credible candidates for asylum while increasing expedited deportations. Adding insult to injury, these newly minted felons are aggregated into misleading statistics about crimes committed by aliens to justify long incarcerations and even more punitive measures. As the Trump administration ended the "catch and release' doctrine of previous administrations, asylum seekers were required to huddle on the southern side of our border for years, instead of within the US, as their cases were adjudicated. The Deplorables joined their Divider in Chief in justifying this with the baseless belief that 99% of all asylees simply disappeared inside the country to rape, pillage and maraud rather than face the outcomes of their hearings. In fact, almost 70% do show up for their final hearings, according to Politifact, while other studies place this as high as 90%. And whether or not they disappear within the country, they are statistically far less likely to commit violent offenses. The fact that refugees tend to migrate to specific, more tolerant parts of the country, only increases the chance they will be invalidated targets of perpetual anti-immigrant outrage by Deplorables, who will vilify them as invaders and as likely illegal Democratic voters living in Blue State America.

Another twisted obsession the Deplorables have had since the Obama administration, is specifically about Somali refugees. Muslim refugees are considered even less worthy of compassion than people from Southern and Central America. Most of the estimated 75,000

Somali refugees living in the Twin Cities of MN today, Settled there after the start of the civil war in that country in the early 1990's. The prevailing wisdom among Deplorables is that Obama purposefully settled 70,000 Somali refugees In the Twin Cities for political effect, despite the fact that during his terms in office only 54,000 total Somalis were settled across the entire US. This is but a single purposeful fabrication disreputable Deplorable manipulators have weaponized against both Islamic immigration and the motives of our 44th president. A recurring theme on the Right is that this completely fabricated factoid explains why Ilhan Omar ran for and won election to Congress in 2016. The theory is that she was a radical Islamic extremist, indeed a terrorist, sent in to mobilize an anti-American Sharia threat orchestrated by the former president. This fairytale is confusing on so many fronts. First, the fifth District in MN has voted overwhelmingly Democrat since the 1960's. There is no reason to imagine Omar not performing well in the district with or without significant Somali and or Muslim support. Indeed she beat her Republican opponent by 57%! As mentioned, most of the 75,000 Somali ex pats currently in the state arrived before Obama was even a political glimmer in anyone's eyes. During his terms in office, a total of only 6,300 Somalis settled in the state. George W. actually beat Obama on this metric with 9,800 Somali refugees settled in MN during his terms. Of the 6,300 Somalis becoming US citizens between 2008 and 2016, obviously far fewer than that total settled in the fifth district. The total population in Omar's fifth district is 718,000 of which 80% represent as White and unlikely Muslim by their racial demographic. Even if she mobilized 100% of the Muslim Somali population with Obama's complete support, we are haggling over less than 1% of the electorate.

How charming is it that a full 30% of our citizens glom unapologetically onto so many fictions to justify their endless bigotries? For anyone predisposed to hate "others" so wantonly, this Somali/Omar nexus is a pure goldmine. It becomes a useful construct for questioning our first black president and perpetuating the conspiracy that he was either an Islamic extremist sympathizer or even a closeted terrorist himself. It endorses the volatile notion that there are places in the country where anti-American immigrants are being radicalized for malign purposes. Making Omar the face of domestic terrorism, threatens the safety of tens of thousands who look like her, or dress like her, at a time when little more is needed to motivate violence against perceived "enemies." It furthers the notion that those we admitted are part of a plot to bring death and destruction to our shores. It rubs the scars of 9/11 into new open wounds to perpetuate the divisive us versus them narrative that captured the nation in the immediate aftermath of that historic tragedy.

We spend less than $1 billion in aid to Central America where the blight of poverty and violence has metastasized, but we spend $20 billion on our border security. This is more than a failure of imagination; it is deliberate pandering to lesser Deplorable angels for electoral capital. Providing for greater safety and opportunity for citizens in the Northern Triangle countries directly would be vastly more successful in eliminating the causes of mass exodus. But, the empathy that required would be roundly denounced by a base of voters consumed by the desire to inflict maximum pain on the "invaders," for whom they have nothing but antipathy.

Unlike the recent past when most of the undocumented coming were single men from Mexico, now the migrants are

138

overwhelmingly families or unaccompanied minors from further away in Central America, indicating that the motives are now more about safety and less about just finding work. Proposing we invert those expenditures to measurably improve the security and viability of their home countries would be an affront to the Deplorables and a poison pill for any politicians pandering to the Deplorables for votes. So, instead, a vicious feedback loop of vilification leading to greater loathing leading to more vilification and more punitive consequences has created a legitimate crisis at our Southern border. The Deplorables frame this as a righteous battle for the soul of our country against lawless invaders hell bent on violating us physically and economically. Really, it is just an unconscionable abuse of human rights totally unbecoming an exceptional country. Thankfully, we heard how a US Federal judge has intervened to prevent the Trump administration policy from indefinitely detaining the asylum seekers without releasing them on bail.

In no way have these poisonous attitudes been more tweaked for effect than through the unconscionable treatment of detained families. A civil society can and should be judged by how it treats the most vulnerable. We expect the United States to be better than most. Separate from any legal disputes over immigration policies, decent people treat fellow human beings decently, full stop. The Trump administration incredulously claimed detainees were treated competently and compassionately despite mountains of evidence and the firsthand experience of concerned law makers, doctors and civil rights advocates who witnessed the deplorable conditions themselves and interviewed the detainees for context. News that the DHS Inspector General had admitted the conditions were unacceptable and opened multiple investigations of facilities and personnel, stretched the administration's defense to the breaking point. As terrified families were herded into woefully small dirty cages to wallow in their own filth and were subjected to the self-righteous cruelty of anti-immigrant zealots among the ranks of our tax funded border patrol, the Deplorables begged for more. Meanwhile, the children in custody were irreparably harmed for political effect, and this simple fact, without further elaboration, neatly separates the Deplorables versus Commendables.

As of October of 2020, it was estimated that 5,500 children were forcefully separated from their parents as a matter of public policy meant to discourage asylum seeking. Recent reports have found that more than 500 of these kids remain separated from their loved ones after years of the policy, with little to no hope of ever being reunited with family. While Trump insisted these children were being taken care of "beautifully," though he could never answer for whether they would ever be reunited with family, virtually every Commendable in the country shuddered over this moral abomination. The Deplorables remained receptive to their hero's lie that these kids were accompanied at the border, not by parents, but "coyotes" and drug cartels. Nowhere in the policy language were legal remedies against third party criminals mentioned implying this was not a principal concern for the administration. For most people, this debacle has shocked the conscience of a moral nation, but for the Deplorables it has reinforced their virulently antisocial, xenophobic impulses. As the egregious violations of human decency mounted, so too did the mindless rationalizations from the truly deplorable. An old theme about the unseen but insidious oppression of white people gathered renewed vigor among those who imagined a Mexican invasion was underway and who blamed the suicidal weakness of liberal America. Holding vulnerable innocents responsible for their own feelings of inadequacy takes a special lack of humanity.

At the height of this abomination, Alexandria Ocasio-Cortez joined 15 other Democratic law makers to tour the conditions at detention shelters in San Antonio TX and shared with the media the unconscionable conditions she and her colleagues witnessed. Her account corroborated a story in *ProPublica* and squared neatly with the Department of Homeland Security's assessment that conditions at the shelter represented a "ticking time bomb." Human rights organizations and immigration lawyers also concurred. For her candor in bringing atrocious human rights violations to the attention of an unwitting public, the rightwing singled her out specifically, as a Latina, for especially vile, bigoted attacks. The abuse of terrified children that broke the hearts of Americans everywhere was never even mentioned, especially among private border patrol Facebook groups, who instead posted graphic sexual verbal assaults against the freshman law maker. Also among the group that visited the shelters was Rashida Tlaib, another female freshman representative, who was subjected to verbal harassment when protestors shouted at her "We don't care about sharia law, go take care of your country."

One comment on the Hannity Facebook page summed up the Deplorables assessment of legal and illegal immigration on our Southern border; "We need 50s and claymores on the border."

"Ok for $5, do you have any idea witch is which?"

"No black faces, but I did see Waldo a couple of times"

Chapter Seventeen

A Soul Sacrifice

"Most people are other people. Their thoughts are someone else's opinions, their lives a mimicry, their passions a quotation."

Oscar Wilde, De Profundis

If Identity is a powerful drug, the consistency of beliefs demanded by the alt-right is truly psychedelic. It's a soul sacrifice, requiring complete surrender to ideas and forces that exist purely outside of our biological natures. Most egregiously, it requires the faithful to surrender allegiance to truth. Certainly the Deplorable's would be horrified to learn that what they believed about vast differences between races, really amount to less than a percentage point of genetic variability. Essentially, we are dramatically all more alike than we are different. Indeed, a construct that has been used for millennia to define and separate people is not scientifically relevant. This early 21st century scientific awakening gives the greatest nod ever to nurture over nature in the debate over the causes of human outcomes. The roots of our divisiveness lie within cultural anthropology. The dividing lines between races are almost entirely circumstantial. The truth we witness today is the consequence of human cultural interactions since the beginning of time. The empathy or antipathy toward peoples who look different from each other, the battles waged, the outcomes of conquests, the economic successes and failures experienced, and the migratory patterns among those who identify this way or that, all have made us what we are today. This truth is attacked viciously by those who would insist it is genetic superiority over cultural relativism that explains so much of the divide and the enduring challenges we face as a species.

It is on that basis that the election of our first African American president in 2007, created one of the most enormous schisms between Liberals and Conservatives ever. This event caused those gripped by irrational fears of a white genocide to become truly unglued. Absent the privilege and unearned advantages all leaders before Obama tacitly conferred upon them, they were horrified by the prospect of being placed on a level playing field to be judged on their skills and merits alone. In the 60's our 36th president, LBJ, who grew up in the Deep South and knew intimately about the politics of racism to divide and conquer, had a good bead on this mentality:

"If you can convince the lowest white man he's better than the best colored man, he won't notice you're picking his pocket. Hell, give him somebody to look down on, and he'll empty his pockets for you."

While the Deplorables continued to look down on the "colored" man, they felt threatened for the first time by the attitudes of a more tolerant society that would ostracize them for it and the backlash from a leader who might punish them for it. A black man being elevated to the highest office would certainly upend their birthright entitlement to the economic and social spoils of their country. Success for African Americans in the minstrel pursuits of athletic and entertainment excellence was accepted for its amusement value, but damned if the Deplorables would be ruled over by the black man. The recent movie, *The Green Book*, captures a time and place, in what's now ruby Red State America, when those attitudes prevailed. It is premised on the idea of knowing and accepting one's place in society.

For not accepting his place in society, Obama would be forever after vandalized by the Deplorables themselves and by whomever coveted their allegiance. Certainly, Obama proved at last we lived in a post racial society, they insisted, and any instance of overt racism from then on was perpetrated by the uppity new First Family themselves and not by his detractors. Evidence to the contrary was simply "fake news" promulgated by an adoring Liberal media. For every instance captured on video tape of enthusiastic haters hanging the president in effigy, for every dog whistled insinuation that Obama was Muslim and not Cristian as he professed, and born in Kenya and not in Hawaii, and for tens of thousands of race taunting memes gone viral in Rightwing chat rooms, one fiction more convoluted than the next emerged to stir the muck. The Deplorables were visibly enraged by our new leader, and convinced themselves he was purely evil, the Antichrist. Obama was accused of being a radical ideologue and an Islamic extremist sympathizer. Rightwing media ominously implored how we should judge the president by the company he keeps, without regard to how tangential the relationships appeared to be. They said Obama "palled around with a terrorist" because he served on a couple of education boards with then professor, but past leftwing radical, and "unrepentant terrorist" William Ayers for his violent activism in the early 70's. They linked the President to controversial comments his pastor had made about terrorist attacks against the country, and despite Obama's repudiations, insisted he must be likeminded in every regard. Obama did not admit to being a Muslim, he did not attend a Wahabi school in Indonesia. Still they painted the picture of a black radical Muslim, hostile to white people, a supporter of both home grown and Islamic terrorism and born in Kenya. What could be considered racist in any of those baseless accusations? Remarkably, 10 years

146

later these themes still prevail on the social media platforms the Deplorables frequent.

No, Obama wasn't a divisive figure who undermined our post racial glory, rather he was a lightning rod for the bottomless rage of sewer dwelling White Nationalists. They projected upon him all of their tragic flaws and fragilities. His nobility lanced their ignobility, and the hate, like so much vile pus, oozed out everywhere. A single mantra welled up inside them "we must take our country back." As we sat complacently, reducing what we witnessed to a curious but insignificant anomaly, the radicalization of the Deplorables was only becoming more widespread. The fear and loathing of "others" became weaponized to the point where the Deplorables determined they could no longer live peacefully with people they once just disagreed with, but now wished to eliminate with extreme prejudice. It is imperative that we no longer assume this is typified by the demeanor of the bigoted few, but of late, has become a well-resourced, significantly trained, and heavily armed terrorist cell that is being activated more frequently than ever.

Chapter Eighteen

Through the looking glass

"If I had a world of my own, everything would be nonsense. Nothing would be what it is, because everything would be what it isn't. And contrary wise, what is, it wouldn't be. And what it wouldn't be, it would. You see?"
Lewis Carroll, Alice's Adventures in Wonderland & Through the Looking-Glass

Through the looking glass, our world has become very strange indeed. As the winds of mass discontent whip tempestuously across the country, there is a growing pressure to choose a side and defend it against "alternative reality" and then shelter in place. But, the universe is governed by the laws of science whether or not you believe in science. Alternative accounts for the events of our time are hardly as fungible as opinion leaders contend. Surely, the space time continuum, quantum mechanics, and the laws of cause and effect make some explanations more plausible than others. Today, as we increasingly express ourselves on social media, it is imperative to recognize how powerful algorithms are used within these platforms to curate a highly personalized experience for users. The objective is to foster the illusion that the world accepts the user unconditionally, however far from normalcy they stray.

There can be no sketchy "rabbit holes" as we understand them, because everything that is, can be everything it isn't in a world created in our own image. The mechanism is constant affirmation. Rarely do people realize *they* are the product social media is selling to third parties with an agenda, as they are herded into homogenous attitudinal chunks of commercial value to the messengers. The system abhors individuality, even as it purports to celebrate it. Users remain unaware as they are sorted into increasingly more receptive cells of likeminded "buyers." This makes it more important than ever to understand the underlying motives of all who communicate with us so we do not "buy" what unscrupulous others "sell."

The alert reader may have noticed I signed this book with the pseudonym of Q. Does this mean I am indeed the enigmatic super patriot with Q level security clearance working clandestinely to save mankind from Deep State tyranny and pedophilia among the world's elites? Maybe. If I am, are you processing my motives and content differently than you might if I was not Q or Alice? How would this shadowy figure, assuming he or she is a single discernable person, write his or her memoir? Would Q think of his fans as compatriots or would Q ridicule them for their weaknesses and inhumanities? Would he love or hate them? Would he feel esteem or pity for them? Would he treat his readers as wonderful snowflakes, each oriented to their world in their own personal ways, or as a hive of fundamentalists buzzing for radicalization? I suspect for his devoted fans, this will all seem pretty counterfeit. I apologize for any artistic license which may confound the reader but, I have dropped many bread crumbs along the way to answer the burning question. Be good little bakers and do your job of completing this dish. If you find yourself offended by the theme of this work, I'm afraid that's an occupational hazard for an author communicating anything to such a bitterly divided public. I will make no apologies for telling the truth as I see it. If along the way I have misrepresented my identity that will be my only willful lie. If I am not really Q Anon, perhaps this book will smoke him out of hiding so he can publicly receive all of the scorn or praise his work deserves. But again, if I am this mysterious soothsayer, what will you make of my obvious loathing for those who held sacrosanct, several thousand unhinged posts dropped onto the world's most dubious message boards?

Is Q Anon a white Knight or a malicious agitator, a purveyor of truth or a master gaslighter? Is he simply a prop to advance a particular narrative, and is the purpose for advancing that narrative objectively knowable? Maybe he is an avatar, simply the face of a think tank comprised of hundreds of likeminded power brokers aiming to bend public opinion one way or another. Maybe he is a cutout for Russian GRU infiltration, strategically injected into our body politic to cause the mass destruction of American institutions. Is the objective of these ideas to build consensus, like WWG1WGA or sow the next jihad among faithful foot soldiers to preserve a white Christian majority? Whatever the narrative advanced, does its author believe in it, or is he simply appropriating it in service to contrary and less apparent objectives? Is the entire *Calm Before the Storm* a harbinger of an apocryphal final conflict between Deplorables and Commendables, or simply an elaborate prank to make fun of such hyperbole? Clearly, each reader will lean heavily upon their own predispositions in concluding these things. For people who believe our country has become an absolute hellscape under the so called Deep State, there may be a sense of real urgency breathing credible life into even the most fanciful and overwrought assertions made. Those insisting the whole thing reeks of an epic put-on, may find delicious satire. One thing is certain, in the age of Trump, we are wise to question what we see with our own eyes and hear with our own ears. If we dare to chase sketchy rabbits down even sketchier rabbit holes, we must contend with the consequences. All of this, and so much more, points up the basic conundrum of this story.

Whatever baggage a particular reader brings to this story, I cannot reveal my true identity. This near real time account of what's going on in our country will surely agitate violent stupid adversaries to become even more violent and stupid. Clearly where the promotion of their interests lie, they know no boundaries. Four entirely fictitious personalities I crafted from mostly fabricated personal details, provoked an alarming number of credible violent threats, including even death threats against my avatars. When cornered, and made to justify the indefensible, society's misfits will reliably lash out against their provocateurs.

The only other breadcrumbs I will provide at this time are these: First, there is no evidence that the person, persons, or entity posting as Q Anon actually has Q level security clearance. Second, we learned from Bob Woodward's new book, Rage, how Jared Kushner explained that you may understand his father in law better if you studied the *Cheshire Cat* from *Alice's Adventures in Wonderland*. "If you don't know where you're going, any path will get you there." The notion of speaking in endless metaphors is central to understanding the purpose of Q Anon's own adventures in Wonderland. The trade craft that confidence artists, charlatans and fortune tellers use to sow compelling narratives for fanatical believers is always in plain sight but remains imperceptible to those who want to believe in magic. When Q posts a crumb that is seemingly validated a day or two later, you should ask yourself is there a plausible alternative explanation for why this rhetorical legerdemain seems so predictive? So much of performance art stems from a few basic varieties of the *Barnum Effect* to describe why really general information can seem personally compelling to the most gullible. As P.T. Barnum infamously declared "a sucker is born every minute." The victims of the skillful application of this sleight of hand will always believe that the "truth" was highly curated for them personally, or for their in-group specifically, instead of the consequence of a mere parlor game. The more urgent their need to believe, the more intractable their beliefs.

Whether I can take credit for the movement or not, one thing is clear, Q Anon is fast becoming the new religion in our more secular society. The fervency with which people must believe the tenets of this faith is no less robust than that of Islamic extremists. You must never forget that for those animated by a zero sum assessment of the world, they will always remain preoccupied with the idea of their own perpetuation, and the superiority of their own kind. No need to be seduced by the convoluted, Q Anon is simply the latest manifestation of the privileged white class reacting to perceived threats against their social and economic status in an increasingly more diverse country.

The Cheshire Cat was spot on when he told Alice that everyone in Wonderland is mad. Granting poetic license to the author, even accepting the suspension of disbelief that fiction requires of us, there is a certain metaphysical order to events occurring in the real world that are routinely violated in Wonderland, and in the world of Q Anon conspiracy equally. For Lewis Carroll, Alice's risky choice to follow the sketchy white rabbit down his rabbit hole, leading to all of her adventures, is certainly an allegory for the outlandish things we talk ourselves into as we burble along through life semi-consciously. Is Q speaking allegorically too, or is he issuing a dire warning about events to come that could alter the course of humankind forever?

Q has coaxed our least intellectually endowed to stumble into an unfamiliar world of his own making, to comfort those seeking answers in a world that confounds them. Quite literally he has led them down a rabbit hole. If his warning were really urgent, would he really have presented his case wrapped in fanciful riddles open to so much interpretation, or would he deliver his message more declaratively? It would be like asking M.C. Escher to draw up your fire evacuation diagram. Whenever the exit looks like it is downstairs,

152

maybe it is upstairs instead? The story of Q is a first person account, in real time, of a gathering threat against humankind, and also his assurance that a highly placed inner sanctum of patriots are implementing a covert plan to restore order. Strangely this story is told and circulated mostly on fringe message boards like 4Chan and 8Chan (now 4 and 8 Kun), which have a reputation for coddling a more subversive anti-establishment clientele of virulent racists and internet pranksters. These boards are the seedy underbelly of mass discontent. Posting in these places is more like hosting a circle jerk among the closest of degenerate friends, messy but purely enjoyable for participants. If Q was a Trump administration insider with a high level security clearance, would he really have vied for attention with Pepe the Frog memes and the half-baked insurrection plots among the Molon Labe crowd? Clearly, he is simply trying to reach conspiracy fanatics with the kind of message, and in the kind of environment they embrace? But why?

The "Deep State" is a construct used by Deplorables to organize against opposition from Commendables. Whether or not a powerful cabal of world opinion leaders really exists, why must we assume their membership comes exclusively from the liberal elites? Clearly it is because that notion can be used by Deplorables to divide "us" from "them" as they define the enemy. The point is, Q's travelogue through the swampy world of all-powerful malign actors reads more like pulp fiction for the reliably delusional than a serious escape plan. "The Storm" is a manifesto about eliminating others just as assuredly as the *Day of The Rope* was for aspiring anarchists when *The Turner Diaries* was published decades ago. It is the tip of the spear, the voice of a movement fed up with being tormented by "others" in a country less committed to providing them with all of the power. Whatever else may be true, it seems, at least, one person understands the desperation believers bring to this pity party and has chosen to exploit the weakness for some purpose or another. If he

153

had some verifiable information to offer, would he toy so relentlessly with the feeble minded or would he just make his unified case?

During the October, 2020 Town hall meeting, moderated by Savanah Guthrie, Donald Trump insisted he knew nothing about Q Anon. The credibility of this assertion was thinner than Slender Man on Keto. It was only a couple of weeks earlier that he articulated how the Anons were against pedophilia and child sex trafficking, remarking how that's "not a bad thing," though by implication, he seemed to be saying that particular disdain, is not universally shared by all, wink, wink. He also said he knew they really seemed to like Donald Trump. More awkward is how observant people had noted how frequently he had retweeted and shared Q Anon content over the preceding 3 years. When he held his MAGA rallies, a fair chunk of attendees brandished enormous Qs, or signs with the ubiquitous acronym WWG1WGA. Should we have suppressed our disbelief that he has never inquired what this yuuuge movement of adoring fans stood for? For well over 2 years, his intelligence agencies had identified the movement as a potential domestic terrorist threat, far graver than the Antifa movement Trump consistently cited as a cause of the nation's tumult. A handful of actual high profile violent crimes have been linked to Q Anon fanatics. There is no question that intelligence about this was regularly shared with 45. And finally, and perhaps most damning, the entire Q Anon enterprise had cast Trump as the hero figure for beating back the New World Order and restoring moral clarity to a country that had lost its way under the scourge of liberalism. Do you really believe a man as fixated on his own press clippings and general acclaim remained unaware for years of his anointment by Q as a world savior? As Barak Obama or Joe Biden would say, "come on man'.

154

As I have said, Trump is a religious figure for his fiercest supporters. He consistently joined forces with reliably subversive rightwing media to sow the seeds of massive discontent over the single issue that has gripped the hyperbolic imaginations of racists, xenophobes, Islamophobes and homophobes. Fear and loathing of "others" became an existential struggle. It was only from their collective narcissism, that they came to wallow so openly in revolt against the very institutions that protect us from chaos. They would rather burn the whole thing down than allow the world they live in to replace them with any number of unworthy others.

Chapter Nineteen

Facts and fictions

"Truth is stranger than Fiction. That is because Fiction is obligated to stick to possibilities; truth is not"

Mark Twain

If we are finally brave enough to admit the Deplorables' Movement is a far larger and more pernicious bug of modern American life than we ever dared fathom, isn't it time we flip on the kitchen light and watch as the cockroaches scuttle back to the dark spaces from which they came? It is incumbent upon all Commendables to consistently ostracize Deplorables, as publically as possible, without regard to dubious anti First Amendment criticisms. Those who resist assimilating American values, or conspire to tear down the pillars of our exceptionalism, can be coaxed back to the murky shallows by blow torch, if necessary, so we may resume our march toward tolerance and equality for all. Commendables must also lobby their members of Congress to enact federal statutes that actually apply to American terrorists. When we battled Islamic extremists, we recognized how perverted and dangerous their ideology was. When we caught them, we locked them away with precious little regard for due process. What exempts home grown extremism from the same aggressive scrutiny? Indeed, if the threat is more pervasive, why wouldn't the same kinds of punishment be even more warranted? We don't condone "cancel culture" in the abstract, but when the tenets of a particular cultural movement are violently at odds with the peaceful conduct of society at large, why would cancelling it be controversial? We provide no quarter for felonious hostility in general, so why overlook it when it is modeled consistently by the Deplorables? These monsters are simply an organized white power movement, full stop. They are the radical angry white men with limited prospects, and the submissive white women who support them, all hell bent on racial and ethnic conquest. Why should Commendables allow them to camouflage their anti-social tendencies as traditional American values, when it is actually counter culture and dangerous? Should we ignore the explosion of murderous violence within their ranks over the last few years simply because they are Americans and are entitled to a different point of view from the mainstream? Must we really accept when this vicious and simpleminded minority insists it is they who embrace the tenets of American exceptionalism, like life, liberty and the pursuit of happiness for all, despite being so openly hostile to all of the "others" that enlightened people embrace, and on which our exceptionalism depends upon? They are neither silent nor the majority any longer.

It is not "others" the Deplorables insist; it is the "illegals" or "thugs" or "Radical Jihadists" or "socialists" or "Antifa" or "Black Lives Matter" or "pedophiles or "cannibals" who secret themselves within groups of "others" they say we must hate and fear. Their antipathy toward non-whites and non-Christians affords them the luxury of indiscriminately tossing out the wheat with the chaff. From the first whiff of different ideas or cultural norms, they are quick to vilify and

157

dehumanize entire populations of humans they regard as threats to white power more broadly. Whatever labels we use to slice and dice this movement into less threatening bites, White Supremacists, Neo Nazis, Skinheads, White Nationalists or KKK members, collectively it's a highly significant segment of society obsessed with reclaiming white power.

Let's dissect a few timely issues, so we may separate facts from fictions in an effort to declaw this movement.

Generally speaking, the Deplorables demand that Muslim Americans accept guilt by association with Radical Jihadist terrorism. Not only must innocent Muslim Americans publically denounce the heinous violence perversely committed in the name of Allah, they are expected to understand why their own reputation must be tarnished by the despicable acts of so very few who hijacked their religious faith. In short, they must wear the shame and responsibility for American deaths with no evidence for their complicity. Never mind how we literally never ask white Christian Americans to shoulder any guilt or blame by association with violence, even when religiously, racially or ideologically motivated. The usual white privilege applies, and the public is admonished for thinking anything other than mental illness is to blame. But, when Ilhan Omar and Rashida Tlaib were elected in in 2018 and reelected in 2020, the Deplorables subjected each to baseless accusations of terrorist sympathy or even terrorism itself. In fact, no two members in Congress have ever been subjected to as many violent threats as these two members of "The Squad" except, perhaps, Alexandria Ocasio-Cortez, another woman of color in "The Squad."

In 2019, as we reckoned with the latest ideologically motivated domestic terrorism by an admitted White Supremacist, we were asked by the Deplorables to lump the El Paso carnage indiscriminately in with another mass shooting in Dayton OH as two equal examples of criminal insanity. In the Dayton shooting, we found a confused young man with a history of disturbing behavior who exacted revenge upon a number of people personally known to him. In El Paso, the perpetrator presaged his massacre with a manifesto explicitly describing the mayhem he would reign down upon Latinx people he described as "invaders" consistent with the prevailing ideology the Deplorables routinely expressed in public, and in chat rooms, and championed by President Trump. Like any radical Jihadist, young Patrick Crusius, identified the target for his politically motivated crime and expressed his specific transformative goal in shooting dead 22 innocent people of Latin descent. His crime was motivated by what he called a "Hispanic invasion of Texas," and he travelled 10 hours from his home in Allen, Texas to enact his plan for separating the country into territories based exclusively on race. Despite the ideological driver, the premeditation, and the political objective for his domestic terrorism, we were implored by Deplorables to accept that he was simply a deranged lunatic and not a foot soldier for the white power movement.

The debate between the Deplorables and Commendables that followed the El Paso shooting, predictably turned on gun rights/gun control sloganeering. But, lost in that tedious squabble was a much more intriguing question. What causes so many in the US to kill total strangers with high power assault rifles, relative to people in other industrialized countries, who simply don't shoot each other? And even rarer among every other First and Second World Countries is the incidence of violence and intimidation, especially against civilians, turned against their own in the pursuit of political aims.

The El Paso shooter killed in the name of White Supremacy, an alarming trend our own DHS and FBI have warned for years is on the rise. Instead of conceding that point, the Deplorables, loathe to own the mayhem, aimed to sort mass murders by political affiliation instead. Because so many recent shootings defied the false equivalency game, the Deplorables reached back in time to cherry pick from all examples of murder within the decade, including examples of standard issue inner city violence, crimes they could hang on perpetrators identified as Democratic supporters. Most vividly promoted were violent crimes committed by people of color.

One of the ways the Deplorables accentuate their biased view that black people are inherently violent and lawless, is by taking great pains to draw a cynical false equivalency between "black on black" murder with the kind of "blue on black" murder they believe the Liberals are obsessed with. Of course Black people kill more of their own; violent crime tends to mostly be intraracial. But, one kind of homicide is not like the other in one very significant way Deplorables are unwilling to acknowledge. By its very criminality, we imagine actual murders committed by law enforcement would be virtually nonexistent. This is why Commendables have so much trouble processing the killing of unarmed black males, on the rare occasions it happens, but don't feel compelled to excuse it as self-defense or accidental when it is not. Commendables certainly don't feel the need to automatically uphold the thin blue line in cases police themselves struggle with it. By contrast, the Deplorables never met a questionable shooting of an unarmed black male by law enforcement they couldn't justify and even ultimately blame on the victim. Even when a rogue cop is found guilty, the Deplorables will insist the thuggish nature of the victim is reason enough to conclude all lives really do not matter.

Unfortunately the prevailing wisdom among our worst souls is inverted with the actual reality our 3 letter agencies and Department of Justice have defined. No one would argue that gun violence isn't a bug of the American experience, but certainly mass casualty domestic terrorism perpetrated by aggrieved white supremacists with an agenda is something more sinister. Right-wing extremists perpetrated two thirds of the violent terrorist attacks and plots in the United States in 2019 and over 90 percent between January 1 and May 8, 2020.

If you are even semi-sentient, you know how anti-immigrant the Deplorables are. Maybe it is more precise to say they are against immigrants of color as recent evidence has surfaced suggesting a major preference for immigrants coming from predominantly white countries over "shithole" countries boasting fewer pale faces. The big dodge, of course, is their insistence that they are not anti-immigrant at all but only anti "illegal immigrant." To exemplify this, they describe the migration of peoples from Mexico, Central America and Africa as "invaders" and insist their motive for coming to our country is to rape or murder us, take our jobs, tap our public assistance programs, vote Democratic, all while silently replacing us with their own brown babies. Immigrants, legal and otherwise, are consistently less violent than our native born population. Rather than accept this inconvenient fact, the Deplorables insist on selecting from rare instances when immigrants, particularly those who are undocumented, have committed gruesome violent crimes. The basic argument they make is "tell that to the families murdered or raped by these animals." Of course, the use of the word "animals" is a big tell about just how easily they will vilify and dehumanize the "illegals" to make their case. Even in cases when migrants are fleeing violence and economic devastation from their home countries, leading them to seek a small chance of asylum at our

161

border, the Deplorables will describe them as criminals. In fact the Deplorables give no quarter to desperate families availing themselves of their internationally granted right to seek asylum, preferring instead to accuse them of trying to either game the system or sneak the worst among them in for nefarious purposes. If all that weren't heinous enough, now they are obsessed with erecting an enormous Commie styled wall at our Southern border as the ultimate "fuck you" to some of the world's most desperate peoples.

One of the most persistent but thoroughly false talking points about the undocumented is how they are sucking up inordinate public assistance benefits from deserving Americans and at the taxpayer's expense. In fact a meme that went viral on Facebook during the recent government shutdown baselessly claimed "18 million illegal immigrants got their government checks this month while federal workers remain unpaid." The most accurate assessment for the total size of the undocumented US population is just under 11 million or 7 million less than the meme presupposes. We know that even legal immigrants who may be entitled to safety net assistance are dramatically less likely to collect this than white Americans. The undocumented are even less likely to attempt to collect government assistance that they are virtually 100% ineligible for. The fact is, it is only for emergency Medicaid and food stamps for their American born children that they would be entitled to any assistance at all. In total it is estimated that not 18 million "illegals" received government assistance, not a little over half that number at 11 million but closer to 400,000 total receive occasional emergency assistance for their American born children only. Of course the Deplorables dispute all these claims, but they also believe that millions of ineligible "illegal" voters commit voter fraud each year, so there's that.

Well at least the Deplorables focus their immigrant outrage exclusively on "illegals," right? In February of 2020, we learned about the Trump Administration's Public Charge immigration rules aimed squarely at reducing legal immigration in the country. In simple terms, the provisions aimed to disqualify legal immigrants from permanent resident status if they availed themselves of public assistance. The Deplorables were ecstatic over this, despite insisting how pro legal immigration they are. Even though they know firsthand how anyone, but for the grace of God, may need a hand up every now and then, they sure don't want that assistance given to brown immigrants over deserving white folk. They will always cheer the deportation of people doing "all the right things to come here legally" simply so they may count on a whiter tomorrow. In July of 2020 the SCOTUS delivered a rebuke of a Trump fan favorite move to rescind the Deferred Action for Childhood Arrivals or DACA program. Again proving that neither Trump nor his drooling cultists approved of legal immigrants; they would gladly send 3.6 million Dreamers, most of whom have known only this as their home, packing for who cares where if it meant re-whitening America.

I have already discussed the immoral abomination of Trump's family separation policy, so I won't dwell on it here, other than to muse about what kind of people would wantonly support ripping young children from the arms of their parents, sometimes permanently dividing families, simply to discourage desperate refugees from seeking asylum. As humans with children of their own, how immeasurably hateful must they be of "others" to so completely dehumanize them in this way? Surely all the protests they have characterized as riots in the country over the demoralizing of an entire race of people would pale by

163

comparison with the revolt they would wage if a single white Christian baby were treated so cruelly.

In the aftermath of so many mass shootings, we may always count on a superficial debate between Commendables and Deplorables over gun rights and gun regulations. This lasts for approximately 2 weeks until the natural order of things is restored in our gun-obsessed culture. Statistically speaking, we know that US gun ownership is far greater than anywhere else on the planet. Indeed, we have over 120 guns for every 100 citizens here or about 400 million for our 327 million citizens in total. In China, which has 4 times our population but also 4 times fewer guns, there are about 50 million or 3.6 guns per 100 citizens. Still, it is foundational that to Deplorables it is not about the guns; it is about the shooters, without venturing any explanations other than the availability of violent movies and video games and the mental ills of our people for the disparity. After all, we only have 8 times as many lethal firearms as China, yet we perpetrate 18 times as many violent gun crimes. One of the most persistent memes embraced by the Deplorables is the notion that gun laws will only infringe upon legal gun owners' rights, as criminals obviously will have no regard for our laws anyway. As evidence, they cite inner city murders, between criminals, that are prevalent even in cities with strict gun laws. Rather than scuffle with the simple minded arguments in favor of unfettered gun ownership in our violent country, I focus instead on a subset of gun violence for its especially pernicious impact on civilized society, mass casualty shootings, particularly those ideologically motivated. If we accept that the objective of mass casualty shootings is inflicting maximum casualties, what weapon would we imagine criminals that are unencumbered by our laws, would use to commit these crimes? Why wouldn't a domestic terrorist, aiming to rid the world of "invaders," not just reach for a fully

164

automatic M16 or hell, why not a shoulder launched RPG 7 or a box of hand grenades and achieve apocalyptic mayhem? Clearly, the reason is because these weapons are illegal for civilians in this country and therefore are not produced and distributed in any significant quantities here. The attention law enforcement has given these banned firearms also makes it quite difficult for the unscrupulous to maintain an effective black market for them. Ah, the alert reader may then conclude how bans on semi-automatic assault rifles here in the States could take a bite out of the rifle of choice for mass shooters, the AR-15, if we had the will. Mass murdering domestic terrorists might still target and kill large numbers of their opponents but not necessarily with the speed and lethality they do now. By the way, no country buys more violent video games than Japan per capita. They have about 377,000 total guns spread across their 126 million people. In 2017, they had 3 homicides and 5 injured by guns.

So, if it is not violent video games or movies, and the sheer number of firearms available isn't directly correlated with shootings, must we conclude the US is just batshit crazy? And, if the US is batshit crazy, shouldn't that be the basis for actually having the very strictest gun regulations on the planet? If our precarious mental health status as a civilization renders us incapable of responsible gun ownership, shouldn't a large percentage of our people be prevented from owning firearms, especially the particularly lethal ones? But, what about murders committed for the calculated purpose of sowing mass terror? Would we imagine these perpetrators to be people with deep seated mental illness documented by extensive records of psychiatric intervention? Would we expect them to have lengthy rap sheets for violent offenses in their past? How often, over the last 10 years of this carnage, have we heard how the weapon used was purchased legally?

Unfortunately, there is no one size fits all for mass shooters. Over the last 10 years, there are only two things they seem to have in common: They are men and they use semi-automatic weaponry capable of inflicting mass casualties rapidly. I'll wait to see what my elected representatives say, but I'm thinking the other industrialized countries may have a better bead on how this kind of violence can be minimized.

A law abiding friend of mine, who is a bit of a gun freak himself, who owns over 20 firearms, including his own AR-15, admitted there was one suggestion I made that he felt could make a measurable impact on the sheer number of guns in our country. If we required owners to pay insurance premiums for each and every firearm they chose to own, just as they must carry a separate premium for each car on that insurance policy, folks would probably buy far fewer firearms. He also admitted sheepishly that many irresponsible, criminal, and mentally ill gun owners would be weeded out over time if they were required to visit a local DMV-like facility annually to pass tests to renew their firearms license. If they were scumbags with a history, they would never want to withstand the scrutiny of having an agency judge them to be a non-convicted mentally stable responsible gun owners like the NRA promotes publically but lobbies against behind the scenes.

Because the gun nuts remain unimpressed by the impact that rampantly available assault weapons and high capacity magazines have on our society, and how attention must be focused only sparingly on glaring examples of mental impairment, they miss an even graver fact. Unlike the kind of inner city gun violence they conflate with ideologically driven mass casualty shootings, they fail to mention that most of these perpetrators who opened fire in crowded spaces did so before they had amassed a troubling mental health history and certainly before racking up a violent criminal record.

So here's our dilemma. When we think about the Deplorables generally, we imagine anti-social outcasts with misdirected outrage issues and seething hate directed at "culprits" who are mirror opposites of who they identify with racially, culturally, ethnically, religiously and politically. We have witnessed their becoming more and more overtly hostile to "others" and more open to baseless conspiracy theories. These forces have been multiplied and amplified within closed echo chambers consisting of equally enraged likeminded haters to sow division in polite society and stir paranoia. They may or may not be appropriately diagnosed for mental pathologies, and they may or may not have criminal records. We are not sure about their consumption of violent video games, and equally violent movies, but imagine these would be appealing to them. We do know they have higher than average gun ownership per capita and feel their Second Amendment rights should be essentially unregulated so they can lawfully own any firearm they choose and as many total firearms as they wish. We also know they are disproportionally from the ranks of current and former military and as such have higher competence in the use of lethal weaponry. Their service makes them susceptible to authoritarian messaging and to believe patriotism and Nationalism are one and the same thing even when modified as "White Nationalism". We have learned from historian Katherine Belew that since the Viet Nam war, a small but significant and enduring antiestablishment white power movement has permeated the ranks of our armed services and have seen in recent years a new rise in violent antiestablishment crime from this wave. How can we identify the unique threat these people pose to our society, and can this threat be neutralized nonviolently?

167

Without the total commitment of the Commendables to sniff out the violent extremists among us, I fear we are rapidly approaching the moment when this dilemma may become unsolvable. I suggest we bring the same level of citizen vigilance to this problem that we brought in the aftermath on 9/11 and resist succumbing to the baseless criticism that there is something inherently unreasonable about informing on rogue anarchists just because they are home grown Americans and not Muslim immigrants or foreign terrorists. We must not assume we will find these threats only among convicted felons. Law enforcement writ large depends upon an informed and engaged public to help serve and protect our communities. It is nothing but counter intuitive to exempt terrorism perpetrated by white supremacists from this kind of citizen surveillance. Social harmony is impossible under the scourge of so much hate and divisiveness. We also have seen the rapid rise of militia groups and other hateful Rightwing terrorist groups who believe in the extra judicial enforcement of their code of societal "ethics." Noteworthy among them are the Proud Boys, Boogaloo Bois, 3 Percenters, and Oath keepers, who have become progressively more unhinged by the rise in counter fascist progress and greater racial diversity in America. Not all Deplorables belong to these white power anti-establishment organizations but virtually all of their violent members are Deplorables. We must make it our business to accept how the threat is as pervasive as it has ever been, however repugnant that may be, and avail ourselves of the same remedies we pursued when it last reared its ugly head.

Chapter Twenty

9/11

"What separates us from the animals, what separates us from the chaos, is our ability to mourn people we've never met."

David Levithan

No event in my lifetime consequentially reordered the American psyche more than the crimes perpetrated against our people on September 11 2001. Nothing brought into clearer focus both the virtue and the curse of American nationalism as starkly as this unprecedented attack against our country. The notion of American patriotism is sacrosanct, but so too is the notion that with great power comes great responsibility. As an unimpeachable standard bearer for freedom and liberty for the entire world to emulate, we must insure these standards are shared broadly without arrogance here and abroad.

More than anything on that tragic day, what seared itself most indelibly in my imagination was witnessing human beings, driven beyond reason, flinging themselves from the highest reaches of the World Trade Center to make peace with the insanity of that day on their own terms. Nothing prepared me for something as incomprehensible. In those moments, the victims were nameless, faceless silhouettes floating against a brilliant blue sky, perfect avatars for the collective "us" versus "them" in the aftermath of an unimaginable crime against humanity. As I watched in somber horror, and felt only the blunt force of pure evil, nothing about each victim's specific identity registered. That was oddly comforting. The essential truth of good versus evil must never be tempered by irrelevant measures of the men and women sacrificed in the name of perverted ideologies. Indeed, how perverse would it be to weigh the tragedy on the basis of the victim's race, age, gender, religion, national origin, employment status or creed? Doing so would make us no better than the terrorists themselves for extinguishing thousands of souls simply because they represented Christian American "Imperialists."

The blank slate that Commendable people see when confronted by "others" is replaced by a repugnant shorthand of bigoted assumptions in the Deplorable's framing. A caricature riddled with infinite flaws and social deformities. These abstractions are supercharged by the fragility of their own identities. As such, the Deplorables are immeasurably comforted by a superiority fantasy that must constantly be fed against manifest reality. In the extreme, the idea of Humanity itself is only awarded to those within the clan. As a result, we suffer through their endless sanctimonious dehumanization of culturally and religiously dissimilar people with the singular purpose of gilding their own wilted lily.

The Deplorables were not content to accept that the attacks on 9/11 were committed by fanatics adhering to a perverse version of the otherwise peaceful religion of Islam as a pretext for mass murder. So, they projected the notion of violent extremism on Muslims writ large.

Unlike the vast majority of the other 2 billion adherents, the terrorists found an irrational interpretation in the sixth pillar of Islam, Jihad, which could justify their blood lust for revenge. Still, the Deplorables consider Islam uniquely monolithic. While they recognize broad variations in religious practice and belief among Christians, their antipathy for Muslims blinds them to the same variations within Islam. Their ignorance of history prevents them from even acknowledging myriad sects of the religion, exhibiting vastly different degrees of fervency. Of course, like so many other abstractions, this is the cornerstone of bigotry in general and makes them truly awful people. Descriptive labels in the hands of willfully ignorant bigots can be treacherous. They demand from American Muslims a blanket renunciation of the supposed tenets of their faith as tests for their assimilation to our country's values. Ironically, they exempt their own religious zealots from the same purity tests. It's as if Christianity was the lodestar against which all others should be judged harshly. When Christian zealots commit atrocities in accordance with their faith, Deplorables insist the crimes must be judged on a case by case basis with no baggage to be borne by other adherents. Our history is replete with examples of violent terrorism, including murders, bombings and arsons at abortion clinics and racist lynching all over the country with no call to condemn the Christian beliefs that motivated the crimes. The Deplorables fully grasp the concept of exceptions to the rule, but are consistently unwilling to grant wiggle room to other groups based on religion, race, ethnicity or creed. By branding all of the Muslims in this country with a scarlet M after 9-11, they created an impossible standard for accountability that could lead only to a dangerous backlash against all Muslims. Rather than modulating the hate, as evidence grew that 9-11 was a horrific exception to the general rule of a peaceful Islam, the

171

Deplorables continued to ratchet up the fear and hostility. In fact, according to the FBI, anti-Muslim hate crimes skyrocketed after 9-11 and have remained at a statistically elevated rate of over 150 incidents per year ever since, never dipping to the low double digit levels that prevailed before the attacks in September, 2001.

How much longer will we ignore the consequences of religious, racial and ethnic hate that has so visibly gripped the Deplorables in the 21st century? Rather than accepting the innate humanity of all people, like the nameless, faceless victims who leapt from the towers, they succumb to the hard bigotry of wholly fabricated expectations, as they create an alternate truth irreconcilable with the remarkable achievements of American idealism. They must be stopped by a show of overwhelming solidarity among the Commendables. We must continue to protest inequality and hate crimes within every state in the country, and we must vote only for leaders who are committed to unity over division and racial equity over white supremacy. A tranquil America with liberty and justice for all requires that we force violent racial hate out of the public square and back toward the margins where it can become a statistically irrelevant curiosity again.

Chapter Twenty One

A "perfect call"

"On July 21, 2019, President Zelensky's party won Parliamentary elections in a landslide victory. The NSC proposed that President Trump call President Zelensky to congratulate him. On July 25, 2019, the call occurred. I listened in on the call in the Situation Room with colleagues from the NSC and the office of the Vice President"

Lt. Colonel Alexander Vindman

Throughout the sordid four years of Donald Trump's presidency, one of the most pronounced dividing lines between Deplorables and Commendables was whether or not they could justify the 45th president's abhorrent policies and frequently questionable conduct. This seemed to hinge exclusively on what skin they had in the game for creating a country that would remain hopelessly divided. So, while the motivations for Republican pols in the age of Trump was transparent, we were left to tease out the thought process of Ma and Pa Deplorable. What forces whipped through TrumpLandia that made denying, or even celebrating, the 45 president's transgressions their raison d'etre. And just as importantly, why does your author feel he must French it up a bit to make this palatable?

For all of the journalistic tripe masquerading as scholarship on the subject of what makes Trump's Deplorables tick, may I remind you, it ain't that complicated. Trump was a cult leader, and his worshipers were cult followers. There is nothing particularly rational in that kind of relationship. It's like asking 'Why extreme ironing?" or "Why competitive wife carrying?" For decades, the chasm between what the Deplorables felt their whiteness was worth as table stakes in the game of life, and what their accomplishments actually looked like on paper, was spreading apart faster than Ebola spreads through a Macaque in the African Bush. They became desperate for a great equalizer, the antidote to Obama's egalitarianism. It could just as easily have been Yosemite Sam who scratched that itch had he made them feel superior to the huddled masses of nonwhites with all their annoying yearnings. In fact, my great fear is that a future leader, maybe Yosemite Sam himself, will emerge and use that same playbook, but with better political skills, and will drive his steely knife right through the heart of our recovering democratic Republic. Like the legendary Phoenix, rising from the ashes, The Deplorables welcomed Trump as an alpha male sent from God to save them from the abyss, otherwise known as white genocide. Not that they were actually heading toward an abyss, and not that their lives became less tragicomic than in their pre Trump past, but the hungry must still satisfy that gnawing hunger for unearned privilege somehow. The point is, a cult relationship thrives on the outrageous, and little was more outrageous than worshiping Trump as a spiritual savior. With his track record of caring for only things named Trump, human or manmade, it's not likely he was consumed by the wellbeing of the wretched refuse of our teeming shores. If you doubt

174

that, check the member list at Mar a Lago for Deplorables. Or consider how he allegedly said "A good thing about the Corona virus was how I wouldn't have to shake hands with so many disgusting people." Hell, it is not even clear he would place the interest of this county above others without assurance they would buy Trump. But for 45, all of the mindless adoration was a pure opiate

When they saw their hero, they didn't see a morbidly obese, psychologically compromised man child wearing an ill-fitting suit, they saw Superman. He was not a woefully incompetent business man who left 10 failed ventures and 6 bankruptcies in his wake, he was a very stable genius allegedly worth $10 billion, or maybe just $3 billion, when the tax man cometh. He was not a thrice married, twice divorced, philandering, pussy grabbing, pornstar banging, serial adulterer, he was a fine family man and servant of Christ. I guess we are all prone to idolizing our heroes but how was it possible to whip this albatross into something transcendent?

It's the fact that Trump's unfavorables were embraced as fanatically as his favorables by the Deplorables that confounded me. Surely this is an oxymoron worth pondering. Wouldn't it be like saying "What I love most about this champion of justice is his purely corrupt lawlessness?" The fact is, love really is blind, especially when that love is based on fanaticism. The excessive enthusiasm, the blind loyalty, the sadistic preoccupation with destroying opponents, the vile rhetoric, the ultra-violent fantasies, these are the dimensions of fanaticism we ignore at our peril. As we watch the Deplorables become more and more comfortable in water that has already reached the boiling point, we must ask what violations of our society's norms won't they tolerate, and even embrace, what warped values will they wrap themselves in as they

175

luxuriate in their morbid fantasy? Will they slip peacefully back into disrepute from whence they came now that their leader's reign of moral decay is finally over? Or like mindless White Walkers at the gate of civilization, will they terrorize our society forever more?

This kind of irrational hero worship was on full display as the circumstances leading to Trump's first impeachment played out. The incredulity of people who insisted they were patriots but placed the exoneration and future reelection of their hero above any measure of American loyalty to the rule of law was stunning. We saw the same dynamic at work during the Mueller investigation, over equally vivid foul play, but not leading to any final reckoning. As it turned out, the events of late 2019 were just a prelude to Trump's final and biggest lie of all. Almost a full year before Election Day 2020, an overtly brash Donald J. Trump secretly knew his reelection would depend entirely upon cheating and at the risk of our country's national security. This was no more of a bridge too far for the Deplorables than colluding with a geo political enemy or obstructing an investigation of giving aid and comfort to that country's goal of subverting American democracy. This was about extorting an ally to tip the 2020 election in Trump's favor, and the smoking gun was a partial transcript from a call between 45 and the President of Ukraine that occurred on July 25th, 2019 for the ostensible purpose of congratulating Mr. Zelensky for his anti-corruption crusade.

So what about this "perfect call?"

- The call was so perfect that when informed that a decorated Lt. Colonel, a Ukrainian expert on the National Security Council, found a shakedown of the Ukrainian president in the transcript, the lead counsel for the NSC said "Oh no, you didn't" and

176

promptly dropped the transcript into a highly secure server reserved for State secrets.

- The call was so perfect that the document that contained words like "Biden" and "Burisma," that Trump referred to as a "word for word transcript", was edited to remove both the former Vice President's name and the name of the company his son sat on the board of as they appeared multiple times.

- The call was so perfect that an unnamed whistle blower filed a complaint with the DNI's Inspector General when he heard other officials say Mr. Trump urged Zelensky to work with Attorney General Barr and Rudy Giuliani to investigate the Bidens.

- The call was so perfect that when the IG sent his assessment of this urgent credible complaint to the acting Director of the DNI, Joseph Maguire, so he could notify Congress as stipulated by law, Maguire claimed it didn't meet the definition of an urgent concern and quashed it.

- The call was so perfect that all of the king's horsemen felt they should attack the credibility of the whistleblower instead of affirming or denying the substance of the complaint, and even suggested that a whistleblower rule was changed and that Democrats on the Intelligence committee colluded with this person.

- The call was so perfect that GOP members of Congress and the president himself insisted the identity of the Whistleblower be revealed despite the grave threat that might present to the anonymous do-gooder.

- The call was so perfect that all of Trump's surrogates glommed onto the notion that President Zelensky insisted he was not coerced by Trump as if the embattled Ukrainian leader had any choice but to deny the facts.

- The call was so perfect that, for the benefit of any who didn't grasp the objective of the exchange, President Trump confessed on the Whitehouse lawn how Ukraine, and China even, should both investigate Joe Biden for corruption.

- The call was so perfect, that two days later, the White House Acting Chief of Staff Mick Mulvaney likewise confessed to the quid pro quo saying it is "done all the time," and we should "get over it." He also said this was mostly about the debunked CrowdStrike server conspiracy. The next day he insisted his words were misconstrued by the media, and the real reason for withholding aid to Ukraine was how our European partners weren't ponying up enough military aid. Then the Chief of Staff went dark until finally resigning.

- The call was so perfect that a Top Ukraine diplomat, Bill Taylor, exchanged texts with other officials involved, including Ambassadors Volker and Sondland, in which he expressed serious misgivings about the US withholding aid for Ukraine over an investigation of a political enemy and Ukraine interference in the 2016 election. Later in his testimony before the House Intelligence Committee, Taylor spoke of a video call from the US Office of Budget and Management that made a direct link between President Donald Trump and the withholding of military aid to Ukraine for political purposes.

The point is not that the party of Trump folded, spindled and mutilated the obvious truth for their own self-preservation, but how legions of Deplorables willfully leeched themselves to the hull of this rotting ship as it began sinking ever faster. Throughout their cult leader's reign of self-serving terror, they artfully suspended all measure of reasonable doubt, not because any of this seemed legit, but because supporting the grift reaffirmed their identity as Trump foot soldiers in the war against decency. Indeed, it is precisely in the incessant gaslighting that they find the greatest sustenance within their malevolent counterculture. Defiantly shitting all over the cultural norms of a progressive society is their personal Nirvana. Long ago they passed the proverbial point of no return and now ride this runaway train to its ultimate destruction.

Not surprisingly, by a straight line vote, the House of Representatives managed to impeach Trump for shaking down our vulnerable ally for his own personal political ambitions. I have a faint inkling throughout of the Deplorables complaining 24/7 about the unfair process and subversion of our Constitution without demonstrating a basic understanding of either the document or the process. Why quibble though, I am sure if the Democrats played this by the book, the Trump cult would gracefully accept how their hero was an unrepentant dirt bag who needed to be removed from the White House at gun point, right? If only the Dems hadn't held their meetings in secret in the basement, with no GOP committee members within miles of the proceedings, we could all remove our noise canceling headphones and find justice impartially. If only the Dems would bring the firsthand fact witnesses, who still wore the afterbirth of this aborted cover up, this wouldn't be the sham it was. It's not like the accused simply ignored subpoenas issued by a co-equal branch of government, specifically ordered by the Constitution to bring impeachment charges, from compelling testimony. Who says It's not just tough titties that this kind of obstruction forced an early conclusion so the 2020 election could be unsullied by scandal? It's not like every document that wasn't about puppies and rainbows wasn't still sitting in hundreds of bankers boxes waiting to be refiled once the law suits were adjudicated within a few short years. What's the hurry, they all whined, after whining as much about how this drawn out process was hurting the Republic? Surely, we could all wait until after the election to resolve the grave matter of jury-rigging the election, right? Generally, when people think in Pig Latin, someone is willfully missing the point.

Against a cacophony of whiny table banging by the Republicans, and their endless slimefukery of honorable public servants, Adam Schiff put 17 witnesses up to corroborate the whistle blower's original complaint. Home schooled fifth graders would have voted to impeach the president, but 195 Republicans and 2 Democrats managed not to do so. After all, nothing spells corruption like B-I-D-E-N, and we all know nothing is more important than identifying who originally called the fire department as the town was burning to the ground. The prevailing wisdom for the nay vote squished around like Jell-O through a strainer but mostly seemed to settle on a single cynical matter. Apparently, the GOP lawmakers felt the process was simply too partisan, and this robbed them of any voluntary control over the muscle in their body that separates right from wrong. Because they couldn't accept the electoral pain that would come from admitting an iota of doubt about their leader, it was unfair that the other side was of sounder mind and could cast their votes unencumbered by fear of a violent backlash from Trump's Deplorables. It would be like saying; "If your case is so weak you can't convince any of us to puree our own genitals in a blender, we must acquit." Yes, it was certainly unfair to expect anyone fearful of the president's rage Tweets to weigh even a scintilla of evidence of irrefutable malfeasance. By the way, in a shock to exactly no one, and to the Deplorables' great relief, the Republican-led Senate settled the matter of this impeachment in record time calling

180

zero witnesses who would either corroborate or refute the evidence presented in the House of Representatives. I am sure, at that moment, a million bananas were outraged to be linked to this Republic.

Chapter Twenty Two

Are you or someone you love a Deplorable?

If you reflexively react to any shady behavior exhibited by your cult leader, as if gripped by Tourette's, with the words "fake news," you may be a Deplorable.

If you respond to every accusation containing the word Trump with the word Clinton or Obama, as in, what about either of these retired public servants, you may be a Deplorable.

If you baselessly call Facebook opponents child molesters but tirelessly campaigned for Matt Gaetz, you may be a Deplorable.

If you insist that Mueller didn't find Collusion, even though he said he didn't investigate for it, and listed ten instances of it anyway, you may be a Deplorable

If you can't fathom why black folks will often use the N word amongst themselves, but can understand why you find satisfaction in calling yourself a Deplorable, you may be a Deplorable.

If you find yourself phoning in death threats to one or more of the freshman lawmakers known as "The Squad," you may be a Deplorable.

If you insist the survivors of the Parkland mass shooting are "crisis actors" who didn't attend the school, you may be a Deplorable.

If spelling homophones (words which sound alike but are spelled differently) is a game of chance for you, with low odds of success, you may be a Deplorable.

If you are certain that the Uranium One approval was a Clinton cash grab, you may be a Deplorable.

If you still argue that Obama was an illegitimate president because he is a Muslim born in Kenyon, you may be a Deplorable.

If you feel that General Flynn, Paul Manafort and Roger Stone all got a raw deal by the Deep State and should have been released immediately, you may be a Deplorable.

If you believe the Mueller report concluded that Trump was exonerated from obstruction of justice even though the prosecutor outlined many examples of it, you may be a Deplorable.

If when Trump asked the Ukrainian president "do us a favor though," you heard "Y'know", as a verbal aside, Like Sean Hannity did, you may be a Deplorable.

If you would bet a buddy $100 that Obama was the original founder of ISIS, you may be a Deplorable.

If you felt black athletes who protested police violence against unarmed black males by quietly taking a knee during the National Anthem disrespected either our flag or our military, you may be a Deplorable.

If you have an unshakable belief that millions of "illegals" actually cast votes for democrats each year, you may be a Deplorable.

If you believe Hillary Clinton will *Frazzledrip* her way into infamy, you may be a Deplorable.

If you are convinced it is the "Deep State" and not Donald Trump himself who is most responsible for the tsunami of legal jeopardy Donald Trump faces now, you may be a Deplorable.

If it has been a year since people just like you stormed our nation's Capital and you are still plotting the next attack to "Stop the Steal," you may be a Deplorable.

If you believe brown immigrants are "invaders" who you may count on to rape and murder your family, you may be a Deplorable.

If you imagine the *My Pillow Guy* Should replace Dr. Fauci as Joe Biden's Chief Medical adviser if *Sleepy Joe* is serious about ending the pandemic, you may be a Deplorable.

If you would swear Trump is a stable genius engaged in 3 dimensional chess against the checkers the Swamp plays, and not a malignant narcissist on the verge of mental collapse, you may be a Deplorable.

If you really can't fathom that Donald J. Trump may have sexually assaulted one or more women in his adult life, you may be a deplorable.

If you want Sean Hannity to pick up where he left off promoting the baseless Seth Rich murder conspiracy, you may be a Deplorable.

If you are waiting with baited breath for tens of thousands of sealed indictments against Deep-Staters to be unsealed at any moment dooming every imagined Trump political opponent to a lifetime sentence in Gitmo, you may be a Deplorable.

If you think the only logical response for every investigation of Trump malfeasance is a counter investigation of the investigators themselves, you may be a Deplorable.

If you believe every lifelong public servant doing their patriotic duty is an enemy of the former Dear Leader, you may be a Deplorable.

If outrage and hate porn on social media is your guilty pleasure, you may be a Deplorable.

If you are so classless that you insist on joking about our former First Lady Michelle Obama secretly being a man, you may be a Deplorable.

If you find the smearing of dedicated career public servants simply to defend the former Grifter in Chief, as sporting as participating in a family soccer match, you may be a Deplorable.

If the Uranium One story has been explained to you in excruciating detail and you have seen the 4 Pinocchios attached to it with your own eyes, but still use it to wage rhetorical war against Hillary Clinton, you may be a Deplorable.

If your go-to response to any claim of racism from team Trump is how the Democrats started the KKK, but can't be bothered with evidence over the last 60 years how the GOP has coopted the White Power movement, you may be a Deplorable.

If you still haven't asked yourself why Team Trump's tireless pursuit of Ukrainian corruption, in a country notorious for corruption, was limited to only people named Biden, you may be a Deplorable.

If you trust Chuck Woolery and the My Pillow guy for Corona Virus guidance over infectious disease experts, you may be a deplorable.

Chapter Twenty Three

Fuck you too

For the last 35 years, I have been conditioned to recognize the Donald J. Trump experience as one fulsomely unapologetic "fuck you" to polite society docudrama. For those struggling to understand his broad appeal, this is essentially it: What vulgar, poorly educated, and uninformed bigot doesn't jones over indiscriminately flinging the bird at every vestige of civilized normality? Saying *Fuck You* to people demonstrably superior in character and values must be so satisfying to people lacking social graces and moral fortitude. Imagine the inferiority complex that comes from years of knowing how normal people either pitied or detested you. "You think you are better than me simply because you have decency, moral clarity, and basic hygiene, well, fuck you!" How liberating it must have been to find in Trump a kindred spirit whose words and deeds were always untethered from moral rectitude. Without the baggage that comes from conscience and accountability, Trump built his empire from one fuck you to another. "Mr. Trump, won't you pay us for services rendered?" "Mr. Trump, it is customary to repay the money we lent you with interest over time." "Mr. Trump, why are you grabbing me by my pussy, just because you are a big star?" Fuck you, Fuck you, and Fuck you, too!!! Today, as anti-intellectualism and myriad phobias have gripped the cult, neither

Dunning nor Kruger could convince the Deplorables they lack the basic competence to be constructive members of the human race. *The Dunning and Kruger Effect* certainly clarifies a question that has blazed through four years of Mr. Trump's dumpster fire term as it perfectly captured both our 45th president and his adoring fans. "People with low ability at a task will always overestimate their ability." Not only do they feel they are supremely competent, but they feel they are supreme in general for their whiteness and for their religious and authoritarian piety. Indeed, when confronted with a rhetorical challenge of right versus wrong, their go to response on social media is "Because fuck you." As impressive as this FuckYoupalooza tactic may seem, the Deplorables warrant scrutiny as their expression of this dogma ranges from harmless snark to unrestrained rage. When their response to Commendables becomes a fuck you bullet aimed at center mass, we know all hell has broken out.

"There is a cult of ignorance in the United States, and there has always been the strain of anti-intellectualism that has been a constant thread winding its way through our political and cultural life, nurtured by the false notion that democracy means that "my ignorance is just as good as your knowledge"

Isaac Asimov 1980

Even a celebrated futurist could not have predicted how prescient this assessment would become in the age of social media, where ratings and affirmation from the like-minded replace actual facts and reason. Between true believers, no communications transgressions matter, no logical fallacies, no lack of context, no ignorance of subject and no outright fabrications. The entire enterprise hinges only on creating dangerous unhinged echoes. For the perpetually aggrieved

187

Deplorables, there is anger and cruelty in public discourse. The idea of "cancel culture" is rapidly becoming something closer to "cancel people" for those lacking the imagination necessary for diplomacy. We must only imagine what the end game looks like to be truly horrified.

Chapter Twenty Four

Trump is the virus Goo, Goo G'joob

"No species in the face of Earth have this little empathy for another living being, as we humans have. We want to fight every logic, every belief, every fact to avoid wearing something which may have the potential to save each other's life."

Sarvesh Jain

There's nothing like a global pandemic to smoke out the truly cray cray. When we learned of the great Covid -19 pandemic reaching our shores in January of 2020, patriotic citizens hoped it would be the latest opportunity to rally around the flag and work collectively to mitigate the harm. What was the alternative? Would we let our inherent divisiveness create parallel realities for how we would cope with a virus that was indifferent to our usual us versus them struggles? Duh, of course that is exactly how we would frame this existential battle. As Covid -19 mindlessly seeks human kindling to feed its flame and spread its seed: It remains unimpressed by political allegiances and outlandish counter factual theories about it. Yet, every assessment of the danger, every analysis of the response, and every prediction for how it might or might not plunder our society; indeed, every public figure we would rely upon, became the usual tug of war between the Deplorables and

Commendables. We could let scientists who have dedicated their entire careers to the study of infectious diseases lead the way on mitigation and cure, but that would hinge on how many of our people accept the legitimacy of science, or trust that it would not be used nefariously against us. Why not let the debate hinge instead on weightier matters like how supportive the policies were of a leader completely dependent upon the self-aggrandizing approval of roughly 40% of our people? Surely, nothing would make Vladimir Putin grin more, like the Cheshire Cat, than seeing debate over the most incontrovertible facts become the latest chinks in the wall of our democratic Republic.

One thing we knew for certain was that Trump would sooner submit to a rectal exam conducted with a chainsaw than accept any accountability for how his team managed this country's pandemic response. I mean, it's not like he had any advance warning about an inevitable worldwide pandemic from either the outgoing Obama administration in 2017 or the guidance from Operation Crimson Contagion in 2019. Just because both urged immediate and far-ranging preparedness and stockpiling of essential materials, including ventilators, didn't stop 45 form from saying, "Who knew anything like this was even possible?" I can imagine the conversation going something like this: "Hey, I used the last roll; you may want to stock up a bit" "No thanks, I will just wait 3 years and blame you as the turds run rampant through the streets."

When his intelligence team attempted to brief him with actual words on a page, instead of with big, colorful, sharpie-enhanced charts, he picked up only on the part that said doing nothing could lead to 3 million dead Americans, an awkward consequence for a man seeking reelection. He had to do something, but that something had to be tuned to the precise frequency that would delight his constituency, whether or not it was a comprehensive and effective plan. Why not blame this exclusively on China? That would check off so many boxes simultaneously that his Deplorables would think it was Christmas 12 months early. Plus, that's where the virus originated, so who else should be blamed? Especially since Obama left the cupboard bare except for only "broken tests" for a novel virus "no one could have predicted was coming" when he left office more than 3 years earlier. The stable genius of the plan became even clearer when he realized the Deplorables could never tease out the exact genesis for Covid-19, whether it was the Zoonotic consequence of exotic animal interaction in wet markets in Wuhan, or it was actually engineered in a lab a mile away. Given the choice, they would always assume the worst about China, a Communist regime they knew would seek retribution for Trump's trade war, no matter how many of its own people would be sacrificed to make Trump look bad. Or how it would crater their own economy making the whole point somewhat moot, but I digress.

Was it a deal breaker with the public when word came that Jared Kushner advised against employing a national response over letting states grapple with mitigation on their own? Surely when the Deplorables discovered his calculus was based exclusively on the craven observation that it was Blue State America suffering the most, and therefore the results could be blamed on liberal leadership, they would be offended by treating the deaths of millions like just another political football. Surely, when *Vanity Fair* quoted Jared as allegedly saying "New Yorkers are going to suffer, and that's their problem," it was a bridge too far for the Deplorables, right? That kind of shell game couldn't possibly pass even casual scrutiny, right? Not in these UNITED States. Indeed, millions of Deplorables could accept that a national epidemic was better handled piecemeal on an intra and not interstate basis. How else could liberal boogeyman be held accountable and their cult hero blameless? And if Governors like Andrew Cuomo and Gretchen Whitmer really needed more federal support, why couldn't they grovel for it, as all good supplicants rightfully should in a Fascist Republic like ours? It was only when poor mitigation efforts in anti-science Trump States exploded into daily record infections and deaths that the Deplorables started responding, "Wait, what just happened?" and the Dear Leader actually donned a mask and resumed giving national Corona Virus briefings. It was at this point Trump was advised, "These are our people."

Since China is a dictatorship, the Chinese clamped down pretty tight on early news escaping from the Republic that might have benefitted other countries. The World Health Organization may also have been too diplomatic as they tended to accept most early accounts of the virus and its transmission and lethality more on face value than what was deserved. All these facts would help create the perfect storm for an administration desperate to say "I don't take responsibility at all."

For the Deplorables, ultimately China was responsible, but for good measure Obama, the governors of exactly 24 states, and all democratic members of Congress, especially Fancy Nancy, were to be held even more accountable for a quickly growing cluster fuck than the Deplorables' hero. But still China loomed largest in the fevered imaginations of conspiracy junkies until other culprits would emerge simply because fevers must be fed.

When matters of accountability are at stake, the Deplorables can always find an earlier or later culprit to hold responsible when motivated to hold their own harmless. When Trump began

192

hammering the Obama administration for leaving only "broken" Corona Virus tests to treat the novel Corona Virus, Covid -19, he was counting on the kinds of leaps of faith only the delusionally faithful can make. Obviously, Obama could not in 2017 have left tests that would be effective in treating a novel virus strain originating three years later. Just as our country's governors could not have foreseen, as perhaps the president should have, the need to fill their stockpiles of supplies fuller than ever in history to meet the Covid-19 outbreak. There was no evidence discussions about this even took place in advance of January 2020. The logic of these obvious things is of no value to the Deplorables who seek only to find a plausible scapegoat that happens to be a Trump opponent. This dumbfukery becomes even more tortured when the blame actually skips potential culprits between those hated from those loved. When interviewed by Jordan Klepper of *The Daily Show*, a particularly daft MAGA circle jerker was still aghast, after 18 years, how Obama was missing in action, always on vacation, and never in the office before 9/11. "I have no idea," he said when asked by Klepper "why do you suppose Obama was not in the Oval Office on 9/11?" The Deplorables will always insist we leapfrog over their leaders as we assign blame for the state of affairs in the country. The economic carnage of 2007 surely persisted through two Obama terms so a heroic Donald J. Trump could bring an unprecedented recovery that brought riches for all over the next 3 years. A Great Depression level relapse could never be related to Trump missteps, unless those missteps could be pinned on Obama era Democratic leadership. Yes, Fancy Nancy was too busy stuffing her face with Haagen-Dazs and Merlot to prevent the spread of the virus and the demise of the economy in 2020. The Deplorables couldn't find a trend line with an electron microscope if doing so would require an honest assessment of shared responsibility.

Hollywood refers to it as the "Willing Suspension of Disbelief" to describe how people are motivated to accept even the most outlandish premise and plot twists, as a narrative is revealed, to justify the high cost of time and money spent watching the movie. Why couldn't an esteemed but eccentric surgeon kidnap a young lady, chop off all her limbs, and stash her in a curio cabinet before the two hopelessly fall in love? Call it *Boxing Helena* and surely the public will plunk down $84.50 to take ma and the kids for an hour and 47 minutes of this gruesome romance. The fabrications and denials the Deplorables accepted in order to forgive the catastrophic failures of the Trump administration were no less staggering an example of the willful suspension of disbelief. It was just as outrageous to insist how the pandemic was masterfully handled by Trump as insisting Dr. Nick and Helena would live happily ever after. The investment of their own human capital in this performance art hardened the Deplorables against any counter narrative. Imagine the bitter taste if all they held to be self-evident was really just a cruel grift? If the love of country and sacrifice they ascribed to Donald J. Trump was just a ploy to achieve and maintain the kind of power that could line his pockets forevermore? What if their trust that he shared their values and was deeply invested in their wellbeing was all just an illusion? Surely they must have known Trump was a showman above all else, right? They most have noticed how he turned Covid briefings into pure spectacle, more resembling his MAGA circle jerks than public service? Hell, he even boasted of his exceptionally high ratings and tweaked each appearance with reliable Deplorable gold like castigating journalists for "fake news." The only thing lacking was an artificially generated laugh and applause track, and who knows if he hadn't suggested as much? What would it have taken for them to grasp how they were witting or unwitting participants in their

194

leader's PSYOPs experiments to find the electoral magic for exploiting their hopes and fears?

Compulsive liars are reprehensible but, it is the compulsive believers who pose the greatest danger to a nation's orderly sense of right and wrong. The Deplorables are the most desperate of drug addicts, and their fix is always a larger and larger dose of hallucinogenic fantasy that life in the real world will never provide. It is very possible the Trump era freak show has permanently rewired their brains in such a way they will never see the con, and for them the dots that connect all the mess that has transpired in the last four years will remain jumbled.

Objectively speaking, the US performed worse than any other country in battling the Covid virus. More people were infected and died here than in any other country on the planet, and fewer were tested per capita than in any comparable first world democracy. In fact, we did so badly, Donald Trump determined he should accuse China of rigging the 2020 election in favor of Joe Biden to distract his Deplorables from actually noticing how the swath of death and destruction could only have occurred if everything had been handled incompetently. In early February of 2020, the Deplorables were comforted to hear their hero boast how under control the "China Virus" was as he predicted that 15 known cases would quickly become zero. In April, when warmer temperatures failed to make the Kung Flu "magically disappear," the Deplorables dug in for the long slog ahead by grasping at every straw that could place blame everywhere but the Oval Office. Five months later, in July, we had 3.2 million cases in the US and 137,000 deaths. By late August that swelled to 5.5 million cases and 183,000 dead. Still the Deplorables persisted in claiming Covid was really no more infectious or deadly than the common flu, and criticism of Trump was a liberal much ado about nothing. We should not, they contended, make the cure worse than the disease by asking people to believe in science and take mitigation steps. After a couple months of committing to a scientific approach to stemming the tide, Trump flung back open the doors to an anemic economy he feared might compromise his chances for reelection in November. Unfortunately, neither he nor Governors across Red State America adhered to CDC guidelines that were to be met as a condition of Trump's greatest economy in history. From that moment on, we proceeded to set daily records for new cases in most of our states and created a steeper curve than we had in March when the CDC was already saying we had lost control.

The Deplorables could not have become more confident in the prospect of a landslide victory for their standard bearer as they were on September 1st 2020 when Trump announced that China was interfering in the 2020 contest to elect Joe Biden. This was the ultimate BOGO as it lashed the two most prominent Trump villains together in a single conspiracy theory that would further absolve Trump from pandemic responsibility and shutter Sleepy Joe's chance to end Trumpism. I only wondered if Trump accusing another of benefitting from election interference was not the most ironically delicious fabrication the Deplorables would blindly accept. It was an article of faith among Deplorables young and old that Biden, for his endless gaffes, obvious mental deterioration, and complicity with his son in the fleecing of America, was already no match for the mighty Donald Trump. This fortuitous news would surely seal the deal. Anyway, this was a card the Deplorables were dealt and so, for the final two months of the campaign, it would be China, China, China they would use to contrast with Trump's albatross Russia, Russia, Russia.

196

As long as Trump could contrast the mayhem that would have ensued from doing absolutely nothing, with the marginal impact of doing next to nothing, he could occupy a mind space the Deplorables would find pleasing. It's a neat trick requiring very little preparation and even less skill to pull off in front of an unsophisticated and adoring audience. Link the stable genius of severely limiting Chinese people from travelling here in January to a warning from the CDC that was stripped of its context, that taking no steps to mitigate against the virus could lead to millions of causalities, and you have all the material you need to confuse the Deplorables ever after. Never mind that the "travel ban," originally inspired by our airlines, applied only to Chinese people and allowed over 40,000 potential carriers to slip through the cracks. Also inconvenient was how our original epicenter, New York, was primarily sacked by the European strain of the virus. Deplorables would accept the brilliance of the plan, applaud how it punished China, and use it to transition from what Trump could do to "Hasn't Trump done enough?"

Trump's cult disciples were stubborn in their resistance to actual facts about Covid-19 and were mystified by the science. I think they believed cases contracted, and the death toll from the virus were entirely separate and unrelated data points. Tell them that the number of cases on any given day is a leading indicator for a certain number of deaths at a future date, and they will look at you with an expression that would make a deer in the headlights laugh out loud. They seem to believe getting a negative Covid test is like a blanket life time immunity. Ask them why they have recently abandoned all safety measures, and they will mention how they have been tested, regardless of long ago this was done or how much risky Deplorable behavior they have engaged in since. They have very nuanced theories for why they, personally, are

197

incapable of contracting the virus. They rarely get the flu, even though they haven't vaccinated against it since kindergarten. No one in their family ever misses a day of work from being sick even when they are coughing up blood. Their regular exposure to every toxin and germ imaginable has given them elite immunity to everything, including herpes. The people outside of their homes who they associate with are the same people they always associate with so, duh! When they spot someone visibly symptomatic, they can always hold their breath for up to five minutes if necessary; no need for a girly mask. Obviously, they contend, only those hacking up a lung and blowing snot bubbles from their noses can transmit the virus, double duh.

Surely, our focus should always be on the number who recover, and not on those infected. That's happier news and could somehow be crowdsourced into a Trump win if we held our nose. After all, no one ever said it would be only 1-3% who would ultimately succumb to Covid-19, and if 97% survive, doesn't that mean it is really just another flu season? Oh wait, you mean 3% is a 10 times higher rate than .3%? Shit! But surely Trump deserved full credit for those who beat the "unseen enemy," right? Why credit medical professionals for anything we could have credited our leader for instead? And even when we saw folks become infected, and soon after succumb to the illness, wasn't it likely this was just another ruse cooked up by the "fake news" media or the Deep State? People die of all kinds of things, why quibble over whether the virus pushed them over the finish line prematurely? And why should Covid get all the credit anyway? In August of 2020, when she and Dr. Fauci let science drive predictive modeling for the Covid virus, Dr. Birx reminded us it was likely our final death toll would surpass 250,000 no matter how conscientious we became. Soon after, we could find neither of the esteemed virologists anywhere but on podcasts and liberal media broadcasts.

When it came to Covid cures, and any particular snake oil the Grifter in Chief was endorsing, for purely humanitarian reasons no doubt, the Deplorables were in want of the proverbial magic bullet. After wading too far from the shore without a credible national response, Trump, too, became pretty focused on miracles. The Deplorables became instantly smitten with hydroxychloroquine against evidence from double blind trials indicating it might actually cause cardiac arrest. Why believe in Science when they heard of a guy who knew a guy who actually survived the virus while on the stuff? Indeed, to prove the universal efficacy for hydroxychloroquine, Trump himself took the potion, ostensibly only to ward off infection but not as a cure, as he got nowhere near the stuff when he actually had the virus and thought he might die from it. When a drug with actual efficacy against the virus, remdesivir, was touted by Fauci, the Deplorables just knew the good doctor, and not their cult hero, stood to benefit financially from hawking this elixir over the other. Not convinced? Trump found a "witchdoctor," Stella Immanuel, to stick her thumb on the scale. Unlike remdesivir, she explained, which contained the same alien DNA all medicines other than hydroxychloroquine and Lysol did, she often used the hydroxy product to cure women suffering from demonic sexual assault in dreams that is always the root cause of female sexual disorders. I am not sure what that means but am sure it will satisfy the Deplorables' thirst for more magic thinking. Still not convinced? Did you see what Chuck Woolery, former gameshow impresario cum Medical Laureate, had to say on the matter?

Once the hydroxychloroquine hysteria finally faded, and the Deplorables declared that only the libtards took seriously Trump's "joke" about injecting disinfectant into our bloodstreams, what new strange trip would America be asked to take on the Trump train? By late August of 2020, over five million Americans had been infected with the Corona Virus, and 183,000 had died. Our economy, which had been the envy of the world as recently as February, lay in ruins with 30 million unemployed and a million more joining those ranks weekly. We tried but failed miserably to get back to normal by failing to understand how normal would be a new normal, subject to new rules, to function even haltingly.

As our gaze lengthened to consider not cures, but vaccines for the Corona Virus, we were again cajoled by an adoring public of Deplorable misfits to believe how evil the race for an effective vaccine itself was. They believed, like so many other anti vaxxer nuts, that vaccines were the surest way to insure our children would be born with autism or an extra nostril, but they also believed and preached how vaccines really weren't very effective anyway. Not like hydroxy. But, the most malodorous new attack was that our beloved Dr. Fauci was in cahoots with none other than billionaire philanthropist Bill Gates, not just to make bank against our country, but to actually implement a well-known NWO plot to control the masses. I listened to a podcast from a Q Anon infected speaker about this very topic. She provided anecdote after anecdote for how intimately Fauci and gates were connected. Because these two men were dedicated to the understanding and treatment of pandemic virus outbreaks, they must be cooking up nefarious takeover plots. How diabolical indeed. While it surely was a bombshell to learn Fauci and Gates were thick as thieves in a matter so dear to each of them, there must be more to the plot, and I instantly regretted diving deeper into the swamp.

Moreover, even though Gates has been an advocate for pandemic preparedness at least since 2015, and has pledged a quarter of a billion dollars through his foundation to develop a vaccine for this latest scourge, according to the Q truther, he is actually directly responsible for the Corona Virus outbreak. What an evil bastard to say with one smug face how we wants to rid the world of evil but with another actually injecting evil into the society's bloodstream for fun and profit. Especially egregious was how Gates said at a TED talk presentation in 2015, "The failure to prepare could allow the next epidemic to be dramatically more devastating than Ebola." The unhinged theory is that because Gates hosted a global pandemic exercise that simulated a worldwide coronavirus outbreak, he must have had advance knowledge that Covid was on its way. As it turned out, Gates did indeed participate, but the host was John Hopkins Center for Health Security. The event didn't specifically address this particular novel coronavirus, but Gates did speak of a very severe pandemic generally. Every serious thinker connected with research and development of global pandemics has been warning for years about the inevitability of a novel coronavirus outbreak. But, with the keen observation that Gates was among the most informed on this topic, and that he participated in symposia that addressed the looming threats, a new conspiracy theory was birthed that could further exonerate Trump and place a Liberal elite boogeyman at the center of this dumpster fire. It might be inconvenient that Gates has already pledged to underwrite up to 70% of the vast cost of supplying a vaccine to underdeveloped nations. Surely he and Fauci will split what remains of the ill-gotten gains. As usual, the suspension of disbelief allowed the Deplorables to overlook their hero being golf buddies with the CEO of the number one generic hydroxychloroquine manufacturer but vilify Gates for his noble cause simply because those dots could be connected in those ways through enough willful ignorance.

When the mighty pharmaceutical companies informed the President they could develop a safe and effective vaccine in less than half the time, Trump heard, "We can help you save your presidency." So, he committed to "Operation Warp Speed" because warp speed was about the speed necessary to find a single good reason to reelect him. Though the skeptical Deplorables were blissfully unaware that CRISPR was not a special bacon order at I-Hop, but a powerful new RNA guided gene editing technology, they still felt, even if they wouldn't take the vaccine unless water-boarded, they could at least credit their hero with the discovery and implementation of this modern miracle. "Duh libtard, we all know Trump is the stable genome!"

After the failed experiment of opening back up our cratered economy, next up was opening the schools. This effort, too, would not be guided by national science based mandates, mostly because the administration knew the states most willing to gamble with the lives of children were now sacked with the virus and could never pass the minimum criteria for reopening. Anyway, though nothing is more precious than our babies, experts have noted that kids returning to actual school buildings, congregating within real classrooms, may spread the seed of the "invisible enemy" to teachers, bus drivers, lunchroom workers and the comorbidly afflicted family members they live with. Especially the middle schoolers and older, who are just as apt as adults to contract and spread the virus, and tend to be far less cautious. Imagine a 15 year old boy, barely more than a dick with a backpack at that age, taking great care to wear a mask for 6 straight hours and socially distance from all the young hotties. Yeah, right. Odds are good that they'll trade that mask for an extra pudding pop by third period. When they return home, still beaming with scholastic enthusiasm, they will wrap their arms around their middle aged mom, a cancer survivor, and hope for the best. Thinking otherwise would be like mainlining an IV bag full of Formula 409. Also, at the risk of being indelicate, it seems most who wear MAGA headgear, don't realize how understated the stats are. The simple math is a mind melt for them, but could it possibly be that our former leader exaggerated when he said Covid was no worse than the flu and that everyone who needed a test was tested? Maybe, as he continued to compare the Covid outbreak to the common flu, he may have suppressed some critical data? Normal people, who wouldn't spend 18 hours in line for the chance to jerk their monkey at a Whitezapalooza event, were not as impressed with these pronouncements. They didn't ask which non-related deaths were lumped into the Covid -19 stats to simply take cheap political shots at the Dear Leader, they were asking a more thoughtful question: Since generally only symptomatic people were tested, couldn't infections have actually been under counted? It seems especially likely in view of the high incidence of virus discovered in those who are tested. When a cadaver is slapped with a cause of death, but no one has any idea if he/she was infected, couldn't that actually trend the numbers upward as well? Clinging desperately to the fiction that Covid was no worse than the flu, committed a math faux pas I'd have received a verbal beat down from my fifth grade teacher, Mr. Beecher. If the math doesn't fit, you must acquit. Also, infectious disease experts parted company with Chuck Woolery when it came to positing how the death toll in late October of 2020 at 220,000 was very possibly as high as 300,000 or more because of something called "excess mortality." This was just a fancy way of saying that during the year almost 200,000 more people than average had died and likely a large share were from the Covid-19 virus.

Now, this is where it really gets weird. In the middle of August we learned how the My Pillow Guy, Mike Lindell, was actively bankrolling the latest snake oil that could have relieved our 45th president of any remaining responsibility if it worked any better than the last magic elixir. This made sense because Lindell was advised by God Himself that oleandrin, a chemical compound derived from poisonous shrubs, was surely the miracle cure anyone leery of a thoroughly tested vaccine sponsored by evil elites might provide. Experts said ingesting a tiny bit of the toxic weed could kill you but "what have you got to lose?" Isn't it always better to stick anything in your mouth that is endorsed by a president desperate for people to stop talking about the Kung flu, and hope for the best? If oleandrin was added to the toolbox, we would have had an awesome set of alternatives to science to choose from that all proved how very deeply Donald Trump cared about us all. If you have any questions, I'd recommend asking Chuck Woolery. Anyway, I am guessing the Deplorables were as thrilled as anyone that this poison pill seemed destined for market by the end of the year.

Once the Red States caught up and surpassed the Blue as new coronavirus epicenters, there was an almost perceptible White House shimmy toward actual science. Trump was even seen wearing a mask one or twice, and he said it was a "patriotic responsibility" for all but him, and anyone he would show respect for, to wear a mask. This lasted about a week until some enterprising Q Anon bread crumber mangled a notice from the CDC which stated that for only 6% of all Covid-19 deaths, Covid -19 was the only cause identified. That did not mean what Trump and legions of his mentally underequipped supporters decided it did. For them the CDC had "quietly updated" the number of deaths associated with COVID-19 to a fraction of what had been reported, a notion they had flirted with from the beginning. It's also not new information; the agency had been providing the same information since May. Imagine how fortuitous it would have been for an administration desperate to shirk all responsibility for the world's highest death toll, if they could simply say the death toll was 96% lower than the almost 200,000 souls reported as of August 2020. And what if they actually believed the storied institution of the CDC, the gold standard for health guidance, agreed that really only 10,000 or so deaths could be blamed on lack of preparedness, prioritization of opening the economy over health consequences, and indifference to science for months as the "Kung Flu" metastasized. Never mind how, from the outset, public health officials always informed us how people with comorbidities were at the greatest risk. And never mind that almost everyone has comorbidities. Surely, the other 190,000 deaths were completely unrelated to a virus that preys on those infirmities. At the very least, the Deplorables could blame the CDC instead of their fearless leader once the new figures were debunked. We knew then it was just a matter of time before breathless rightwing freak-out messages accused the CDC of misleading the public about the severity of Covid-19 by insisting the CDC said it was only 10,000 dead. I mean really, as patriots, shouldn't we have agreed to remove the last vivid example of Trump incompetence, and accept that it was the scientific community and not 45 that willfully distorted reality?

Unknown to the Deplorables was a covert plan hatched in September of 2020 by the Trump administration to quietly seize control over how the scientists and the CDC framed the pandemic and reported its findings to a concerned public. In addition to mounting public feuds with all of the infectious disease experts, Trump installed his long time lackey, Michael Caputo, as a top official at the Department of Health and Human Safety to sow general confusion and undermine the CDC with conspiratorial accusations of Deep State opposition to the President. This, of course, was pure meat and potatoes for the Deplorables, who had imagined for almost 4 years a massive coup against their duly elected hero. At a Facebook Live event in early September 2020, Caputo made outlandish and false accusations that career government scientists were engaging in "sedition" in their handling of the pandemic and that left-wing "hit squads" were preparing for an armed insurrection after the election. Allegedly, the CDC was harboring their own resistance movement, not to counter reams of recent misinformation to provide our citizens with good health and peace of mind, but to undermine the president, especially if the death toll could be inflated. And to presage a violent backlash from the left over his aims to quell this insurgence, Caputo directed this thought to his fans "If you carry guns, buy ammunition, ladies and gentlemen, because it's going to be hard to get," A week later, Caputo took a 60 day leave of absence from his post. He cited mental and physical health issues. If I were a betting man, I'd bet we never see Mr. Caputo again.

What happened when an unprepared but cocky Donald J. Trump thought he could leverage interviews with the investigative reporting legend Bob Woodward into pro Trump pablum ahead of the 2020 elections? Of course, he got burned alive. The new book, appropriately titled *Rage*, hadn't even reached the bookshelves or

Kindle before damning audio excerpts reached the mainstream media. In an exchange about the pandemic from an interview at the end of January 2020, Trump revealed a surprisingly detailed understanding of how deadly the corona virus was. And, on February 7 he confided "this is deadly stuff." "You just breathe the air and that's how it's passed, and so that's a very tricky one. That's a very delicate one. It's also more deadly than even your strenuous flu. This is more deadly. This is five per — you know, this is five percent versus one percent and less than one percent. You know? So this is deadly stuff." Hearing the recording in the unmistakable Trump tone and tenor, I wondered how the Deplorables would square this honest assessment, behind closed doors, with the endless prevarications Trump used publicly thereafter to downplay the threat. Comparing the virus to influenza, ridiculing mask wearing, promoting untested miracle cures, saying repeatedly the virus would miraculously just disappear, and creating no coherent policies about social distancing would seem at odds with his early understanding of the threat. Saying he took no responsibility for the outcome, despite being pretty well informed of the likely outcome, seemed almost criminal to most Commendables. The Deplorables' response leaned exclusively on Trump's vow to "always want to downplay" the virus as a sign of true leadership under pressure. Trump obliged them with a new meme when he said he didn't want to "jump up and down" creating panic. Certainly, the Deplorables could make bank on this after the anointed one had spent the entire year whipping white people into fits of hysteria over all of the liberal plots to bring anarchy and violence to their neighborhoods. When the liberal vision for America is a violent socialist dystopia, why should anyone care about something as quaint as a deadly virus that could actually kill them? Especially when they are sure only a fraction of the number of reported casualties can be attributed to Covid-19. And when William Barr compared the attack on civil liberties, this pandemic has imposed, as second only to slavery, who could argue with that?

So, as a leader, what do you do when it becomes apparent you shit the bed and far more than the rosy prediction of a 100,000 death toll was eclipsed by August? When your election hopes depended exclusively on an economic resurgence, there was no turning back for a better do over on starving the contagion. No Mulligans allowed on this course. No, instead this leader tried to fit the last Jenga block into his own teetering legacy on this issue. So Trump grabbed hold of a doc from the Fox, Scott Atlas, who was neither an epidemiologist nor an infectious disease expert but did speak Deplorable. Trump said of Atlas at the time, "He has many good ideas and will take the administration efforts to combat the pandemic to a new level." The good doctor had argued that the science of mask wearing is uncertain, that children cannot pass on the coronavirus, and that the role of the government is not to stamp out the virus, but to protect its most vulnerable citizens as Covid-19 runs its course. In other words, Atlas promoted an "if you can't beat it, let it infect us all" approach that had just the right ring to an administration in a real pickle over this disaster, and an adoring public of Deplorables still unimpressed with science. Yes my friends, very quietly the administration had pivoted to a herd immunity strategy that they would pursue with or without the very vaccine that makes such a strategy efficacious. Perhaps this was awkward, considering that the herd must represent more than 60% of our population, and without an effective vaccine administered to the herd, we imagine 2-3% of those 200 million people will give their lives to this cause. Maybe this was not completely thought through by 45 considering his bar for unqualified success in handling the pandemic was saying less than 2 million could die from this "plague," and a conservative guess for casualties from seeking herd immunity without a vaccine was 4 million. And maybe referring to it as "herd mentality" instead of "herd immunity" was the biggest tell of all about his stable genius. I am betting my last donut that 9 out of 10 Deplorables had no idea they wouldn't see the first hint of the vaccine until months after the election.

Since we changed nothing about our mitigation efforts, we would have landed somewhere just north of 250,000 dead by Election Day and nearly 400,000 by the end of the year. We knew there will be no coordinated national plans to whittle this down. Our kids would be returning to schools all over the country, creating tens of thousands of new super spreader epicenters. The reopening of the economy, at the insistence of the Dear Leader, ever faster as Election Day neared, would create many more opportunities to spread the seed of a virus biologically predisposed to gobble up all human kindling in its path. By all means, why not expose the entire population to a deadly virus months before widespread distribution of the vaccines to create herd immunity, which is based on accelerating, not decelerating the curve as another desperate measure to escape responsibility and blunt criticism for a botched response? If only there were a country or two we could have compared notes with on this strategy. In the final months of 2020, as we drew near to Election Day, and the incumbent's chance at an encore performance dwindled to almost none, I imagined how this madness would only intensify.

Can we remember a time when Donald J. Trump ever didn't make everything about himself? After playing down the virus for 9 months, who was the least bit surprised when Donald and Melania Trump finally succumbed to the Wuhan Flu? As it turns out, mask less bravado is not the best strategy for warding off infection, and on October 2, 2020, we learned Trump had had too much contact with all those "disgusting people," or maybe just with the Gold Star families he seemed intent on blaming for the illness. Anyway, this turn of events could have provided 45 with some much needed reflection about the indefensible way he had conducted himself throughout the pandemic. It could have coaxed an ounce of empathy for the plight of others from a man who had shown no empathy since early childhood. It could even have prompted him to plead with a jaded base of Deplorables to take this as the serious health crisis it was, and not an overwrought hissy fit by Democratic cucks with an evil agenda. We know from insiders who spoke off the record, his immediate response was to ask if he was going to die from this, demonstrating at least a modicum of normal humility. But within hours he was checked into Walter Reed Hospital where a dedicated staff of ten esteemed doctors provided a level of preventative immediate care and 24/7 attention that 7,237,043 Covid -19 patients before him never experienced as they lay gasping for their next breath and praying a single doctor managing an ICU full of other souls, who were already physically compromised, wouldn't let them die. Allegedly, he was administered an aggressive treatment plan that did not include hydroxychloroquine, or bleach, but did include remdesivir as well as an experimental anti body cocktail regeneron. The Deplorables still insisted hydroxychloroquine was the bomb and hoped they would have chance soon to unleash that whoop-ass kraken on the Wuhan Flu.

Trump recovered pretty quickly from symptoms of the virus and even before he was cleared by two days of consistent negative tests, he chose to preen for an adoring crowd of Deplorable well-wishers by taking a slow ride around the block in his presidential motorcade driven by his devoted secret service agents. Apparently this was a compromise, as Trump had originally demanded he be released from Walter Reed the moment the regeneron cocktail made him feel better than he had in 20 years. A couple of days later, he returned to the White House in a highly produced pomp filled spectacle to document his win over the Wuhan Flu. It was a stunning attempt to transform his medical ordeal into a show of superhuman strength, without so much as a nod to the millions who had shared an experience with Covid that bore no resemblance to his own nor an acknowledgment of 220,000 dead Americans. Within seconds of waving to those assembled below, he removed his mask and stepped inside the White House. We still don't know when exactly he contracted the virus.

But wait, there is more. After assuming his bout with the Covid virus provided him with life time immunity, Trump was quick to revert to his old tricks of downplaying the dangers of infection to adoring fans who would never receive the care or treatment he did, and in fact would stand a far greater chance of joining over 220,000 dead souls than he if infected. Instead of being chastened by his own experience and acknowledging his superior treatment, he inspired them to new heights of incoherent hero worship by telling them "don't be afraid of the virus." Don't be afraid of what, struggling for survival as your circulatory and cardiovascular systems shut down as you lay alone and terrified in your hospital bed, without the comfort of friends or family, and gasping for air? As it turns out, that lack of empathy paled by comparison with Trump's enthusiasm to rejoin the campaign trail by appearing at a dozen or more super spreader MAGA events buoyed by the confidence he couldn't become infected again but generally unconcerned for what could happen to thousands of souls who would rather scarf down a plate of dogshit than don a mask for the festivities.

There was no universe, either parallel or perpendicular to this one, in which it was true that 7 days from the 2020 election, we were "rounding the turn" or indeed, that Trump had "ended the pandemic. In fact, trend lines drawn in late October indicated we had achieved our highest ever spike of the 3 main spikes traced since the beginning of the pandemic. We knew, even if the Deplorables remained oblivious, that record numbers of infections would produce an accelerated death toll which was hardly the stuff of "rounding the turn" or "ending the pandemic." In fact, this was why we surpassed projections on end- of-year totals substantially while the Deplorables insisted it was time to stick a fork in it with or without inoculation. Talk about "herd mentality." For Trump and his legions of deplorable cultists, it was hoped the record numbers wouldn't stretch their lies so thin even they couldn't defend them. What would a self-serving malignant narcissist, fearing indictment and incarceration after the 2020 election, do about this? Lie even more, of course. So, with exactly no evidence to support it, Trump told his millions of emotionally dependent and intellectually inferior supporters that no one was really dying from Covid anymore. Problem solved, right?

At the very end of October 2020, mere days before the election, we learned of a study conducted by economic researchers at Stanford University that concluded 18 Trump campaign rallies in the summer had ultimately resulted in over 30,000 Covid -19 infections and 700 deaths. We can only imagine how a tsunami of final stretch MAGA celebrations may have doubled or tripled that body count. Most of us were aghast at this fact as we found it incomprehensible that the leader of the free world would be so indifferent to the toll this increasingly voracious pandemic was taking, especially as it begin to mingle with flu season to make detection and treatment even more complicated. We

212

found it morally indefensible that this was simply a turn out the vote gambit with exactly no empathy for the hundreds of thousands of useful idiots who may have been sacrificed at the altar of Trumpism down the stretch. Presumably, his victims remained ignorant of the consequences even as they drew their last ragged breaths in late November and early December. For them the pandemic was always premised on paranoid delusions about the Deep State and awkward examples of what "civil liberties" actually meant. But, Donald J. Trump was fully cognizant of the threat and apparently indifferent to the toll it might take on his supporters.

The Deplorables all believed that everything about the pandemic had been overblown by liberals whose only objective was to vanquish their hero and drag the country kicking and screaming toward socialism. For them, only a firsthand experience of the corona virus tearing a loved one down to his studs, registered any coherent impression at all. Until then, every scientific fact seemed as convoluted and jury rigged by liberal elites as anything else that simply would not coalesce around their limited imagination about right and wrong. They simply would not be the proverbial sheep led to slaughter. So, they stood vigil, in the final hours, against facts and common sense like millions of Bobble Head dolls insanely nodding approval to their Alpha hero. This is how Trump, as a televangelist grifter, spread the gospel as preached by tens of thousands of haters before him about the inevitability of a perfectly divided nation of winners and losers. But, till the bitter end, while he remained acutely aware of the risks of Covid, that his disciples were encouraged not to be. For all four years of his presidency President Trump had been obsessed with the size of crowds who would visit him wherever he spoke, even as these became super Covid spreader events. The crowds still remained overwhelming white

213

and overwhelmingly riddled with the kinds of grievances bigoted white people have always had.

On the last Friday before the election, Trump delighted his MAGA crowds in a few locations by baselessly accusing doctors of inflating Covid case counts and death tolls. To a crowd of thousands, as loud and as electrified as ever by the spectacle, Trump said, "Our doctors get more money if somebody dies from COVID....You know that, right? I mean, our doctors are very smart people. So what they do is, they say, 'I'm sorry, but everybody dies of COVID.'" No, Mr. President, not everyone dies of Covid, just 231,000 as of that date with no end in sight. Yes, Trump is the virus, Goo, Goo G'joob.

As I am putting the finishing touches on this book, in early February of 2021, the US stands at just shy of 27 million cases and over 460,000 deaths. We ended the previous year on a pace of adding roughly 3,000 deaths a day to this grim total. We have transitioned to a new administration that will make mitigation and vaccination on a national scale priority one with the objective of creating actual herd immunity by the end of this summer. The fumbled handoff between 45 and 46 put added pressure on the ambitious goals but most in the new administration seem confident we are finally on our way to ending this scourge. The backlash from the Deplorables was immediate and hardly diminished by the loss of their de facto leader. It would appear they remain undaunted in their plan to oppose the "Deep State." I suspect this may take the shape of all out resistance to vaccination to undermine our goal of achieving herd immunity. Surely the Deplorables would never allow President Biden to celebrate a victory that their hero deserved.

Chapter Twenty Five

Where is this all heading?

"It was dark now, and broodingly sluggish. Like something supine waiting to spring, with just the tip of its tail twitching. Leaves stood still on the trees. An evil green star glinted in the black sky like a hostile eye, like an evil spying eye.

Cornell Woolrich, Angels of Darkness

For the Deplorables, it is seductive to believe in tidy explanations for why life has become so challenging, or even unrecognizable in the early 21st century. Ironically, the fairytales they believe in are anything but tidy. They only ring true if the cat's in the cradle or the dish ran away with the spoon. But, rather than become skeptical over such flights of fancy, they roll them right into the mix, and then spend endless hours kneading them into perfect alignment with other bits of dumbfukery as they burble merrily along. Consider the ludicrous notion that there is any reason to still believe in Donald Trump as a hero figure. How exhausting would this be if the explanation must remain tethered to facts and reality? If only you reviewed and tallied up the receipts as they were created in real time, it would be impossible. If you spent even an hour replaying the actual history of the man's words and deeds for decades before his election, you could scarcely imagine such devotion. You would have to believe there was some kind of cloak of invisibility that worked only on Deplorables as you watched him coddle our enemies and emulate ruthless, fascist dictators in broad daylight. How broad would your definition of patriotism have to be for it to capture what you have witnessed over the last four years? Why have his adorning cultists always been willing to place Trump's dogged preoccupation with personal aggrandizement above the needs of a needy country unless they regarded this enterprise as merely another Trump vanity project? Even the folklore of his rags to riches rise to fortune crumbles under any applied scrutiny. Why are the Deplorables unwilling to spend a moment questioning the accounts of their hero's greatness? No, this man is not noble or righteous by any reasonable standard. But, if you believed this grifter was fashioned by God himself, as an imperfect but powerful talisman for healing what ailed the country, how much fervency might be welling within you at this consequential moment? Worse, what if you were certain the only force that might beat back the unholy perversions of a shadowy cabal of powerful elites, hell bent on lording over us all, and creating a one world alliance, was Donald J. Trump, what then? The augmented reality of this moment for believers is stunning.

Where most of us saw pure incompetence, dastardly deeds done wrong and total, almost catastrophic failure, it is crucial to remember the Deplorables saw stable genius, unquestionable patriotism and the ultimate plan to make America white again. Don't underestimate how fraught with peril these times have become, or you will never be prepared for what's about to happen. Don't confuse empathy with sympathy. You can remain opposed to everything the Deplorables stand for, but understanding how they think and why they do what they do has real survival value. Surely, it has become evident they are weighing the events of our times in vastly different ways than the Commendables are.

If you believe in omens, this moment in time is either a good or bad one. One fear is that, rather than accept what is manifest, rightwing conspiracy will drive the Deplorables to more and more fits of anti-social behavior, violence and even domestic terrorism. Certainly, as we looked at the facts on the ground, mere months from the coming election, we must have considered that the likelihood that the transition of power would be anything but peaceful or dignified. This was no longer about basic disagreement between sides. A new regime would be considered an existential threat, glowing with urgency, and requiring a desperate response. When the Donald was asked about our almost 250 year tradition, enshrined in the Constitution itself, about an orderly transition between outgoing and incoming presidential administrations, he said "We're gonna have to see what happens, We want to get rid of the ballots, and we'll have a very peaceful — there won't be a transfer, frankly. There'll be a continuation." Was that a prediction or threat? Is it in fact true that dead ending or suppressing millions of legitimately cast mail in ballots was the only way to appease this tyrant and his malcontented cultists? As those votes came predominantly from minority districts, the Deplorables would scarcely criticize efforts to hold back the "barbarians at the gate." Contending without evidence that even in person voting was subject to cheating, if voting machines could be jury rigged by powerful opponents, was premised on the idea that no fair election could possibly advantage Joe Biden over the Chosen One. Surely by now, you realize no tactic is ethically suspect if it advantages the losing Deplorable team. "Mr. President, will you only accept the results of the election as legitimate if you win?" Stating that of course he and his team will accept the results of a "free and fair" election, after so visibly describing what is not free or fair in their conception, is the kind of gaslighting that has sustained this counter decency movement for 4 years. If you are feeling déjà vu from 4 years earlier when Trump, chastened by awful polling several months before Election Day, spoke of a "rigged election" until our ears bled, it's not by accident. Could we afford to look at this as anything but the leader of the free world activating Deplorable terrorist sleeper cells?

When the hypothetical possibility of life without Trump became a certain destiny, would all of the pent up hostility spill over? After years of dehumanizing their opposition, would the Deplorables resist primal urges that conspiracy hawks had tweaked for a decade or more? False prophets like Alex Jones, had already foreshadowed how a violent response might be required to take back their country. Even from the halls of Congress, the message throughout Trump's presidency had been how the unhinged liberals cared only about destroying the duly elected 45th president. The 2nd amendment was now spoken of, not as a right but as a remedy. The occasional unhinged social media posts predicting the next civil war, became a constant drum beat, finally reaching maximum volume as people frustrated about the Deep State response to "violent rioting" in our streets inspired them to respond in kind. Black folks, mistreated by law enforcement since Jim Crow, were vilified in rightwing chatrooms, not as citizens demanding equal justice, but as murderous Marxist thugs. BLM protestors were always accused of choosing the wrong place and the wrong time to make their grievances known. But now, Deplorable attacks disingenuously focused more on violence and destruction that they claimed typified the

218

protests as sides clashed more frequently. They held their own anarchists harmless for agitating otherwise mostly peaceful events. The Deplorables, though always confused, were wide eyed when it came to whom they would blame for the chaos. Urban unrest is the fault of liberal leadership despite the GOP's flight from urban America fifty years ago. Who they wonder, is always trying to take away their guns and religion, but this liberal scourge?

Speaking of Alex Jones, we know his ratings depend entirely upon stirring up the crazy. We learned recently how he claimed to have received a highly secret report that "Maoists" were beginning to stockpile a vast arsenal of WMD, including McVeigh's weapon of choice, Ammonium Nitrate, and even chlorine gas agents, as preparation in our major cities for a war against patriots like the Deplorables. If that sounds like the kind of pulp fiction that has always agitated useful idiots, it is. In fact, when we imagine the story could have just as easily been plucked from the pages of the Turner Diaries, it's because it could have. In response to this purely made up plot, he exhorted his fans to immediately take action by saying "The best thing to do in a defensive way, is to kill as many of them as possible". Though we might prefer to assume that purely incendiary dumbfukery like this would fall on deaf ears, will it? No one begins life as an unhinged Monster, but as the unhealthy echoes of hate surround him throughout a difficult childhood, can we imagine a man becoming another Timothy McVeigh? I think we can, and must.like an inert gas, only requires a half turn for release, shouldn't we be prepared when the Deplorables among us are torqued like this to incite terrorist violence? When professional agitators paint the scene for a final showdown, we must pay attention, however revolting we find the tactic. Don't lull yourself into believing no one actually thinks like this. If we have learned nothing, we have learned that even unbelievable carnage can be made seductive when the malign makes bedfellows with the ignorant.

Speaking of the ignorant, it seems as if the Deplorables were blissfully unaware how the Republican Party had lost its conservative groove in the age of Trump to become little more than the party of white grievance. After the first year of Trumpism many Conservatives couldn't find a principle other than hero worship their party still stood for and yet we heard the insistence the party of Trump was about fiscal responsibility and limited government. Imagine how envious and enraged they must have been for the overwhelming outpouring of love and admiration most in the country expressed upon the passing of several monumental liberal figures over the last couple of years. Their antipathy for the legacies of civil rights giants like Elijah Cummings and John Lewis was revealed vicariously by a president too small to even pay respects to either gentleman as they lay in State. The distinction may have seemed subtle, but I wondered if Trump really had any choice in the matter. The commendable causes each of these men devoted their lives to was like pure kryptonite to the Deplorables. Even tacitly acknowledging their powerful role in creating a more racially hospitable America would seem like a gut punch for Deplorable people diametrically opposed to equality for all. Clearly a president entirely reliant on his base for reelection, as these hopes continued to flicker, could not chance alienating people for whom Cummings and Lewis represented insurmountable road blocks to white supremacy.

Chapter Twenty Six

Adrenachrome, Frazzledrip and Wayfair, oh my!

"There's only one source for this stuff... the adrenaline glands from a living human body"

Hunter S. Thompson

The Deplorables are outrage savants. They have a genius for the sordid and vulgar possibilities in all things. It's a dodgy gift, which allows them to see the worst things they project on others as if the wretched thoughts hadn't been stewing in their own juicy imaginations for years. Where most see puppies and hopscotch, the Deplorables find cannibals and pedophiles. Where Commendables pray for world peace, Deplorables imagine anti-American globalist plots and the next Civil War. Commendables wonder what hope there is for consonance between us and them when truly outlandish conspiracy theories are more comforting for Deplorables than pedestrian explanations based on facts. Why do some insist on decoupling from Occam's advice to seek the simplest most linear explanation, instead of always building fanciful Rube Goldberg contraptions? Why is there so much discomfort with the way truth is normally construed? Yes, of course, it is from the pain of cognitive dissonance, but why do they exempt themselves from even the pretense of critical thinking? Simply put, it's because critical thought doesn't get the cake baked anymore. Only unhinged pablum is sticky enough to hold these fairytales together now. The big lie is a cheat code for true believers that helps them leapfrog over all non-conforming details. Even if few outside the outrage bubble believe all the gauzy new confections, at least these lies may "trigger" the libtards. As long as these "alternative facts" remained elastic and serpentine enough, who on the team would discount them?

The Clinton/Trump presidential contest in 2016 was vicious. One thing that addled the usual campaign dynamic between the rivals was a raft of disinformation from both foreign and domestic miscreants that managed to scrape at old wounds and create many new ones. General distrust of the Clintons, as reliable Republican foils, has always made it easy for many to imagine the worst of them. "Is there anyone Bill hasn't raped?" "Didn't Hillary disembowel a former body guard in front of his wife?" So, when the Deplorables learned of Hillary Clinton using a private server as Secretary of State under Obama, they became predictably unglued over it. But it wasn't until Russian Intelligence used Wiki-leaks as a cutout, to disseminate thousands of hacked DNC emails that a metaphorical cattle prod zapped their amygdalas. "Now we've got that bitch right where we want her, let's "LOCK HER UP, LOCK HER UP."

Buried within the trove of Clinton dirt, was a few back and forth emails between Clinton's campaign manager John Podesta and the owner of a local DC pizzeria, seemingly about organizing a pizza party for staff members. With help from intrepid Q Anon fanatics, this email exchange became an active crime scene as they felt they were witnessing obvious signs of two men trading in the language of pedophilia and child

222

sex trafficking. What else could he possibly have meant when he inquired about "cheese pizza"? And when talk turned to hotdogs for the kids, surely Podesta meant hotdogs were the kids.

Complicating matters were additional emails between Podesta and Marina Abramović, a performance artist and Podesta friend who was inviting Podesta to a *spirit cooking* dinner. Apparently for the outrage savants, spirit cooking is more like a satanic blood ritual and less like a casual dinner party for the woke. With this, a new rabbit hole tempted tens of thousands to embark on a mission to #savethechildren from the horrific fetishes of a shadowy cabal that reached all the way to the House of Windsor and beyond. This had been fertile ground for the Christian Right and Republican Party for decades; it just needed a new shot in the arm. No doubt, they felt, that filthy Jew pedophile Jeff Epstein was the social lubricant that kept these wheels turning. Beneath their phony piety about Israel, the Deplorables have always imagined the Jews were at the root of all cultural evil. Epstein's longtime friendship with Donald Trump was a detail that committed cultists would muddy up as necessary.

This bizarre new conspiracy theory relentlessly circulated to the fringiest of rightwing freak out sites until it was also picked up by the anarchist journalists in more mainstream places to serve up new hate and outrage porn. Several unnamed sources were mentioned, including allegedly highly placed members of the NYPD, claiming the emails clearly pointed to a sex trafficking operation and "people are going to jail for this." One young North Carolina man, 28 year old Edgar Welch, consumed by outrage over this evil, made his way to Comet Ping Pong to end the madness. After terrifying the patrons by brandishing his AR-15 and firing a single round into a closet door,

223

believing it was an entrance to a basement below where children were surely secreted for satanic cruelty, Mr. Welch surrendered peacefully to DC police.

While Commendables were relieved that the overwrought imagination of the gunman didn't result in death and destruction, surely we were unnerved by what could have been. This man had predicted the confrontation between good and evil would be very violent. As such, he had tried to recruit accomplices and told them the mission would require "sacrificing the lives of a few for the lives of many," according to court documents. He received a four year prison sentence for his misguided rage against a threat that did not exist.

Alex Jones, notorious Infowars conspiracy psycho babbler, whose mission is "seeking the truth and exposing the scientifically engineered lies of the globalists and their ultimate goal of enslaving humanity" was forced to issue an apology after promoting Pizzagate for weeks. He had said on his show many times "you have to investigate it for yourselves."

Ah, but there is more. Once the Deplorables get their snaggle teeth on a bone, no one is going to pry it loose with truth alone. For months after Pizzagate, progressively more unhinged Q drops led millions of amateur sleuths to take a deeper dive, as the matter so many found so fathomable about Hillary Clinton must certainly still be true. If she could kill dozens of former aides, surely she is capable of making preadolescent fricassee of our babies. The stickiest conspiracy theories are ones that validate a group's collective anxiety. What could make them more anxious than the Clintons, who are well connected with so many the Deplorables find reprehensible? Hillary is, after all, little more than the subterranean demon child of Illuminati luminaries. Duh!

At the tail end of the 2016 campaign, we may recall how FBI Director James Comey mysteriously announced he would reopen his investigation of the Clinton Servergate "scandal." Apparently a number of emails between her and her longtime aide Huma Abedin were discovered on Abedin's husband Anthony Weiner's computer. Weiner had been convicted 5 years earlier for sending sexually suggestive material to a minor, so it didn't take much to tweak the hyperactive imaginations of the Deplorables yet again. As it turns out, this material was no more incriminating than the original stuff, and the story mostly petered out on its own. That is until a purely fabricated allegation that a disturbing video was found on Weiner's laptop in a file titled "insurance" surfaced in 2018. What particular fiction could be so monstrous to salt the raw nerves of people already dedicated to hating Hillary Rodham Clinton? Welcome to Frazzledrip.

The "snuff film" video, allegedly still circulating on the dark web, was conveniently far too grainy to make out faces or even to clearly see what was transpiring, but allegedly featured Clinton and Abedin drinking the blood of a child as they wore masks made from the skin of her surgically detached face. Or maybe it was a tea party for Clinton's own grand baby with party masks and Kool-Aid for all. As I said, the lighting was bad. Supposedly reliable sources, including a NYPD investigator, who viewed the film, called the content "worse than any nightmare." Anyway, in a side by side comparison, it appears the grainy screen capture of Huma Abedin wearing the girl's face, may have been the image a popular supper club used to promote their restaurant. Who's to say? Both were creepy as hell and maybe the supper club is in on the crime anyway. Surely some Democrats somewhere are disfiguring and torturing children before drinking their blood at this very moment. Even more inconveniently, authorities never arrested either

225

Clinton or Abedin for this horrific crime that was gift wrapped on video. No word was made of any parents connected to the young girl who may or may not have recognized their child's face on the body of a 70 year old former presidential candidate. What self-respecting Deplorable could possibly question the veracity of this story?

The Deplorables believed a great reckoning would come swiftly in the age of Trump. All of the God awful progressivism of the last 60 years could be dumbed down to a simplistic theory, viciously at odds with reality, but scary enough to mobilize millions of social underachievers. This would hinge not on any lucid analysis of facts, but on piqued anxieties in an age of diminishing returns for the Deplorables. No pulp fiction could be too lurid, no illusion too macabre, to energize their retrograde movement. Finally, they could tear the whole of liberal democracy down with ruthless abandon. With the aid and comfort of their perversely acidic leader, they would triumph over the evil of progressive liberalism. For the Deplorables, it's always the same song and dance. They must overcome the despair and angst that comes from opposing human progress, and this always is made possible by a willful distortion of reality.

Speaking of pulp fiction, what could be more fulfilling for the maladapted than glomming onto the kind of "Gonzo Journalism" the late great Hunter S. Thompson popularized in the 70s? Surely, narratives driven by sensationalism over objectivity could rub raw personal emotions when bland truth might deaden the receptors instead. This response, of course, depends upon how amplified the counter narrative can become. The Deplorables' Movement has more than enough foot soldiers to amplify outrage.

In Fear and Loathing in Las Vegas, Thomson riffed off of the science behind a neuro-chemical compound called adrenochrome, which is essentially epinephrine, an oxidized form of adrenaline, to create a plot twist for his protagonist Raoul Duke. For Duke, adrenochrome represents the promise of the greatest high imaginable if he dare to cross the Rubicon of inhuman depravity. In Duke's estimation, imbibing adrenochrome would require violently extracting the substance from the adrenal glands of a living human, preferably a young one. The Deplorables knew what Thomson did. Nothing is a more powerful hate lubricant than imagining what truly awful things "others", as in other races, other religions, other parties, are capable of doing.

For Deplorables this was a perfect metaphor for the moral degradation of today's liberal America. So, Q Anon appropriated this fictional account of satanic decadence and amplified it at a frequency only the unhinged Deplorables could hear.

The Deplorables have always had a preternatural concern about the harm liberals intended for children and families. Any dislocation from the original idea of a nuclear family was a liberal plot to undermine the fabric of society. Women working in the workplace indicated deeply decaying traditional gender and family values. Education had long since become indoctrination against family and American values. A woman's right to choose a moral abomination. The blurring of traditional gender identity, exposing our children to the prurient whims of immoral pedophiles, or at least, oversexualizing the innocent. Within this context, it is easy to imagine how overwrought they became as unifying theories for liberal depravity surfaced. It can be quite seductive to imagine what moral perversions the opposition is capable of when casting aspersions, and how hyperventilated this reckoning can become under duress. As war time combatants have always known, it is only through dehumanizing the enemy that the complete annihilation of other humans can seem palatable.

So, after the Pizzagate debacle, Q Anon managed to tweak the basic premise of an opposing campaign's moral degradation into something more all-encompassing. Q found the incoherent fears and plumbed these pressure points for political capital. It wasn't just Hillary Rodham Clinton and her degenerate coterie of cannibals; it was a shadowy cabal of all the liberal Elite power brokers across the entire globe who were feasting upon the blood of our children for evil immortality and immoral world domination. Besides the usual Jewish suspects, the Rothschilds and George Soros, highly visible members of academia and Hollywood, as well as the mainstream media, were all identified as active co-conspirators. Adrenochrome, harvested from the living bodies of pedophilia victims, before they were cannibalized, was the keystone that bound all of the liberal heretics together. Clearly, the Anons insisted, these monsters must be eliminated with extreme prejudice as expeditiously as possible before they become omnipotent. It was just a matter of time before Donald Trump would fill Guantanamo Bay with this inhuman filth. Accept the flight of fancy, support the mission, and after the calm, soon will come the "Storm." The only hope for white power will come from eliminating the opposition to reclaim a "moral majority." WWG1WGA.

Convincing adherents that the political ruling class was a swamp badly in need of draining was step one. Expanding upon the idea of a liberal curse that encompassed all of the trappings of a decadent society was the next priority. This is a vast leftwing conspiracy after all. And, of course, the final piece of the puzzle was to rally around Donald Trump as the unlikely savior figure.

So, what did the intersection between the Deplorables' skepticism over the Covid-19 pandemic, and adrenochrome abuse look like? It was an article of faith among the Deplorables that Covid-19 was a liberal hoax and that it was leveraged for control over the world's population to create a New World Order and a villain for their hero figure to vanquish. The Q Anon faithful imagined adrenochrome was the drug of choice among the Hollywood liberal Elite. Deplorables were asked to imagine Hillary Clinton toiling and troubling over a steamy cauldron of human brain stems to harvest hormones from human adrenaline. Now it must be accepted that Hollywood treasures like Tom Hanks were also addicted to the stuff. Remember, all of liberal society is in this together. Apparently, Hanks caught Covid-19 from a tainted batch of adrenochrome. In fact, the reason why so many in Hollywood look haggard these days is not because they skipped hair and makeup, but because there is a worldwide shortage of adrenochrome. Rumor had it Hanks was on the lamb and hiding in Australia until accounts of his return to the States surfaced. Then it was alleged the plane's captain was undercover FBI who had apprehended the actor. No explanation was forthcoming to why an organization that had become so vilified by the breadcrumbers since Trump's election, was to be trusted on this particular leap of faith, but on no others. Maybe soon we will be treated to an explanation for why Hanks and his lovely wife, Rita Wilson, have surfaced many times since on TV from their home in Los Angeles. If that detail cannot be solved for, I suppose the Deplorables will turn their sights on Oprah, Ellen DeGeneres and Celine Dion who they believe are equally gripped by adrenochrome

229

dependence. Shhh, be very quiet as they continue hunting those wascally wibtard wabbits.

As we have seen, the panic over sex trafficking and pedophilia by the super-rich and politically powerful is a bug at the core of the Deplorables' Movement. It has become the cornerstone of the unified Q Anon conspiracy theory and as such, has spread with evil abandon across the whole rightwing Freakosphere. Nothing has vilified all of Liberal America as much as the emphatic accusation that they are evil incarnate. And nothing has fed the appetite of the Deplorables for a final confrontation with their tormentors quite like this unhinged fantasy. The collective effort to engage in this malign enterprise is nothing new, and is almost expected, when it comes to bare knuckled politics obsessed with "winning" at all costs. But, what should we think when the tactic strays from the political arena to popular culture? Why is there such an obsession among Deplorables with the financial and legal ruination of entertainers when simply tuning them out and not buying their product seems so much more logical. Cancel culture is one thing, but willfully seeking to destroy people with whom you disagree seems sadistic for all but genuine sociopaths. And yet this is becoming a more go to reaction; The Deplorables aren't content with simply boycotting the NFL, the NBA, the NHL and even NASCAR; now they want to burn these institutions to the ground for daring to support inclusiveness and racial tolerance. Soon enough, their idea of culture will be watching owls fuck from the safety of their porch swings.

A bizarre spectacle is wading into corporate America. It's perfectly reasonable to withhold purchases or patronage of companies for which you have no allegiance or even those with whom you have political differences. But, when pure fantasies are concocted to tar a

230

particular company with baseless accusations of heinous criminality for no particular reason, this is another alarming sign of hate and fear run amok. In 2018 another unhinged Q inspired conspiracy debuted on Twitter before spreading rapidly to most corners of the social media universe regarding the online furniture and homewares company WayFair. An alert Twitter poster observed that certain high priced items, mostly cabinets and dressers, were promoted with names that purportedly matched reports of missing children all over the country. The theory was that WayFair was actively selling and transporting abducted children to pedophiles who presumably were in on the scheme. It was also suggested that the SKUs for these items linked to images of children on a Russian search engine called Yandex, and served as a visual product description for buyers. "Anons may have busted a human trafficking ring from a seller on WayFair. Selling $10K cabinets that are worth $200 with names of missing children," wrote a Q Anon adherent on Facebook. Begging the question of "Why would they" that would occur to virtually anyone not addicted to this gunk, an Instagram poster asked "When will the mainstream media talk about WayFair trafficking?"

As I am sure you already predicted, nothing ever came from these heinous allegations as only one of the missing children, for whom the merchandise was allegedly named, remains missing. When an independent investigator searched on Yandex, no images of children could be found. I know, who in America uses a Russian search engine? And, of course, are there really hundreds of thousands of people for whom this dreck resonates as the number of posts, shares and likes suggests?

So again, I'd ask you to imagine what kind of persons would traffic in this lurid filth, but ones secretly battling with their own obsessions and perversions, and thrilled to project this pathology on their perceived enemies. I am sure much of their cognitive dissonance comes from this kind of internal struggle with their own prurient fixations. And when you learn that these kinds of people are 100% committed to ridding the world of their polar opposites, would that get your attention?

Chapter Twenty Seven

It's all about cruelty

"Dragon kind was no less cruel than mankind. The Dragon, at least, acted from bestial need rather than bestial greed."

Anne McCaffrey, Dragonflight

What happens when the Deplorables become jaded by the usual bukkake? They just find new heinous ejaculates to douse each other with. Vicious fictions, under intense public scrutiny, tend to split off into even more grotesque lies, each more overwrought than the last. The sketchiest rabbits among us are sent scrabbling down even sketchier rabbit holes in search of a less temperate reality within which social anarchy seems increasingly less extreme. Clueless Deplorables, racked by immeasurable rage, lash out against civil normality. The Deplorables try on and invent more tortured metaphors every day to coax a reluctant reality into alignment with their parallel Machiavellian universe. In an age of fading religious fundamentalism, the Deplorables need a new myth that makes them the good guys, the defenders of morality. As the usual social opiates, well past their use by date, are in rapid decay, more potent hallucinogens become necessary. New fixes require progressively higher octane. The centripetal force from opposition to their maladaptive folklore, closes in upon them. The fear and loathing they have becomes frothier. The tribe is restless in search of a new mythology that feeds their delusions of moral grandeur. The myth of a great crusade against child sex abuse by liberals gathers up decades of self-righteous revolt into a single destructive touchstone. Liberals aren't just wild eyed and unrealistic; they are messengers from hell, led by satanic elitists, who will eat your baby alive or drink her blood if something isn't done about it soon. They will take your first born and drain him of adrenachrome to achieve evil immortality. Taming the Deplorable beast is like playing whack-a-mole with flaming bags full of dog shit. When you think things can't get messier, just wait. Their sadism is not easily quenched by small social and political victories; they are aiming for a major liberal blood bath. Are the Deplorables being literal when they say so, as they are swaddled in the warm embrace of Parlor and Gab? I assume we will understand more clearly once violence runs rampantly through our streets.

This is all about the capacity for cruelty the Deplorables have toward those they have no empathy for. As they remain apathetic to any real principles, it is opposition itself, obnoxious and raw, which girds their loins. Now is the time to cauterize this wound and protect the rest of us from infection.

So far, we have spoken only of Deplorables and Commendables as if these two labels captured all of humanity. That dichotomy was used strictly for dramatic effect to make this an easily digestible story of good versus evil. The largest share of our people are neither of these; they are what I will call the Redeemables. The Redeemables are society's lymph nodes from which disease is either contained or spread by people who are neither entirely commendable

234

nor entirely deplorable. They are the Everyman, conservative in some ways, liberal in others. A little bit country, a little bit rock and roll. They are those for whom the wavy line of the past can be straightened as they react to the pull of a righteous future. They are where the action is, and are in fact, the real "silent majority" in our country. They define the margins of a governable union. As this country demands enlightened change to regain our righteous footing it is only from the ranks of Commendables and Redeemables, that this is possible. It will be from an active partnership between those already committed to the principles that make this an exceptional country, and those struggling to do so, however much they may have strayed in the past, that we will defeat the Deplorables for good. This idea has only become strange in recent years as we have allowed others to insist that we pick and defend a partisan side.

Chapter Twenty Eight

The test

It turns out, verbal fluency is a good predictor of IQ and effective cognition. As such, various measures of it make it into neuropsychological assessments of the premorbid (before cray cray). We generally expect adults to create coherent sentences with a little more than 30,000 words to choose from. People who stand in line for hours to jerk their pickles at super spreader MAGA events may have fewer words at their disposal but allowances are made for "the best words" repeated often. A distinction is made between active and passive vocabulary, because no one is big enough to get away with saying words like Churlish or factotum without getting stuffed into a broom closet. Anyway, when the Deplorables are encountered in their natural habitat, they are remarkably unable to correctly use homophones – words which sound alike but are spelled differently. Nothing says "huh?" like the pure crap shoot of word selection when alternatives are available that sound alike. Some people are said to be verbal and some visual thinkers and some presumably are neither of the above. If you fear Deplorable creep and want better for you and your family, may I recommend taking the homophone aptitude test here? Just like the cognitive function test Trump took, the entries get progressively harder on a scale from simple minded to almost like thinking out loud. The last few even feature sentences with more than one choice between homophones to control against excessive cheating.

I will _____ (sea/see) you at the MAGA rally next week.

Truth _____ (hurts/hertz) doesn't it Libtard?

Did he say Covfefe _____ (allowed/aloud), or was it in a Tweet?

Biden is for free stuff and open _____ (boarders/borders).

Surely you don't _____ (bye/by/buy) what the fake news is selling, do you?

No challenge is _____ (to/too/two/2) great for our stable genius president.

We _____ (one/won) the popular vote by whatever number of Illegals cast votes + 1.

Who will ____ (lose/loose) the election, Trump or sleepy Joe?

____ (are/our) ____ (vice/vise) president is a servant of Jesus Christ.

_____ (ate/eight) years of Obama was more than I could ____ (bare/bear).

My heart skipped a _____ (beet/beat) when Trump's _____ (plane/plain) _____ (flu/flew/flue) into JFK International.

When Mexico sends _____ (there/they're/their) people, _____ (their/there/they're) not sending _____ (their/they're/there) best.

Realistically if you got fewer than 10 right, I'd skip Mensa orientation week.

Chapter Twenty Nine

Stand Back and Stand by

After so much breathless anticipation, we finally got to watch the Donald and Sleepy Joe square off in the first of three presidential debates on September 29, 2020. This was a TV spectacle, reaching tens of millions, which made the Apprentice instantly seem less ridiculous. Deplorables from every nook and cranny of Red State America could finally watch their hero eviscerate an overmatched dementia sufferer in front of 80 million Americans. You see, approximately 20% of the American public was simply "heart sick" over how the DNC, and an opportunistic Jill Biden herself, foisted the mentally diminished former VP on an unsuspecting public as a pure Deep State ploy. This act of cruelty was emblematic of the immoral Democrats. The Deplorables literally pleaded with Biden's "handlers" to show a modicum of human decency, as their side would, if only Trump were a blithering idiot and petulant man baby incapable of running the country himself. However, within seconds of the opening bell, Trump become a babbling brook of incoherent gibberish as he prattled on whenever it was Biden's turn to speak over the objections of his opponent and the moderator. Clearly, the leader of the free world came with a loaded diaper and plenty of colic to prosecute his case against himself, and did a pretty fair job of shitting the bed publically.

Many of the former president's handlers admitted that this was a Trumpian tactic to confuse and overwhelm his opponent. What they didn't anticipate was the mess a man untethered from truth or sanity could make of a conversation he dominated. After watching a sitting president fling his own feces around the stage for an hour and a half, the Deplorables were convinced this was the kind of powerful leadership that Made America Great Again, and chalked it up as another win for a leader who never tired of winning so much.

At some early point in the race, a really misshapen turd was dropped into the Deplorables' feedbag, and they were delighted to gobble it up. The theory was that Biden's candidacy was a thinly veiled ruse. Even if, by some remote chance he won the contest, it would not be he who took the reins, but his running mate, or even Fancy Nancy. Leave it to the dastardly Dems to bait and switch that way. Clearly Biden, who lacked both the stamina and mental acuity to be President was a cutout for AOC or Bernie to swoop in, accept the nomination, and begin to make this the kind of Socialist Republic only pedophiles, people of color, and Jews would embrace. I think the President himself may have seconded and thirded this point during his debate rant when asked about something completely unrelated.

As it became more and more apparent, to Trump at least, he would sooner win a Big Mac Eating Contest than reelection, the former Grifter in Chief began roasting the truth, like so many weenies and marshmallows, over an open dumpster fire. This made his little Deplorable campers positively giddy. But, generally speaking, candidates who expect to win reelection, don't begin inoculating supporters against defeat months before Election Day by insisting the results will be rigged against him. In fact, if you feel you are hearing a faint echo from 2016, when an equally chastened Donald J. trump was convinced Crooked Hillary would win, you are. The dulcet tones of that dodge was like Don Ho singing *Tiny Bubbles*. Mary Trump would be the first to explain how her uncle had no choice. Admitting he lost to a superior opponent would be like having his hemorrhoids lanced by a machete. Miraculously, a second after that contest concluded, the notion the 2016 election was a sham was replaced with the insistence that Trump's win was not only never in doubt but was the most bigly in history!

In 2020, Trump was even surer he would lose in November. There are only so many poorly educated white male sociopaths to absorb defections among every other constituency on the Trump Train. Apparently it also had occurred to Trump that far more Democrats would vote by mail during a murderous pandemic than Republicans. This is mostly because, in the age of Trump, Republican voters placed white angst above actual thinking. This gave the 45th president two excuses for how he could lose to Sleepy Joe but insist he was not a complete putz. Everyone, other than the election officials in every state in the country, knew for a stone cold fact that voting by mail is always rife with massive cheating. No less than zero Republican investigations conducted over a decade or more had established that fact. If election fraud was rampant among "illegals" and dead people for in-person voting, it must be twice as bad when offenders don't even need to show up. If Trump could cobble this together with the random notion that voting machines themselves would be hacked by China or Venezuela, he would have the Deplorables at "Stop The Steal." Hell, they might even be more surprised if Biden lost.

Whatever else was true, it should be noted, that Trump was perfectly willing to accept the results of the 2020 election the very second it was called in his favor but not a second sooner. In a real sense, he was not running against Biden at all, but elections in general, for their nasty habit of crowning superior combatants. Suggesting how the "Corona hoax" led to massive mail in voting was the perfect foil as both tickled the Deplorables in ways they dared not admit to being tickled.

So, after hobbling an already beleaguered US Postal Service to compromise a timely and complete counting of the vote, Trump also asked his Deplorables to descend upon polling places and watch the other side try to cheat. Team Trump called them an army and encouraged an overly aggressive, camo clad, locked and loaded presence to discourage cheating only among those who would vote against him. To make the point exceedingly clear, open carry where permissible in swing states was encouraged. Earlier, he had recommended his supporters should cast their votes twice, by mail and in person, to "test" for cheating. That apparently was a tactic the Attorney General at that time, William Barr, was not convinced was illegal. Wait, what?

Back to the debate. After mostly jousting with himself for an hour to insure that suburban women, of all creeds and colors, would vote for Murder Hornets before him, Trump was presented with a golden opportunity not to look like the anti-Christ. The moment was focused on all of the racial upheaval in the age of Trump. The moderator Chris Wallace joined Biden in goading the president into actually denouncing the white supremacists; specifically, in this case, the Proud Boys, a violent neo-fascist racial terrorist group mostly committed to co-opting peaceful protests and turning them into riots. "Will you ask them to stand down?" both Wallace and Biden asked? After several dodgy seconds, contemplating how his base of white supremacists might react, Trump rose to the occasion and firmly stated "Stand back and stand by." I am not a cunning linguist, but even I could detect the difference between asking bad guys to stand down with asking them to stand back, whatever that means, and to stand by. According to the Meriam Webster dictionary, when Trump suggested violent anarchists "stand by" he meant, *be ready or available for immediate action or use.* Then he chased this with a shot of "whataboutism" by insisting most of the violent agitation in Trump's America came from Antifa and BLM. When Biden explained how Trump's own FBI considered Antifa more of an idea than an actual organization, the Divider in Chief went tangerine ape shit and denounced his own premier law enforcement organization over the kinds of groups the FBI has identified as our greatest domestic terrorist threats. "This is not a Rightwing problem, this is a Leftwing problem," he insisted as millions used their Google machines in real time to see if a single murder was ever pinned on either Antifa or BLM. Within an hour, Proud Boys leader Henry "Enrique" Tarrio dropped this on Parler "Standing by sir," proving the president's veiled message was more transparent than millions of Deplorables would admit the next day. Even giddier was Joe Biggs, another well-known Proud Boys leader, who took Trump's comments as a call to action. "Trump basically said to go fuck them up!" he wrote on his Telegram channel. "This makes me so happy." Anyway, what could possibly have GONE wrong when the Leader of the Free World activated terrorist cells all over the country to help him restore order and bring home a victory in November? Buckle up, Snowflakes. Despite protestations to the

242

contrary, the relationship between Donald Trump and white Supremacists, Militia groups and multiple white nationalist groups was not strictly a one sided affair. While Trump may not have openly coddled them, he clearly found utility in their allegiance to him.

Speaking of fringy Rightwing terrorist groups, and their extra judicial and counter decency tendencies, we learned, about a week after the first debate, of a failed plot to put a bright red exclamation point on Deplorable-styled depravity. On October 8, 2020, the FBI announced the arrests of 13 suspects accused of plotting to kidnap Gretchen Whitmer, Governor of Michigan, and otherwise violently overthrow the state government. Incensed over Ms. Whitmer's aggressive measures to stem the rising tide of Covid infections in her state, these champions of civil liberty picked up where they had left off months earlier. These gentlemen were among a larger group of angry Trump-loving "patriots" who stormed the State Capitol back in April of 2020 so they could brandish their loaded long guns and hurl menacing threats toward Whitmer and her staff. They were trying to impress upon Madame Governor that they would not stand for the kind of liberal fascism that would place public health above their right to live like mindless Neanderthals or MAGATs generally. The October surprise was allegedly to snatch up the governor at gunpoint from her vacation home in Northern Michigan, bring her to a remote location, try her for treason, and, pending the result of that "trial," execute her for her crimes against the will of President Trump. You see, it had been made abundantly clear for months how Blue State leaders were using the Covid hoax to control and otherwise make constituents dependent upon liberal government. When their hero in the Whitehouse said explicitly they should "take back their state," who were these humble servants of American freedom and justice to argue? The stable geniuses who masterminded the plot were the two founders and leaders of the Wolverine Watchmen, another paramilitary militia group promoting rightwing political violence. Pete Musico, the de facto leader bannered his Twitter account with the same "Don't tread on me" image that has been used to accentuate antiestablishment anarchy for decades and was allegedly 100% in favor of locking Hillary Clinton up, as endorsed by our Conspiracist in Chief during all 4 years of his presidency. On YouTube, Musico regularly ranted about the "deep State." On Gab, the social media platform of choice for virulently subversive racists and xenophobes, Musico allegedly ranted about how "they were killing white people in South Africa."

Another member of the Wolverine Watchmen, scooped up by the FBI in connection with the plot, was Eric Molitor. Molitor heaped gobs of praise on another kindred spirit in the war against equality for all, Kyle Rittenhouse. Remember Kyle? He was among a number of vigilantes obsessed with protecting America against the notion that black lives matter. On August 27th 2020, the 17 year old Illinois man, illegally toting an AR-15, was patrolling a BLM protest in Kenosha, Wisconsin when he shot two unarmed protestors dead and grievously wounded another. The Donald remembered Rittenhouse, too. To illustrate how it was Antifa and BLM that stoked endless racial violence, and not any number of white power groups he claimed to know nothing about, Trump admonished anyone who might view Rittenhouse as anything but a victim of the liberal mayhem gripping the country on his watch. Trump twisted every ounce of evidence to erroneously conclude that this juvenile American "patriot" acted purely in self-defense when he killed the two protestors.

If you are sensing an interwoven pattern here between White Supremacy, domestic terrorism, Q Anon fanaticism, men obsessed with inciting a racial civil war, and the rabid approval of our 45th president, you are very observant. This is all part of a movement, growing ever larger and more ominous, that has been torqued to a catastrophic breaking point by political leaders more obsessed with coddling the most subversive elements among us for electoral capital, than any commitment to American idealism.

Speaking of the Proud Boys and election meddling, on October 20th, 2020, we learned of highly threatening emails sent to Florida Democrats allegedly from the Proud Boys info@officialproudboys.com address advising them to vote Republican, presumably to influence the election in Trump's favor. Less than 2 days later, a hastily arranged and unprecedented news conference was delivered by the Director of National Intelligence, John Ratcliffe, to warn the public about the plot. Ratcliffe was joined on the podium by FBI Director Chris Wray, though Wray remained silent throughout the barely coherent statement. Ratcliffe spoke of a highly concerning plot by Iran to interfere in our election by linking the rightwing anarchists, the Proud Boys, to efforts to undermine confidence in election security and hurt Trump's reelection. Wait, what? Yes, this Donald Trump loyalist, appointed to the top intelligence post in the Spring of 2020, alleged that when emails reached the inbox of thousands of Democratic voters advising *" You are currently registered as a Democrat and we know this because we have gained access into the entire voting infrastructure. You will vote for Trump on Election Day or we will come after you. Change your party affiliation to Republican to let us know you received our message and will comply. We will know which candidate you voted for. I would take this seriously if I were you,"* it was meant to hurt Trump's chances in the election. Ratcliffe also seemed obsessively concerned that this ruse be attributed more to Iran than Russia, the country we usually associate with Trump promotion in our elections. Was it really Iran, or was it Russia using their ally Iran as a proxy, or was it a 400lb guy in his bed that wanted to coax a few thousand more Trump votes out of Democrats in a Swing State to help Biden? Whichever is true, it seemed very odd that the DNI director addressed this at all, considering how there had been oodles of other manifest signs of foreign interference leading up to Election Day that he never informed anyone of. Why the excessive desire to get out right behind this, like an elephant poop scooper at the circus, just a couple weeks before an election that seemed hopelessly tipped in the Democrat's favor? A casual stroll through TrumpLandia on social media after the announcement made it clear. With all the baseless rightwing attacks on Joe Biden landing with a thud, Team Trump was sure as hell not going to let something two thirds of our people would find credible about the Proud Boys become linked to their man. There was no conceivable way the Deplorables would ever imagine foreign interference could very well be the sliver of a diminishing chance to MAGA more, so this revelation must join all others as a plot to help Trump's opponent instead. Ratcliffe simply obliged an adoring public of American truth deniers.

In the aftermath of the foiled terrorism and murder plot of Governor Whitmer, the Commendables might have expected their president to unreservedly condemn those who would undermine American righteousness in the name of hate. Instead, at multiple MAGA rallies, Donald J. Trump egged on his venomous supporters when they chanted "lock her up" about Michigan Governor Gretchen Whitmer.

If you ever wondered what WOULDN'T Trump and his merry band of Deplorables do to win an election, the answer is, basically nothing. While we the people would rather drag our pupils over broken glass than cast a MAGA vote to aid and abet the candidacy of the Grifter in Chief, the Deplorables would donate both kidneys to the cause. Rudy Giuliani, who had become unrecognizable to many who worked for him in 2001, became another foot soldier in turning out Deplorable enthusiasm and votes. Giuliani, it turned out was a massive proponent of the "rubber and glue" defense that is used whenever one is credibly accused of wrong doing, and must be exonerated, simply by saying "I'm rubber you're glue, whatever you say bounces off of me and sticks to you." When Trump was caught with his hand deep within the cookie jar extorting Ukraine for dirt on his rival, Rudy G masterminded something so simplistically sticky, The Deplorables are still posting it online. Apparently, Biden himself was the one actually corrupt, and wasn't it he, too, who extorted our Eastern European ally years before? Biden was also corrupt because his son Hunter served on the board of a Ukrainian gas concern that was, at one time, long ago, investigated for corruption. Sticky indeed. Once they had this bone to gnaw on, the Deplorables would never release it over mere facts alone. When it was reported that Biden was instrumental in withholding a loan guarantee to Ukraine in accordance with the wish of many in Ukraine, all of our European allies and our own policy on Ukrainian corruption at the time, they just heard "he quid pro quoed first."

Next, was a blind owner of a computer repair shop in Delaware allegedly handing over to Rudy a laptop he claimed Hunter Biden had

247

dropped off a year earlier but never reclaimed? In addition to containing damning proof that Hunter and Joe Biden were related to each other by blood, an email or two from the laptop may have exposed that Joe Biden actually did know a thing or two about his son's business dealings. Clearly, for Deplorables everywhere, that was case closed on the matter of Joe Biden's s anti-American collusion with Communist China. If that allegation didn't warm the cockles of MAGA-obsessed Deplorables, claiming the hard drive contained 25,000 photos and some videos of Hunter Biden torturing and raping young children would surely seal the deal a mere few weeks before election day. Especially considering how a Steve Bannon- owned Chinese website purportedly uploaded the heinous evidence. A breathless Rudy Giuliani, who had remained unchastened by his Lev Parness-assisted Biden dirt dredging before, began begging the Conservative hate and porn outrage media cabal to amplify this new dirt louder than the old dirt, and in time to affect the outcome of the election. 99% of the free press took a hard pass for the scandal's thin sourcing and complete lack of a coherent narrative. Only Rupert Murdock's *New York Daily News* tabloid took the salacious bait but then couldn't answer to a skeptical public about its veracity. Still undeterred by the diminishing returns his bombshell was driving, Rudy apparently convinced Fox News to play along with slightly less salacious dirt from the laptop.

Tucker Carlson, who is always game for breaking down baseless nonsense into gooey bite sized pieces for his dimwitted Deplorable fans, agreed to sit for 45 minutes of live air time with Hunter Biden's former disgruntled business partner, a huge Trump fan, for an in depth analysis of whether Joe Biden was ever in on emails he and Hunter shared about a Chinese Oil business opportunity. Carlson managed to capture his largest viewership ever, as 7.5 million

248

Deplorables hung on every word Mr. Bobulinski said about Biden's web of corruption. Maybe for some it was inconvenient that the New York *Times* had reported earlier how Bobulinski was working with Trump's campaign to pitch the story to the *Wall Street Journal* before they settled on giving it to the *New York* Post. We already know the WSJ had opted out of the mess and said there was no credible evidence of wrongdoing by either Biden. This nourished the latest "our news" versus the "fake news" fantasy that makes Deplorables glow like demented fireflies. Surely if no other media would touch this hazmat, it must be the real truth. What more reliable evidence do the Deplorables need to disapprove of Joe Biden's vision for America than seeing how some disreputable publication felt they could make bank on a Biden hit piece no one else dared to run?

Listen Deplorables, I get it. Your hero's legal reckoning is near at hand. After years of baseless protest that Trump was the victim of a massive Deep State Liberal takeover plot, it is now clear his chance of remaining unincarcerated after the election in 2020 is hanging by the thinnest ribbon of gristle. The DOJ's legal opinion was the only thing that prevented his indictment for multiple crimes spelled out in the Mueller Report. Well over 1,000 former DOJ officials concluded as much. He was not exonerated by that report, his crimes were simply passed over to other legal bodies, including the US Congress, for future consideration. Massive tax evasion, possible money laundering, and multiple campaign finance violation cases are already brimming with evidence and will certainly be consummated soon after Trump leaves office. Most of your fellow citizens simply did not believe this was all a coup against a duly elected president. Instead, we see how the whole Trump experience has been one enormous power grab thinly premised on a seductive, but deeply cynical slogan, "Make America Great Again" as if American exceptionalism and Trumpism were ever remotely related. I predict you are not comforted by these facts and indeed will react in violent ways to truths which must finally be accepted.

As Election Day stands only 3 days away and you begin to contend with the reality of life after Trump, what will you do next? Assuming the cheating already underway can't produce an outcome that two thirds of country opposes, you will soon lose the thinnest veneer of political legitimacy you had received from the bully pulpit. Will you find a new champion for your endless white grievance, or will you keep hate and perpetual outrage warmed over until a new Fascist king is crowned? Sadly, one of our political parties has accepted you on your own terms, as a monster they helped create, and now must treat as a cost of doing business. But, their waterloo has come and will surely mire them in disrepute for years to follow. We don't imagine you will ever honestly reckon with how maladapted you have become in these UNITED States. How far will you separate yourselves from the plurality of public opinion and viciously defend an indefensible minority opinion that is anathema to everything we hold dear? Are you actively plotting the next Civil War that you have spent the last 4 years enthusiastically predicting? And if instead, you win by the slimmest margin imaginable, how much more will you plunder the idea of American exceptionalism over the next four years? Clearly I am not a fan, or I may have devoted more time to addressing you directly. I just wanted you to know, some of us are onto you. We know you are not just a curious satirical anomaly in an otherwise orderly society. We know your ranks have grown in number and urgency over the last decade. We know your idea of conflict resolution is based on violent militancy, and you are plotting at this very moment to make your demands felt. We know you mean to bring great harm to many people

250

in this country with whom you feel you simply can no longer coexist. Because you are the discrepancy between how things in America are supposed to work and how they actually work, the bug and not the feature, you have become the greatest threat to the Homeland. We once hoped you were not all beyond redemption. But, you are not redeemable, are you? Not in the respect that you could peacefully assimilate to a tolerant nation that soon will be a majority minority country. As such, I think you know where you will stand.

Chapter Thirty

3:53 AM 10/2/2020

"Hope Hicks, who has been working so hard without even taking a small break, has just tested positive for Covid-19. Terrible! The First Lady and I are waiting for our test results. In the meantime, we will begin our quarantine.

Donald J. Trump @realDonaldTrump

On October 2nd 2020, the Corona Virus Doubter in Chief created an instant meme that could have made Bad Luck Brian blush, as he and FLOTUS became the $7,389,996^{th}$ and $7,389,997^{th}$ US victims of the Covid hoax. Allegedly, this was the fault of soldiers and law enforcement officers who met with Hope Hicks. Like her boss, she is a sucker for a man in uniform. Or is that, a man in uniform is a "sucker and a loser?" Only the Cheshire Cat knows for sure. I know, I know, if only there were some commonsense precaution folks could have taken to minimize the transmission of the Invisible Enemy, the Wuhan Flu. But, unless you want to become Venezuela, or look like a liberal cuck, we really must just grin and bear it. It is what it is, after all. So instead, before this incident was over, the First Family, Hope Hicks, Chris Christie and 3 other law makers had contracted the virus. "Who knew?"

The odd part of this particular outbreak of the virus was determining causes and effects from an administration that insisted there were almost none of either when it came to Covid-19. So, who infected whom and when did it happen? Even more burning of a question is, did Hope Hicks infect the first family or did the president beat her to the punch? The corollary question is even more intriguing; was Trump banging Ms. Hicks?

Like Malort being the single worst adult beverage you can swill, we knew it would only be a matter of hours before Q would weigh in. Channeling one of his very earliest posts from October of 2017, which announced how Trump must isolate himself to protect against the "bad optics" of going after Crooked Hillary publicly, it was ordained that this was performance art. Finally Q admitted 45 was basically a grifter. The president's Covid diagnosis was just a ruse to distract his enemies while he quietly moved Mrs. Clinton into her 4 x 4 concrete slab at Gitmo. Certainly, he had not actually contracted a virus that all Anons knew was a Liberal hoax. And even for those who acknowledged that tens of thousands of people had died from Covid, we were reminded how Trump insulated himself against the virus by taking massive doses of hydroxychloroquine anyway. In his Tweet, Trump announced "We will get through this TOGETHER." For those hopelessly addicted to pure nonsense, the Q Anons broke the word *TOGETHER* into syllables to coax out these 3 bread crumbs: **to-get-her** as a sure sign he was signaling the Storm was, at long last, at hand and Hillary would be first to fall! By the way, my friend, who is a psychologist, has a license plate reading "THERAPIST." I can't wait to confront him with **The-Rapist.** Whatever else was true, we knew Trump did not test positive for Covid on any of the dates floated by spokespeople. More stable genius!

Amidst a thicket of Christian prayers, another Deplorables dodge emerged and quickly became a celebratory meme to pinball all over Conservative social media. Without even comparing notes, they all simultaneously arrived at this sentiment expressed word for word thousands of times over on October 3rd 2020 "Mr. President, I am literally sitting here crying and throwing up at this news. You are the bravest man I have ever seen. I named my first son Donald after you. If anything happened to you, I don't know what I would do. Thank you for ending racism." Should we credit a Lithuanian bot farm, a particularly committed cultist, or the Babylon Bee for this odd contrivance? Yes. I couldn't resist jumping in. "I understand the love and devotion you have as I have named all eight of my children Donald J. but still wonder if you were really crying and throwing up at the same time? Personally, I just peed myself over the news." #MAGAmess. Strangely no one questioned my sincerity. Yes, my thoughts and prayers were with the First Family that day, but personally, I prefer presidents who don't get sick from a hoax.

Chapter Thirty One

Election Day

After four years, which felt to most like it lasted longer than the Ming Dynasty, at last Election Day 2020 came. This would give the plurality of our people a chance to atone for trying to transform our buoyant democracy into a Russian styled Kleptocracy. Or simply to say "Lock Him Up, Lock Him Up." Finally as a people, we could emphatically state this is the United States of America and not just a Trump vanity project. But, as I have telegraphed throughout, this is not principally about the former Autocrat in Chief or his failing brand. Viewing every tragicomic thing that happened as if it were just the waste water churned up by a radioactively malignant leader was a useful construct to make this story relatable to normal people. But, to folks who would sooner step inside a Super Collider than take a step in a Deplorable's shoes, Trump simply dog eared a regretful chapter of our shared experience, but was not the driving force behind it. That force remained purely unintelligible to the ethically grounded Commendables among us. The Deplorables are wired in a completely chaotic way that gives most Commendable sorts the heebie jeebies. We only pretended to understand the movement because we are terrified with what the obverse of our reality might really look like. It is this essential truth that makes Deplorablism a curious but vile thing for all who measure society with a moral compass.

The Deplorables would rather throw themselves head first into a chipper shredder than admit they made a mistake in 2016. Enterprising journalists remained tethered to the "rational man" theory of explaining stuff as they sought to find remorseful Trump voters for human interest pieces but could find very few. Was it remotely possible the Deplorables, who did not rely upon rational calculations to make a rational decision then, would find a new religion 4 years after baking their original sin into the most impenetrable coating imaginable? No, the Deplorables would acknowledge their awful decision, was awful, about the same time they would agree to stick their face inside a Waring Blender and push the Puree button. As we struggle to imagine the kind of fanaticism that allowed them to defend the President's record across any number of extraordinary failures, psychologists are quick to point out how this cognitive dissonance has only grown under the pressure of rational opposition. Indeed, the president's appeal over 4 years needn't have any causal connection to his performance whatsoever for Deplorables to remain as rabidly supportive of their alpha hero today as they were in 2016. Their enthusiasm for casting a vote for the embattled 45th president of the United States would remain more of a referendum on themselves than Trump. And it was about opposition to their liberal tormentors too.

For months before Election Day we knew the voting experience would be unique because it would occur during a raging infectious pandemic. Folks who believed in science, and sought to conscientiously shield themselves and others from unnecessary harm, would avail themselves of reasonable alternatives to same day voting on

Election Day itself. The Deplorables, egged on by The Glorious Leader, the Grifter in Chief, sought a pretense for a loss he would surely face, uniformly agreed that shoe horning themselves into crowded polling places on November 3rd, made better sense. After all, it was the only lawful way to cast their ballot and prevent against the kind of massive Democratic voter fraud they were sure always occurred though never saw evidence of. Also, clearly, they weren't afraid of no Wuhan Flu.

Trump seized the moment to distort a perfectly rational freedom of choice matter into another us versus them struggle by insisting vote by mail on a broad national scale was ripe for voter fraud without any empirical evidence. The vote would be stolen even as it was counted by machines not equipped to fold, spindle or mutilate anything, let alone, the ballots cast. It almost seemed like maybe he wanted to disenfranchise voters who would surely vote against him. I know, I know, why was I always so cynical of this president's motives? I forgot how he did this all for love of country without even drawing a paycheck and how his family could have been doing so many other things than grifting off the American public. His Deplorables knew that inner city black and brown people could never be trusted to behave lawfully at the polls. They also knew that dead people and "illegals" are reliable Democrat votes that must be ruled invalid with or without evidence they actually were cast by dead or illegal people. From the moment Trump said the Democrats would use mail in voting to steal the election, an interesting dynamic was birthed that would dog so much of what was to follow. You see, the legislatures in many swing states like Pennsylvania, Michigan and Arizona were controlled by Republicans who rejected the early counting of mail in ballots and early voting ballots that would favor Joe Biden. This strategically set up an awkward

257

moment on Election Night when Trump would declare victory in those places with over 40% of the vote still left to count. But wait, it was even worse. As he lumbered up to the podium a few hours after the polls closed, he did his best Vlad Putin Tribute by admitting he was not impressed by the democratic right of all to cast a vote. He actually stated that the vote counting should immediately stop in states he was leading but continue in perpetuity where he trailed. Surely he didn't mean to exclude the votes of mostly urban and suburban Americans, did he? Would it seem valid to scrutinize and remove Philadelphia's ballots from the tally of Pennsylvania's votes or Detroit's from Michigan's votes?

The Deplorables found this all reasonable and would only become more and more agitated as reality failed to comport with their hero's claims of a fraudulent outcome and 45 insisted they should become more unglued about it. One thing they remained clear about was they must "Stop The Steal." Over the next few days on social media the meme was consistent, as Trump voters remained flummoxed by a fact even home schooled teens grasped. As the vote count continued in states long after Election Day, surely the mail in voting and early voting numbers would favor Biden. Remember, 9 of 10 Trump voters dragged their corpulent bodies over shards of glass to vote in person on Election Day only. Those votes were counted first. Did they really think votes tabulated after those totals were counted would be more favorable to their white power cause? Did they think razor thin margins on November 3rd would hold? Somehow the obvious always confounds people who must rely on the opposite of obvious things to get along in life. For 4 days straight every vote total that increased disproportionately in favor of the opponent was to be vilified as an "irregularity" or something fraudulent. Team Trump and their adoring

258

cultists seemed to be vying to one up each by leveling baseless allegations of one horrific example after the next of election malfeasance against election officials who had exactly no reason to jury rig a vote they would need to have certified in the coming weeks. We could only have imagined how many of these officials would face credible threats of violence against them as we had already witnessed in Arizona and Pennsylvania. We are still haunted by what Gabe Sterling, a top election official in GA said at the end of November about this: "Someone's going to get hurt, someone's going to get shot, someone's going to get killed." This marker laid bare the clear and present danger it was when leaders rigged reality to insist, against evidence, of a rigged election. Eric Trump, who Saturday Night Live parodies as the dumb son, as opposed to the coke snorting heir, wasted no time in putting up a video that had already been debunked, of election officials allegedly burning ballots for Trump. Rudy Giuliani, still smarting from getting Borated, was seen in a bizarre internet video doing his best Carnac the Magnificent impersonation by reading random scraps of paper that proved Trump had already won the presidency simply because totals on November 3rd said so and it was "Totally impossible!... Illogical!... Irrational! ...That the same thing would happen in all five or six places where there were close votes."

It was almost as if rules of logic and math didn't apply in TrumpLandia. Some Deplorables insisted that election officials in Arizona admitted foul play when they said they preferred ballots that were filled in with Sharpies. Apparently they heard instead, "we will reject Conservative ballots filled in with sharpies" with no explanation why. Team Trump launched meritless law suits wherever possible. Some of these hinged on what they claimed were attempts to prevent their poll monitors from having "reasonable access" to observing the counts in progress within swing states. What they may have actually meant was the citizen poll watchers Trump deputized were kept out of vote counting centers where actual bipartisan representatives were allowed in. Perhaps this egregious act of defying the will of the Deplorables was out of an abundance of caution for the vote counters as angry and violent protestors were demanding to flood into these rooms. On a lighter note, we learned how the Deplorables turned on Fox News for having the gall to level honestly with their viewers about the election outcome, and would seek media which more appropriately lied to them moving forward.

As I complete this chapter, it is Saturday November 7th 2020, and Joseph Robinette Biden has just been declared the 46th president of the United States. Within moments of the announcement, Trump accused Biden of "rushing to falsely pose as the winner," immediately making the ghosts of both Barnum and Baily blush.

Sadly I predict this will be the day history records the beginning of the next Civil War in America. Though Biden ultimately won the contest handily, capturing both an electoral college plurality, and the highest total popular vote in history, commendable people remain dismayed that over 70 million people still sided with Donald J. Trump seemingly for no reason other than to thumb their noses at liberalism. It is the irrational premise of this irrational choice which haunts us. If pure fanaticism can fuel such a counter decency movement to such monumental heights, are we as a people, now exactly split in half over every reckoning of what is right and wrong about our country? 160 years ago, a schism between commendable and deplorable people plunged us into 5 years of a struggle for the soul of a nation. It is a quaint notion that our country ever actually resolved the differences our first

Civil War was waged over. Realistically the South may have been chastened by the experience but were they actually defeated? Was the idea that all men were created equal really consummated in 1865 when the Confederate army laid down their arms and the secessionists surrendered? Was it settled that the United States would become a free society with equal opportunity for people who had endured moral and physical violence for centuries before? It wasn't long after the first Civil War that the South came back with the same demand to accept their country only if on their own terms Tragically two months after our 2020 election, people still hopelessly at odds with what would Make This Country Great Again, set out to settle an old score.

The same grievances against nonwhites and non-Christians prevail today, only slightly obscured by the political incorrectness of open hostility and by modern laws that prevent it. The seething resentment the Deplorable have always had for non-whites may have become less visible over time but has remained just as palpable in the 55 years since Jim Crow laws were repealed. With the tacit, and sometimes even explicit, approval of a White Nationalist leader, these unhealed wounds only became rawer. The threat of a new Civil War has always hid in plain sight as the notion of white supremacy has come under attack. We came very close under the Obama presidency of poking this bear again. For all four years of Trump's presidency, the idea of another Civil War between ideological rivals has welled up to the point of certainty among the Deplorables. Nothing throws them into fits of unrestrained rage than the kind of level playing field that will no longer advantage them in an increasingly diverse nation. Donald Trump made it abundantly clear to them that certain people in the country are more intrinsically valuable and deserving than others, and as such has permissioned the kind of racial and cultural anarchy that will surely fuel a major us versus them struggle. When he told them their ideological rivals have stolen this all from them, it was as if he personally set their homes on fire and dared them to do something about it.

Now that the ad hoc leader of the Deplorable movement has just been vanquished, must we remain naïve for what is about to happen? We could wait in vain for a concession speech that would signify the peaceful transition of power, or finally accept it was never going to happen. Within that void, those of us wishing to embrace our better angels and heal a deeply divided country paused to wonder just how one sided that prayer was. On Saturday afternoon in early December of 2020, after all the "Sound and Fury" that signified nothing but contempt for a free and fair America, the Trump supporters descended upon several cities to protest, crying "Stop the Steal."

Chapter Thirty Two

Deplorables Attack!

"When the rest of the world watches the news from America, they see a third world dumpster fire. A failed state."
Oliver Markus Malloy, *American Fascism*

As we paused to briefly savor the return to normalcy a Joe Biden electoral victory promised, we were aggressively jerked back to a more checkered reality. There is nothing like a violent insurrection launched against our own country, leaving five dead and countless others wounded, to forever sully our opinion of a couple thousand social arsonists, and the millions of Deplorables who support them. Our desperate desire to find unity after experiencing the greatest disunity since the Civil War was met with an equal backlash of violent rebellion. So many of the perpetually outraged Deplorables actually insisted upon even greater divisiveness in the wake of defeat. We were bludgeoned by the stark fact that the only historical precedent for an attack upon our nation's Capital occurred over 200 years ago and wasn't perpetrated by our own people, but the British during the War of 1812. Indeed, the very idea that such a bloody insurrection attempt could happen at the behest of our own vanquished leader, and with the support of his closest confidantes, is an abomination that will forever relegate the domestic terrorists, and those who incited the wreckage, to blasphemous ignominy. We watched for years as militant rightwing White Supremacists eclipsed even Islamic extremists as the greatest threat to the homeland. Still this attack managed to shock the conscience of most decent Americans.

While we Commendables were thrilled that a plurality of voters chose a more harmonious path forward, we were loath to accept how an unprecedented number of other citizens voted against progress. Indeed, it was disheartening to discover more white voters than ever supporting the status quo. We certainly had hoped that empathy for "others" could finally be seen as an opportunity and not a threat, especially after months of protests from those marginalized others seemed to galvanize so many people regardless of race. In the push me – pull me reckoning of zero sum assessments, must the Deplorables still insist that diversity and tolerance comes at their own expense?

The Deplorable terrorists came from all corners of the country to protest a free and fair election that was symbolically at odds with their own white fragility, and many resorted to seditious violence to draw a brighter line between us and them. 5000 or so gathered for a rally only a half mile from the Capitol. Of them, at least a thousand stormed Capitol Hill itself while millions of Deplorables around the country joined them in spirit. It seems, ever since Obama's election in 2008, they have stewed within the juices of their own unhealthy ethos, raging about losing the battle for racial power in America and even about white genocide. As they became increasingly overwrought by their dwindling majority and the conviction that America looked less and less like the country they grew up in, they became more receptive to a kind of anarchy that promised a great do over. MAGA.

The Commendables were shocked to find unanimity among the Deplorables, whether they participated themselves, or simply supported the cause, for approving of such a bloody insurrection waged over a moot point. Basic human decency in a civil society requires we all reject waging violence against our fellow citizens, especially when the violent backlash is over the consequences of an election that was never legitimately contestable We were also buffeted by a certain depraved indifference for the lives of those who are sworn to serve and protect. The closest thing to condemnation we found among the Deplorables came when they insisted on falsely equating what happened on January 6, 2021, with what had happened throughout most of 2020, during BLM protests, to conclude that all riots should be condemned. That analogy was tortured beyond recognition by malcontents desperate to justify anti- American chaos. For those of us with an ardent faith in our democratic Republic, who have become more critical in recent years of the deteriorating American condition, this betrayal is the most visible face yet of irreconcilable differences.

The public face of the Deplorables' movement is a red herring. The "issues" they debate with Commendables, in the mainstream, are simply constructs used to organize opposition to liberalism and tolerance generally. Their authentic selves are only revealed to kindred spirits in places where conspiracy theories are more comforting than reality for their ragged souls. Their attack on our Nation's Capital was not about the economy, immigration, legal or otherwise, abortion, or even whether we are at heart a Capitalist, and not a Socialist, country. This was exclusively about a remarkably large group of mostly white

265

men who imagine their place at the top of the food chain is under attack, and are willing to do anything, including armed insurrection, to "take back their country." As it finally dawned on them that their standard bearer would soon be displaced by a leader more committed to egalitarianism and inclusion, all of their uncontrollable rage bubbled up to the surface.

For the last 10 years, we watched passively as the visible fin of this movement cut through heretofore less turbulent waters. We remained only marginally aware of the larger bulk of the predator lurking below the surface. Some things are so grotesque we instinctively suppress our awareness of them. It took actual blood in the water to wake up. We simply could not imagine how diametrically opposed so many were to the basic values we embraced, as Americans. We were seduced by silver tongues to accept that most of the Deplorables' allegiance to leaders and causes we didn't embrace ourselves were about kitchen table economics or the kind of culture wars we have always relished debating. Surely, only a small number were purely indecent anarchists committed to burning down the pillars of our democracy in favor of Fascist Authoritarianism. We naively assumed that all were in favor of life, liberty, and the pursuit of happiness for all. How could we possibly have known that the Deplorables would always reject the notion that we all deserve equal access to American exceptionalism?

The Q Anon faithful imagined that the siege of the US Capitol would trigger what they called "The Storm," the fantasy that all of Trump's foes would be executed in an apocalyptic final conflict. Their success in overturning the certification of the vote would assure Trump held onto power and could complete his righteous mission. Many adherents were captured in photos and video inside and outside of the

266

Capitol building all dressed in the ubiquitous branded apparel of the cult. When Trump called for protests over the certification of the new president, this was a sign the moment they all prayed for would finally come. One Trump supporter killed in the melee, Ashli Babbitt, a 14 year US Air Force veteran, who served four tours of duty defending her country, wrote a disturbing post on social media the evening before. "*They can try and try and try, but the Storm is here and it is descending upon Washington in less than 24 hours.....dark to light!*" She defended her country during tours in Afghanistan and Iraq but became so radicalized over the usual MAGA nonsense, she turned against her country that day in January 2021.

The baseless allegation that the 2020 election was stolen from Trump was consistently amplified within the Q Anon echo chamber and championed by Q Anon associated attorneys Sidney Powell and Lin Wood, who joined Rudy Giuliani's feverously preposterous allegations in failed court cases in every battleground state. You may recall these attorneys also are infamous for defending Michael Flynn, Trump's pardoned former NSA, who is also a Q aficionado. On Parler, which tends to coddle subversive rightwing agitators, and has become a landing pad for Q forums, many posts about the insurrection seemed to revive the fading hopes for a final reckoning before the inauguration. The agitators relentlessly ginned up purely destructive conspiracy theories to undermine a peaceful transition of power, more relevant for a hobbled America than ever. Most chatter promoted the preinsurrection rally and were shared broadly by general Trump supporters; Militia men, violent White Nationalist groups, and of course Q Anon supporters. Because Trump served as a validation for their unhinged fantasies, we always feared violent retribution could come in the aftermath of his political demise. The only reckoning left

267

was how much life this movement would have in the years AT and how many more people would die.

"I predict within the next twelve days, many in our country will die," ominously commented Q Anon believer Cleveland Grover Meredith as he made his way to Washington D.C. all the way from Colorado. On route, he texted associates to advise he was "3.5 hours from target practice...ready to remove several craniums from shoulders...and so ready to FK SOME TRAITORS UP." When he was arrested, he allegedly told authorities he was thinking about heading over for Pelosi's speech and putting a "bullet in her noggin on live TV." Q agnostics were driven to the confrontation by more militant instincts about what a Biden presidency meant for the country they claim to love. For both factions, chatter intensified steadily for two months on the less-moderated Social media platforms over what this moment meant, how it would be planned for, and how it was permitted by their leader himself. This happened in plain sight for anyone willing to confront it.

As if we really had to remind ourselves, we find that these sentiments were only considered extreme examples of Deplorabilism, in the sense of how pornographically vivid the lust for violent retribution was. Everything else was basic food stock for the movement. On the Hannity Facebook page we found this from MG: *"The Democrats are being allowed to take the country over, folks better wake up and realize what their (sic) doing. They have taken your VOICES, rigged an election, and you know Joe Biden would never have been elected. Pelosi and her thugs rigged the whole thing. It makes my stomach sick at what their (sic) doing. Free speech is censored and the Democrats are bringing a coup against Pres Trump. If Biden is inaugurated, The USA is no more....IT will be Communist."*

268

FB added this about the Democrats targeted in the insurrection: "*They have declared war on all of us! We all should think the same like Nazi Germany!!! Just so happens we learned from that history. It will not be repeated!!! We will not be disarmed or led by train to a camp. We will not get a vaccine!! We will shoot and die before we live that way!!*"

Speaking for the domestic terrorists, who stayed at home but were just as agitated, TP shared this rather tortured analysis of the heightened military presence planned for the inauguration: *"Pretty sad when the GREATEST COUNTRY ON EARTH has to hide behind the military!!! If the election hadn't been stolen there would be no need!! Americans are not going to stand for the few speaking for the silent majority!! I don't believe our great soldiers will turn their guns on American patriots!! The Storm is coming...USA"*

TM dropped this simple bread crumb: *"Prepare to be blown away on the morning of the20th. Trump will be President. Remember my words."*

These kinds of hyperbolic screeds exemplified how fervently committed the Deplorables were to counterfactual folklore about Liberalism writ large, and the attack on our Capitol specifically. Each cast an enormous storm cloud over anything resembling human decency. Beyond the fear and loathing for others that is endemic to their movement, we are now convinced significant mental illness also exists among the most faithful. The mass delusion, the malignant narcissism, the paranoia, and the purely anti-social tendencies on full display would objectify afflicted individuals as a danger to society. This danger is only amplified as millions have coalesced into more and more of a single evil entity. It is critical to remember, Trump is not the only player in the MAGA saga who is gripped by debilitating narcissism. This, and so many more psychopathologies, are chinks in the Deplorables' armor too. Pathological narcissists are driven largely by catastrophic neediness which makes them abusive and dangerous. The desperation revealed in these comments is primal. These are not the philosophical musings of moderately aggrieved thinkers. This feels more like a plea from the tormented for mindless Armageddon. It is time to accept, what the Deplorables have always known: The divide between us and them is mostly irreconcilable. But, unlike the Deplorables, who would settle this through violent insurrection and civil war, we choose to peacefully shelter in place within the main of society, while banishing those who will not abide by American values back to a place of dark disrepute.

It is time to admit this moment was inevitable. The heart felt sentiment that filled every nook and cranny of the insurrectionists' dark souls have been beating furiously since the first Civil War. Their cause was not vanquished in that bloody fight it was only held temporarily at bay for the sake of a weary nation.

Chapter Thirty Three

The Deplorables' Foot Soldiers

"Within the domestic terrorism bucket, the category as a whole, racially motivated violent extremism is, I think, the biggest bucket within that larger group...and within the racially motivated violent extremist bucket, people subscribing to some kind of white-supremacist type ideology is certainly the biggest chunk of that"

FBI Director Christopher Wray 2019

There is a division of labor that typifies membership in any anti-establishment terrorist cult. Some members themselves actively participate in the lawless acts of senseless violence to achieve political and social ends, while most others, though equally fervent adherents, allow their more militant brothers and sisters to do the dirty work as they cheer the team on from the comfort of their La-Z-Boys. This division of labor hinges less on ideological commitment than risk tolerance and the degree of radicalization, each of which can rise or fall over time. It is critical to acknowledge that it is from the ranks of the presently noncombatant members that radicalization can metastasize under circumstances we all must vigilantly watch for. The same kind of CIA tradecraft that was applied to Islamic extremism could help us unearth the conspiratorial forces which can activate otherwise dormant hostility. But, until law enforcement has the same set of tools, and Congress the will, to hold Americans as accountable for their terrorist violence, this detection will remain more challenging than it should be.

Upon identifying leadership figures among the perpetrators of domestic terrorism over the last decade, the FBI could walk backwards, in a manner of contact tracing, and arrive right at the doorsteps of current and future rightwing terrorists. As these American Jihadists represent the most dangerous current threat to Homeland security, this should be an immediate priority. But, one thing that complicated this task in the age of Trump was how we never imagined the "Enemy within" could be the enemy within the Whitehouse. Anyone who remembers the forensic analysis of Bin Ladin videos after 9/11 for signs that terrorist cells within the country could be activated, will remember how every gesture, odd turn of a phrase, cryptic reference to a date, or even the surroundings could be combed for evidence of an imminent attack.

It happens to be an article of faith between the Q Anons that Trump's public briefings and Tweets were replete with coded messaging. To believers, these were breadcrumbs and actual instructions on what the faithful should do when called upon, if only they could solve for the hidden messaging. It was the premise of the ubiquitous WWG1WWA message of interfaith unity. Perhaps this is the one thing Q purports that isn't just gibberish. Anyway, if we imagined that Trump may have been a de factor leader of domestic terrorism over the last four years, we would need to scrutinize his massaging as forensically as we did Bin Ladin's. Even now, it seems unlikely anyone will have the political will to approve that investigation.

So instead, we look at the faces of rightwing fanatics who served as foot soldiers for the Deplorable movement. These are the people Trump never explicitly denounced throughout 4 years in office and seemed to rely upon to sow maximum chaos whenever the preverbal shit hit the fan. They were the Deplorables to whom other Deplorables paid homage and for whom other Deplorables made endless baseless apologies. They were the "patriots" rightwing media lauded as victims of leftwing marginalization. Not only have their names surfaced again and again over 4 years of domestic mayhem but, they have always imagined they were doing the 45th president's bidding. They were the leaders of the "kraken," an unsubstantiated claim of democratic voter fraud, and the leaders of the bloody insurrection at the Nation's Capital that followed on January 6, 2021. These are the people that have splintered the domestic threat we face as a country from one, nurtured overseas and brought to our shores by Islamic Jihadists, to dozens of groups, born and bred in these United States, and sewn together only by their insistence on white supremacy in America. They all have felt, to one extent or another, that they had become exiled to the unacceptable margins of society. In Donald Trump they found new legitimacy and an opportunity to tip their innate violent tendencies against those who had sought to marginalize or replace them. And in the Turner Diaries' 14 words they have found an enduring kinship. "We must secure the existence of our people and a future for white children."

The Proud Boys is perhaps the most visible face of far-right, neo-fascist, white nationalism in America today. Besides having an outsized presence at the Unite the Right Rally in Charlottesville in 2017, they achieved their greatest notoriety when they became a subject of debate between Donald Trump and Joe Biden in September of 2020 in which the 45th president infamously stated how they should "stand up and stand by" instead of "stand down" when asked to denounce one of his most enthusiastic support groups and reliable partners for social anarchy. They promote and regularly engage in political violence. They believe that men specifically, and traditional Western culture in general, are under attack in liberal America. They see themselves as working to defend against cultural changes that are destroying a male dominated white Christian society. Like so many other white nationalists, they countenanced the looming threat of the next Civil war splitting the country along racial and political lines. The group, which has been banned from virtually all mainstream social media for their embrace of violent extremism, was founded in 2016 and designated as a Terrorist group by Canada on February 3rd 2021 for their involvement in the storming of the US Capitol. Several of their members have been indicted by the US Department of Justice.

The Proud Boys led many anti-Antifa and anti-BLM themed events over the spring and summer of 2020, as BLM protests became the regular and visible thread of a growing social justice movement in the country. These accelerationists brought extreme violence to otherwise peaceful protests, especially in Portland, OR, considered to be the whitest city in America and home to the most prolonged series of protests against systemic racism and police brutality in 2020. Most of the deaths the rightwing blame on the BLM protestors occurred in that city and were disproportionately instigated by the Proud Boys and other neo fascist, white nationalists. The Proud Boys' role was basically to agitate otherwise peaceful marches into the politically charged illusion that pro black and anti-fascist sentiments were the biggest threats to domestic tranquility in the country. They managed to convince the 45th

274

president of the United States and all of his staunchest Deplorable supporters that they were right.

On December 12th of 2020, the Proud Boys became the subject of a hate crime investigation in Washington DC for allegedly vandalizing two black churches and setting BLM flags on fire during a rally there. Videos posted on Twitter show a group of people identified as Proud Boys marching with a Black Lives Matter banner held above their heads, then cheering as it is set on fire while chanting "fuck Antifa." Members were also wanted for questioning in 4 stabbings and one shooting at the same event. In the aftermath, the group's leader Enrique Tarrio called for his members to "violently disrupt Joe Biden's Inauguration."

Social media posts discovered by the FBI found that a member of the Proud Boys, arrested on Wednesday February 3rd of 2021, indicated that he and others were planning in advance of the insurrection attempt to organize members to overwhelm police barricades and breach the U.S. Capitol on Jan. 6. In court filings, U.S. prosecutors alleged that 30 year old Ethan Nordean, AKA Rufio Panman, and other Proud Boys were motivated to avenge what they perceived was an insufficient police response to the stabbing of one of their members who attended a December pro-Trump demonstration in D.C. Several video accounts of the violence outside the Capitol captured these men beating Capitol police that day. Nordean faces more than 30 years in prison if convicted on the four counts he faces.

The Boogaloo Bois aren't as Trump obsessed as most Deplorables because they believe Trump is pro blue and they, most assuredly, are not. They are united by a love for guns and a hate for cops. Ideologically, they are obsessed with bringing down the pillars of

275

civilized society and plunging the country into bloody chaos. We find them showing up whenever nihilistic anti-establishment moods can be stoked to violence. Some say Boogaloo, like Antifa, is more idea than movement. The Boogaloo Bois seek to exploit existing grievances against those they imagine are opposing political or social provocateurs. Over the last many years, they have looked for any provocation against "civil liberties," including gun control measures, BLM protests, Covid-19 lockdown measures, or even the controversy surrounding the next presidential inauguration, to spark violent conflict. Their ideology is reminiscent of extreme rightwing terrorists of the past like Timothy McVeigh, as they typically become activated by what they perceive as government overreach. They appear to be committed to violent revolution and a nationwide insurrection leading to what they call *Civil War 2: Electric Boogaloo.*

They show up heavily armed and dressed in their signature Hawaiian shirts to exploit any event that has the potential to stir up division. They are the agitators Commendables think of when they watch otherwise peaceful BLM protests become suddenly violent and destructive. Some members even hurl Molotov cocktails at law enforcement to edge those events toward chaos. Three members were allegedly involved with the plot last summer to kidnap and kill Michigan Governor Gretchen Whitmer.

We have already touched on former US Air Force Sergeant and Boogaloo Bois affiliate Steven Carrillo, who ambushed and killed a federal security officer and a police officer within the space of a week in June of 2020. Allegedly, when he shot and killed the officer, he scrawled the word "Boog" on the officer's cruiser in his own blood and next to that the phrase, "Stop the duopoly" referring to our traditional two-party political system.

Notwithstanding Carrillo's high profile association with the Boogaloo Bois, the number of current and former military among their ranks is relatively small. But, eavesdropped discussions on social media in recent years have detected an increased interest in recruiting current and former military for their combat expertise.

Unlike the Boogaloos, who are proudly anti-establishment, the Oath Keepers stash their obvious antigovernment leanings behind a thin veneer of American "Patriotism." This group explicitly recruits their ranks from current and former military, law enforcement, and first responders, who all took an oath to "serve and protect the Constitution against all enemies foreign and domestic." The sticky antiestablishment wicket for this militia group is their belief that many among our current protectorate have abdicated their oath in service to a federal government coopted by the New World Order. In their estimation, this shadowy international conspiracy aims to co-opt current police and military to violently strip Americans of their right to keep and bear arms so they may be enslaved in concentration camps, leading ultimately to the destruction of America's Constitutional Republic.

You may recall it was the Oath Keepers predominantly who were the "supporters" of Cliven Bundy at his infamous standoff with the Bureau of Land Management and other federal agents in 2014. This incident rekindled much of the anti-government fervor from the 1990s to shape how the Deplorables would define the "Deep State."

The Oath Keepers were particularly active in a tumultuous 2020. They participated in many anti Covid-19 lockdown protests at

State Capitols all over the country. They were quite reliable in providing vigilante "security" for local communities and businesses, "under siege" and under protected, in their estimation, during the Black Lives Matter protests that spread in the wake of the killing of George Floyd. And toward the end of the year, they warned of the looming threat of a takeover by the "Marxist left" during the 2020 election. In response to this threat that noted conspiracist and rabble rouser Alex Jones of *Infowars* promoted a month earlier, The Oath Keeper's leader, Stewart Rhodes, promised Deplorables, hungering for a final reckoning, that violence against liberal targets was coming. He said this in an interview with Jones, "We have men already stationed outside D.C. as a nuclear option in case they attempt to remove the President illegally, we will step in and stop it....we are prepared to go in if the President calls us up." Call them up Trump did, and attempt to stop it, they did.

Justice Department prosecutors found the Oath Keepers' fingerprints all over the planning and implementation of the riot at the Capitol. The militia group used their vast reach and significant resources to turn out the hate and even paid the travel expenses for many "soldiers." But, what most captured the Feds' attention was social media communication from another leader of the group beginning at least two months before the Capitol siege occurred. Jessica Watkins, a military veteran, who played a significant reconnaissance role in the insurrection attempt, began indicating online and in texts, how she was explicitly waiting for direction from the 45th president before committing to the plan. In a text on November 9th she said, "I am concerned this is an elaborate trap. Unless the POTUS himself activates us, it's not legit. The POTUS has the right to activate units too. If Trump asks me to come, I will. Otherwise I can't trust it." By the end of December, Watkins was able to resolve her dilemma and was clear about the mission. She had what authorities called "a single-minded devotion to obstruct through violence...the certification of Joe Biden's presidency."

Q Anon has been the velvety ribbon of pure nonsense that has loosely bound together so much of what has threatened our democratic Republic over the last 4 years. The Anons are not the tip of the spear, they are the connective tissue and social lubricant that moves waste from the irritable bowels of the affected throughout the digestive system of their body politic. They wouldn't beat a Capitol Hill police officer to death with an American flag pole like the Boogaloos and Oath Keepers would with a wink and a tip of their red caps. But, they would baselessly accuse the officer of violating small children if doing so removed him as a threat. They are the Deplorable Movement's worker bees spreading endless non sequiturs to keep hope alive that the world will soon be reordered in their image. They also provide a narrative that has been used to cross pollenate and agitate so many other Deplorables who are fiercely militant.

The Anons are essentially a monolith that weighs every idea for its utility in worshipping their cult hero. They will make strange bed fellows with anyone who will accept Donald J. Trump as their lord and savior even when they disagree with them on everything else.

For four years they propped up all of the pro-Trump rhetoric that brought the Deplorables to their Waterloo moment on January 6th 2021. In fact, they shaped the conspiracy that Team Biden fraudulently stole the election before joining a thousand other arsonists to express their deep dissatisfaction that common sense prevailed when they stormed the Capitol. Ron Watkins, who some believe may be Q Anon himself, was the former administrator of 8kun, where the Q faithful mingle daily to swap conspiratorial bread crumbs. He amplified the

279

shadowy musings about rigged Dominion voting machines that could be used to switch Trump votes to his challenger as the ultimate Deep State "fuck you." The idea was to flag the attention of Trump himself and his servile conspiracy-obsessed minions for a November surprise. Watkins wanted to discuss this plot personally with Rudy Giuliani. But first he needed the approbation an actual media outlet could give this limp biscuit. So, on November 12th he showed up at *One America News,* a Trump fluffing propaganda network. As if by divine providence, Trump himself began a Tweet storm a day later that would last for over two months about the Dominion cheat. He alleged that Dominion machines "DELETED" more than 1 million Trump votes in the US.

The President's personal attorney Rudy Giuliani joined Sydney Powell and Lin Wood, two Q adherent attorneys, on a quest that placed the Dominion lie at the center of over sixty failed court cases to validate the "Stop the Steal" meme.

The Anons joined hundreds of thousands of other Deplorables on social media to discuss the glorious Rapture that would come to D.C. in the form of a final protest to "Stop the Steal." In their hero's support of a mass protest against the certification of Joe Biden's election victory, they saw an undeniable sign that the "Storm" was at hand. According to *USA Today* almost 1500 tweets between Jan1 and the day of the insurrection, from accounts with known Q Anon ties, featured ultra-violent language about what posters felt would happen on January 6th. On *Parler* a malicious rumor was planted that counter protestors planned to kill Trump supporters at the rally and that they should arrive heavily armed and ready to fight back.

Traditional media still struggle to adequately explain the Q phenomenon. While the Anons are exceedingly radical in their belief system, they are far less physically aggressive than most radical rightwing arsonists. Because the Anons are more PSYOP terrorists, who exploit mental and emotional fragility to achieve their aims than violent American Jihadists do, media coverage of their antics at the Capitol was less proportionate than their presence warranted. They were as much of a thicket in the halls as any other group, and two among them died for their misguided enthusiasm to "Stop the Steal."

Rosanne Boyland was a 32 year old recovering drug addict when she succumbed to Q Anon fanaticism. At 34, two years clean, she joined the mob at both the protest and the Capitol siege, mostly just to express solidarity. She came bearing a "Save America" sign and the Gadsden "Don't Tread on Me" flag, once a symbol of the American Revolution, but now increasingly just a rightwing extremist dog whistle. Just after the mob breached the Capitol entrance, Ms. Boyland was trampled to death as her comrades beat back the Capitol Hill police on their way to kidnap and/or kill particular members of Congress and the Vice President who were the visible totems of resistance to Donald Trump.

Seconds after the mob breached the outer doors to the Speaker's Lobby, a hallway that led to the House chamber, 35 year old Ashli Babbit was shot and killed by a Capitol Hill police officer as she was first to traverse the shattered window panes. She was among many Q Anon acolytes at the Capitol that day, convinced that storming the Capitol was symbolic for "The Storm" their prophet had spoken of for 2 years. "Landing in DC. Here to do God's work. Save the Republic. #StoptheSteal." Were Tweets she exchanged between Jan 4th and the

281

day of "The Storm." Babbit was a US Air Force veteran, born and bred in California, who served in Iraq and ironically received the *Global War on Terrorism Expeditionary Award* for her meritorious service in protecting the Republic. For Babbit the Capitol insurrection was not just symbolic; it was a pivotal moment in the war for the soul of a country she was always sure she would fight and die for. For weeks before the terrorist attack, Babbitt was active on Twitter retweeting the president's baseless accusations of voter fraud and amplifying all of the Q rhetoric from Trump attorneys Sydney Powell and Lin Wood to a fevered pitch. Within the convoluted Helter Skelter of all these posts were the unmistakable basic food group Q warnings that had already agitated millions beyond reason.   In responding to a Tweet by Kamala Harris about ambitious Covid vaccination plans, she responded: "No the fuck you will not... No masks, no you, no Biden the kid raper, no vaccines...sit your fraudulent ass down...we the ppl bitch!"

The media is always titillated by sideshows. Rather than plumbing deeper for an explanation of how the radicalized belief system of the Q faithful contributed to the mayhem, they made a spectacle out of Jacob Chansley, AKA Jake Angeli, perhaps best known as the Q Shaman. Instead of reporting how so many came to the Capitol looking ridiculous by design, dressed like Superman, Lady Liberty, and even Honest Abe, many also sporting war paint and obscene   t-shirt messaging, Chansley emerged as the ludicrous face of a movement. Chansley came shirtless, in red white and blue face paint, and pocked by multiple weird tattoos as he strode defiantly through the halls of Congress adorned in a fur headdress rimmed by buffalo horns and carrying a spear. He joined dozens of other accomplices in the aftermath of the terrorist attack in making it abundantly clear this was done at the behest of the President exclusively. After everything we have learned about the participants, it is far more likely they were simply paying homage to a leader who gave shape and "purpose" to deep wounds they always intended to avenge.

And so they all came. They came to vanquish an enemy they felt was committed to their destruction in favor of unworthy replacements. They came convinced liberal leadership would strip them of their First and Second Amendment rights and enslave them, as others had been enslaved before them, as lesser, more servile, Americans. The time was nigh for a bloody new civil war to re-stoke the angst of a people still grieving over the results of the last one. They came to the Capitol bearing the Confederate battle flag and the Gadsden flag, both powerful relics of a racially intolerant and revolutionary past. They came bearing any makeshift weapons of destruction they could carry because opponents stood to foreclose on their existence and the future of their white children. They came to beat to death a thin blue line of resistance as a reminder that law enforcement in America exists to serve and protect them against the invasion and incursions of "others." When those others could not be disenfranchised of their votes, more violent means of suppression were to be imposed. When the law exists to restrain these immoral yearnings, it becomes the enemy, too. They came because fascism in the service of white supremacy was a lesser evil than antifascism in service of a multi-cultural and multi-racial ideal. For the Commendables and Redeemables who have had an unflinching awareness of the evil that has always existed, but has crested over the last four years, we see in this terrorist attack a prelude for worse acts to follow.

Chapter Thirty Four

The Three Lies of the Apocalypse

"If you tell a big enough lie and tell it frequently enough, it will be believed."

Adolf Hitler

The Washington Post famously concluded that during his single 4 year term in office, Donald Trump told 30,573 lies of various sizes and shapes and degrees of relevance. As you might expect, thousands of these were the kind of inconsequential "white lies" used pathologically to protect his self-idealized image against the fragility of obvious mediocrity. To chronicle the rise and ultimate fall of the Deplorables, we focus on the 3 lies that did the most to stir them to heights of unspeakable hostility and paranoia.

We may think of it as a modern phenomenon that is aided and abetted on Social media but, the malicious use of "Fake News" has been around for centuries as a tool to move public opinion and insulate more fascist regimes against criticism. What makes it more pernicious these days is the difficulty of determining to whom fake news may be attributed when it rears its ugly head. Is it State sponsored propaganda, or does it originate in the fevered imagination of private social agitators?

Maybe it is one thing and then coopted and amplified to become another thing. For the Deplorables, the concept of "Fake News" has been both a tactic and a dodge. When applied to any communication critical of the movement's standard bearers, "Fake News" is to be summarily dismissed as an "Enemy of the People." No need for even the pretense of debate between reasonable people. If it is anti-Deplorable, or anti-Trump, it is "Fake News." And, when it can be used to spread and amplify misinformation that is useful to the cause, even when the cause itself is disreputable and malicious, "Fake News" becomes a rhetorical device to achieve consensus. When that happens, "Fake News" is considered the real truth.

The first lie that brought us to this rickety moment in American history was when Trump persuaded millions of people that only he was telling the truth by dubbing every criticism from the mainstream media "Fake News." This single lie has nurtured most of the wretched fictions that have tipped the Deplorables toward violent anarchy. We may assume Trump's only real motive for this lie was to cast himself as a hero figure who would "Make America Great Again" without constructive opposition. But for the Deplorables, it was the irritant that salted their open wounds after years of feeling marginalized by the society's elites. The Fourth Estate, which has served as a check and balance to our three branches of government as another significant source of social influence, would be violently opposed in all cases in which the media stood on progressive America's side. There was simply no way the Deplorables could tolerate any institution that would aim to hold their movement accountable to decency or even the rule of law. For the Deplorables, this has fed a violent alternative interpretation of the "Day of the Rope" from *The Turner Diaries* to hold American race traitors responsible for the state of the union.

285

As the Mueller investigation of Russian interference in our 2016 election began focusing more intently on whether the Trump administration was complicit in Putin's plan to undermine American democracy, another cleft emerged between Deplorable and Commendable people. Even when the Deplorables admitted Russia attacked us, they were never going to hold their cult leader accountable. When Trump called a matter of national security, as defined by every one of our three letter agencies, a "witch hunt," focused on removing him from power, it fed an alternative "reality" that prompted a call for investigating the investigators instead of team Trump.

This "hoax "was just another Deep State plot to disrupt patriots form making America white again. The enthusiasm Deplorables had for tarring and feathering every perceived opponent reordered the country, in their estimation, into two camps, those who sided with the President and "Never Trumpers." This was the classic "us" versus "them" zero sum assessment that made all of their usual grievances fester even more. The expression, "lock them up," which originally applied only to Hillary Clinton, was applied to virtually every face of the resistance. When a particularly Trump compliant AG announced he would appoint John Durham to Special Counsel for the Department of Justice to investigate the origins of the Trump-Russia collusion probe, the next major lie of the apocalypse was born. Edged toward incoherent glee that finally their liberal tormentors would be destroyed, the Q Anon wing of the Deplorables hatched a baseless new meme that the Durham Report would lead to "The Storm." This would be the cataclysmic moment when all of Trump's evil opponents would be rounded up and imprisoned at Guantanamo Bay and their hero would be freed to continue saving the world against the shadowy cabal of pedophiles who plotted a New World Order. After 18 months of investigation, in order to find support for Attorney General Barr's claims that Trump was targeted by politically biased Obama officials to prevent his election, Durham found no credible evidence of this plot. Thousands of sealed indictments against Trump opponents went poof, and the Deplorables flooded social media with post traumatic distress over the nothing burger.

Oddly for a figure so overtly enamored with himself and his rock star appeal to Deplorables everywhere, Trump showed very early signs of fearing he would lose his reelection bid in 2020. Months before Election Day, he began beating the same drum he did in 2015 by positing how the only way he would lose in 2020 is if the election were rigged against him. Outwardly at his MAGA rallies he was supremely confident, but inwardly he feared that presiding over a catastrophic blunder on the Covid-19 pandemic and the cratered economy his incompetence engendered were the proverbial kisses of death. And so, the third lie of the Apocalypse was simply to inform millions of Deplorables months before a single vote was cast how the election would be "stolen" from them. Within the impenetrable bubble the Deplorables ensconced themselves in to hide from "Fake News," it took little time to erect many barely plausible explanations that could vie for affirmation on Parler and Gab. At the time they probably never imagined how much help they would get from rightwing cable media, the President himself, and scads of devoted hangers on in sharing and amplifying this fabrication beyond reason for so long. Anyway, nothing galvanized the perpetually outraged Deplorables more than how the Trump Train could be derailed so easily if they didn't take drastic action.

A mixture of so many combustible lies, constantly agitated, created a pressure cooker environment for the Deplorables that was destined to explode into violent rage. The bipolar roller coaster of perceived victories followed by soul crushing defeats must have been unbearable for them as they traversed the last four years of American history together. Slithering back into the world of disrepute after flirting so briefly with legitimacy must have been difficult. I have no first hand familiarity with the kinds of murderous intentions emotionally vulnerable cultists experience when asked to act on their impulses by a cult leader, but I must imagine they would be quite intense. Likely, mental illness is also clawing away at their sense of a normal self-image in an age of diminishing returns. The whole thing seems like hypnotic suggestibility among people with a dissociative identity disorder; a healthy personality split into many unhealthy pieces under the weight of unresolved trauma. Will life after Trump return them to the moderately aggrieved state they lived in for years before reaching the brink of Armageddon, or have they become an unrestrained geyser of violent rage? We are still piecing that together, as they have not surrendered yet.

Afterword

To my readers who have braved almost 300 pages of an emotional roller coaster ride, and accepted my occasional rhetorical excesses, we arrive mercifully at the actual point of *The Deplorables.* When I signed this work Q, it was not to establish the irrelevant question of my identity; rather, it was to posit how everything that has occurred in this country over several years of turbulent social unrest has been governed by the questions Deplorables and Commendables choose to ask and how each have answered them. Within this context, Q stands for "Question" and here is my parting one. Is ignorance really bliss?

You may recall the prophetic words of Isaac Asimov from 42 years ago when he addressed a "cult of ignorance" in America; *".....there has been a constant thread winding its way through our political and cultural life, nurtured by the false notion that democracy means that my ignorance is just as good as your knowledge."* The entire theme of *The Deplorables* has been to point out how diametrically opposed Commendables and Deplorables have become over what Makes America Great. The idiom "ignorance is bliss" describes the struggle aptly for both sides in the fight as most people find it immeasurably more comforting to deny at least some realities over the hard scrabble of modern American life. Few bother to sort the events of our time into what may have existential survival value and what may remain subject to idle conjecture without dangerous consequence. Equalizing the venomous with the innocuous will certainly complicate our threat assessment. So we lie to ourselves or, at least, suppress what we find most discomforting. In *The Deplorables* we have focused on the fairytales, baseless conspiracies, and malicious lies that either comforted or agitated the Deplorables, but what of the Commendables? Perhaps the most dangerous lie of all that has circulated among decent people is simply the denial of the visible signs of evil coalescing again among society's lesser angels for well over a decade in plain sight. As decent people have remained willfully ignorant of the aims and behaviors of the indecent, the dangers to society have been exacerbated beyond reason. Nothing has interrupted America more than this failure of imagination.

You simply will not get a good whiff of what is actually occurring in front of you if you rely exclusively on the mediated reality that comes from partisan arbiters of truth. It is time to inoculate against agitation from malicious provocateurs and acquaint yourself directly with the granular metadata that underpins everything. Most people cloister themselves, beyond the reach of opposing views, on one side or another of the manageable center; the only place where plus sum outcomes are possible. Media, both traditional and social, fosters confirmation bias and creates a blind spot where ignorance really does seem more blissful but where real dangers do lurk. Their ratings depend upon obsequious bobbing for approval. In these places, key details will always be manipulated or omitted for partisan effect and the vulnerable exposed to greater exploitation. Modern obscurantists always have an agenda that people either gravitate toward or away from, but will rarely make it transparent. Commendables and Deplorables differ dramatically in their tolerance for being manipulated. If you want to be on speaking terms with the objective facts of the world around you, become very intolerant of willful ignorance and those who exploit it. In addition to availing yourself of sources of knowledge not filtered through partisan media, you should also embrace Occam's razor; in judging two competing narratives, choose the simpler explanation that accounts for all of the facts. This is the principle most frequently abused by people trying to manipulate the truth.

For decades the Right and Left pendulum points that defined the state of our union were narrowly spaced apart to describe the country as either a Center Left or a Center Right America. Then came the Obama presidency. From then on, the rightward arc of the bob began swinging wildly beyond its original limit to capture a new strain of racial animus from the Deplorables. The harmonic motion of the entire American enterprise was distorted into something new and grotesque. The distance between sides grew so vast, the Deplorables and Commendables barely recognized each other. Instead, Deplorables now believe their only relief will come from eliminating the opposition entirely; a consequence made acceptable through extreme dehumanization. Still, the Commendables, who could easily have recognized this if ignorance were not so blissful, imagined the danger was managble in 21st century America. The murderous intent of the Deplorables simply could not be fathomed by Commendables unable to harbor that kind of animosity toward other living beings. This failure of imagination has left good people unprepared for what will surely follow.

Where Commendables find the Deplorables objectionable and impolite, the Deplorables find Commendables pose an actual threat to their survival. The bad guys lack the capacity to disagree with rivals constructively, so they will disagree destructively and will imagine these encounters are more consequential than Commendables will. If you have ever experienced road rage directed at you by an unhinged fellow motorist, you can begin to get a sense of the raw emotions you are unintentionally toying with simply by coexisting with Deplorables. You may be blissfully unware of the savage intemperance you have inspired through some minor faux pas. There is significant survival value in not underestimating how asymmetrical encounters with the opposition have become.

Now that I have your attention, I would suggest you steel yourself for even more turbulent and violent clashes ahead with people who can imagine no better remedy than a fistfight or worse to settle the differences they have with you. For the last four years, their antisocial impulses were moderately tempered by an optimism that they were gaining ground on their objective. But now, as the country's march toward equality and tolerance resumes, they soon will find society inhospitable again, and whatever restraint existed will melt away under newly overheated embers. Just as US intelligence has identified white supremacist terrorists as the principle threat against the Homeland, and a new administration accepts that assessment, the Deplorables will imagine their opposite ranks represent the principal threat they face. No longer will anti-fascist groups divert the attention of national security advisors. Their scrutiny of all the groups which have upset the nation's tranquility for years will create an equal and opposite backlash from Deplorables simply unwilling to accept responsibility for undermining our democratic Republic. Commendables must imagine the Deplorables, now on tenterhooks, are bound to react like any wild animal backed into a corner, by lashing out even more aggressively.

Not only must we imagine that the fight is coming our way whether we like it or not, but now we must actively recruit the single largest group of people in America, the Redeemables, to our side. These people are inherently receptive to the notion of bettering themselves and atoning for past mistakes. When they find themselves drifting toward the "dark side," Redeemables are drawn to the light. They are perhaps the least likely to accept their own willful ignorance as they always seek to know more and be more. Any number of extreme events that have occurred in recent years may well galvanize the Redeemables as a force for restoring decency.

If you identify as either Commendable or Redeemable, it's time to get off your ass. For all who truly love her, America is a work in progress. By all means join together in large crowds within every state in the union to petition whenever the nation becomes less uniquely virtuous than advertised. Until she offers liberty and the pursuit of happiness equally for all lives, acknowledging that all lives truly do matter, our work remains undone. Until all of legal age may cast their equal votes fearlessly and uncompromised by barriers erected to limit their participation, our work remains undone. Until our legal institutions treat all men and women as if they were created equal, our work remains undone. Until the wretched refuse and tempest tossed from the immeasurably less fortunate world around us are offered by America a hospitable chance for life, liberty and the pursuit of happiness, our work remains undone. And when you march at rallies, large and small, all over the country, steer clear of the Deplorables; who will do everything imaginable to turn your peaceful redress of grievances into violent skirmishes to undermine all uniquely American causes for which they have complete antipathy.

And finally, if you are either a Commendable or Redeemable who identifies as a Republican voter, I suggest you withhold your support until the party proves it is ready to govern again. For the last 12 years the Republicans have become the "party of no" simply because saying no to the opposition turns out votes from an unprincipled and unthinking constituency born and bred to regard "others" as a threat. The GOP has become a tripwire to activate the pent up hostility of monsters they have spent years creating in the laboratory of public opinion simply to draw a more visible line between parties. They used culture wars, like flaming torches, to torment the Deplorables who have always wallowed in self-pity and perpetual cultural grievance. When it became apparent that opening their tent wider to a more racially diverse America was anathema to the Deplorable core of their base, and wasn't likely to work anyway, they set out to surgically suppress the vote of certain Americans. This may have seemed to be in their rational self-interest until the monsters they created began pillaging and plundering our polite society. Now, the party must answer to a country weary of so much strife.

When asked to condemn their outgoing leader, Donald Trump, for inciting a riot at our nation's Capital, Republicans have been inconsistent at best. At first their Congressional leaders suggested Trump was indeed largely responsible for the death and destruction but should not be held accountable in an impeachment trial in the Senate. They hid behind a manifestly untrue reading of the Constitution they said would hold no leader subject to impeachment upon leaving office. In plain sight, they pandered to Deplorable voters they knew would become violently incensed if they did not hold the cult leader harmless. And then, when the impeachment ship sailed without a conviction for the 45th president, these same "leaders" said they would certainly vote

294

for Trump again if he ran for the highest office in 2024. Unless you approve of anti-American anarchy becoming a plank in the party platform, how will you cast a vote for the GOP or their standard bearer again? Until they stand for things again and not just against things, what are you voting for anyway? As of now, the GOP has made it clear they are a party that is focused on seizing and holding power against the will of the American people.

As a nation we stand at the proverbial crossroads. Will we find compatriots among all, regardless of political affiliation, who will reset our country upon its exceptional course, or will we surrender to the Deplorables who insist it is only white Christians who deserve our abundant riches and warm embrace? The Deplorables are right about one thing: A consequential fight for the soul of this country is already in progress, and will likely become far bloodier before order is restored. Will you stand on the side that finds comfort in what Lady Liberty represents?

As I finish this Afterword, I am weighing the initial response people, both Commendable and Deplorable, have had to the start of the Derek Chauvin murder trial. Clearly this moment is swelling with considerable energy from both sides and has become watershed for the country.

As we read the angry posts online from Deplorables lamenting the unfairness of holding officer Chauvin responsible for the wanton disregard for human life he showed his victim and America, we wonder what skin the Deplorables have in the fight. Why is this issue so personal for them though they are neither the victim nor the perpetrator nor associated in any discernable way with either? Is there really no longer a universal appreciation for right and wrong? If the skin they have in this fight is simply white skin, as in a desperate need to reclaim white privilege they believe they have lost, will this just be another fistfight between Commendables and Deplorables? When the vile comments fail to comport with their need to insist publicly that "All lives matter," may we safely assume the Deplorables were lying to paper over deep seated grievances? Must we deal gracefully with the transparently racist trope about "Angry black men" that reared its ugly head for the defense in this trial and was amplified by the Deplorables? Surely we have struggled with this meme since the end of the Civil War. And, while defense attorneys will always flip the script to make victims of their clients, pay close attention to how the Deplorables have used the same script to vilify George Floyd as if this trial was about his worth and not whether or not the accused is guilty of a crime

As the Deplorables all presupposed Chauvin would ultimately be exonerated, they began furiously speculating about the riotous mayhem that would occur in the aftermath of the verdict. This was interesting considering how we have seen this film before for the last several years. More intriguing is to ponder what mayhem will surely follow a guilty verdict.

Deplorables Glossary

Alternative Reality: The Deplorable's antidote for "fake News"- or anything antithetical to actual reality that can be contorted into a defense of Trump's awful behavior. It also refers to the legions of empty talking heads who insist you should never believe what you see or hear over their own sponsored propaganda.

Cheeto Jesus: The conception of Trump as a Jesus figure who will restore the natural order of white supremacy to this nation and the world more broadly.

Commendables: The opposite of Deplorables and the protagonists in a drama your author imagines will continue to play out. The Commendables are committed to everything that makes this country exceptional, the idea that the United States is inherently different from other nations for our belief in liberty and equality before the law.

C.U.N.T: An acronym referring, not to a grossly inappropriate word for female genitalia, or an Irishman's good natured retort after a pint or two, but to **C**ant **U**nderstand **N**ormal **T**hinking which refers to an inability the Deplorables have for grasping even basic logical arguments when they disagree with the premise. It also refers to clinging to debunked talking points long after the use by date. Think Benghazi or Birtherism or the "democrats are the party of the KKK". You literally can't dislodge this orthodoxy with a thousand megaton MOAB.

Deplorables: Originally coined by Trump's 2016 presidential election opponent, Hillary Clinton, to describe a sizeable chunk of the Donald's key constituency. The label is emblematic of people who are the very dregs of our society. Endlessly bigoted and misinformed, mindlessly authoritarian and consistently aggrieved over perceived attacks to their white Christian identity, they are conspiracy addled useful idiots who pray at the altar of their Cheeto Jesus.

Dumbfukery: The repeating of fallacious talking points without any discernible incentive provided by talking heads with enormous monetary or political incentives for spreading propaganda. Example: Sean "Hannity has about $40 million reasons a year to spout that dumbfukery, can you give me a single reason you believe it?" The word is purposefully misspelled to underscore how dumb the tactic is.

Fake News: For Trump's cult zombies, anything, no matter how evidently true, that doesn't toe the dear leader's line delivered by the news media particularly. It is always the opposite of State sponsored messages coming from the last Authoritarian regime. Think Goebbel's Nazi propaganda. Fake News is also a charge leveled at "libtards" on social media for any comment they make.

Freakosphere: The entire ecosystem of counter culture material in the public eye meant to freak out the barely literate Deplorables and encourage their activism.

Fannities: Fans of Sean Hannity's TV, radio and Facebook goo.

Gas-lighting: Asinine mind games deployed simply to corner social media debate opponents into making seemingly hypocritical statements that are only hypocritical if stripped of all context and nuance. It is

298

psychological manipulation directed at non-believers to sow doubt in their opposing views.

Nitzing: Named after David Francis Nitz, a former marine and current sociopath from Jacksonville Florida who weaponizes gas lighting and baseless ad Hominem attacks of the most heinous variety to wear down his intellectually superior opponents. This tactic is rampant on social media against liberal "trolls".

Otherism: The very oxygen the Deplorables breathe. Used 24/7 to dehumanize, marginalize and discredit all who are not generally white Christians or part of the true believer's sect. "Others" are those who would replace Deplorables in any contest in which the rules applied equally to all participants. "Others" are attacked viciously for their "otherism" and are subject to the vilest invective and death wishes/threats regularly.

Outrage Porn: The vile hatful slop the Deplorables gleefully wallow in 24/7 on reliably anti-social and anti-intellectual Rightwing social media sites to share their endless grievances among kindred spirits. Like actual porn, this behavior is highly addictive and surely leads to greater moral decay.

Process Crime: Any major crime(s) committed by people in Trump's orbit, not directly linked to "Russian Collusion". It is a tiresome canard used by the Deplorables to illustrate how purely innocent their cult hero is of any malfeasance. "Process" refers to due process, the main tenant of our judicial system and a process crime refers to attempts made to undermine fair treatment under the law. The most common process crime is perjury which the Deplorables will happily accept and enable if the perpetrator commits it in the service of protecting the Dear Leader.

299

Redeemables: The vast majority of the American people, who are neither entirely Deplorable nor Commendable but have the capacity to tip in either direction based on the prevailing winds in society.

Scooby Dooism: Refusing to acknowledge the obvious willful ignorance of things accepted just because. Even though Scooby and the gang revealed how the alleged apparition was always actually a wing tip wearing local businessman in disguise, they began each new episode as true believing ghost hunters.

Suspension of disbelief: Borrowed from Hollywood to explain how people can justify the high price of admission at the movie theater. Related to Scooby Dooism but principally focused on implausible alternative facts accepted as true to make even more implausible cases. Think of the Pizzagate narrative linking Trump's 2016 nemesis Hillary Clinton to child sex trafficking.

The calm Before the Storm: Specifically relating to Q anon articles of blind faith but more generally used to describe baseless conspiracy nonsense required to accept alternative reality. The premise is that everything we see with our own eyes and hear with our own ears about Trump's criminal enterprise is purposefully contrived to conceal the covert battle waged by patriots to beat back the New World Order led by George Soros, the Illuminati and Snow White, all hell bent on controlling the world. According to their prophet, Q Anon, The actual targets of special Counsel Mueller's investigation are Hillary Clinton, Barack Obama, George Soros, John Podesta, the world's pedophiles and the Obama's dog Bo. At this moment we are told sealed indictments targeting liberal boogeymen number 63,000.

Trumpanzees: A particularly heinous species of Trump fanatics fond of flinging their own feces around with reckless abandon. Self-indulgent, poorly educated, and dumber than boiled tofu, these animals are hateful philistines who would set the planet back millennia if not beaten back by civilized tribes.

War Zero: Appropriating valor and unearned street cred from past military service that was motivated by all the wrong principles. Example; I served in Iraq because I loved shooting "rags".

Whataboutism: The asinine and supremely juvenile habit of responding to every criticism of Trump with "what about _____" (fill in the blank with any/all liberal boogeymen). Though the Deplorables would never accept such deflection from their own lazy eyed children, they believe it is a purely reasonable tactic in adult conversations.